AFRICONOMICS

AFRICONOMICS

A HISTORY OF WESTERN
IGNORANCE

BRONWEN EVERILL

WILLIAM
COLLINS

William Collins
An imprint of HarperCollins*Publishers*
1 London Bridge Street
London SE1 9GF

WilliamCollinsBooks.com

HarperCollins*Publishers*
Macken House
39/40 Mayor Street Upper
Dublin 1
D01 C9W8, Ireland

First published in Great Britain in 2024 by William Collins

1

Set in Sabon LT Pro by HarperCollins*Publishers* India

Printed and bound in the UK using 100% Renewable
Electricity at CPI Group (UK) Ltd

This book contains FSC™ certified paper and other controlled
sources to ensure responsible forest management.

For more information visit: www.harpercollins.co.uk/green

For JG: my IR

'You Europeans, you Europeans, we fear you. If it pleases you, you will help a man. If it doesn't please you, you give no one help. And no man can tell when it may please you.'

Elenore Smith Bowen, *Return to Laughter* (1954)

CONTENTS

Introduction 1

1 A KING WITH HOLEY STOCKINGS,
  OR MEASURING WEALTH 17
2 LEARNING TO BE FARMERS 43
3 GETTING PEOPLE BACK TO WORK 71
4 MONEY PROBLEMS 104
5 UNEQUAL DEVELOPMENT 135
6 FINANCING FREEDOM 168
7 HELPING YOU TO GET RICH QUICK 193
8 WOMEN ARE NOTHING MORE
  THAN SLAVES 217

Epilogue: How to Think Differently
About African Economics 241
Acknowledgements 253
Notes 255
Index 277

INTRODUCTION

I was getting a lift back to Roberts International Airport in Liberia. It was the end of 2008, and I had just finished a term spent digging through archives. I had been searching for material for the PhD I was writing on the history of Liberia and its neighbour in West Africa, Sierra Leone. A Liberian friend was giving me a ride. As a recent returnee from the United States himself, he had heard my accent and had helped me out when I first arrived, allowing me to tag along to parties. He introduced me to well-connected friends with family archives stretching back to the nineteenth century, and others who might know where to look for documents in the national archives. Making conversation as we drove out of Monrovia and the flat, green countryside opened up in front of us, he asked what I made of the two places I had been researching. 'So, what are the big differences you've seen between Sierra Leone and Liberia?'

My research was really focused on the early nineteenth century – the foundation of anti-slavery colonies for formerly enslaved people, and early Back-to-Africa movements. But I'd walked around both countries having conversations with people and had been struck by some differences. For example, football was the sport I saw played everywhere in Sierra Leone's capital, Freetown, in the streets and on the beach and in the national stadium, while in Liberia's capital city, Monrovia, there were a large number of busy concrete basketball courts – a difference that might be explained by the British and American origins of the two former colonies. A more serious difference was the scale of the presence of international aid workers and advisers in the two countries. There were plenty in Freetown, to be sure, but Monrovia was on another level.

Sierra Leone's decade-long civil war had ended six years earlier, in 2002; Liberia's civil wars, which had begun in 1980, had ended in 2003 and its first post-conflict elections took place in 2005. The reconstruction in the two countries was unfolding differently as a result of the nature of the wars, their impact on the capital cities and their effect on the wider population. This was hard not to notice, even for a bookish historian of the nineteenth century who was just there to read in archives and libraries.

But as I walked through central Freetown, white Land Cruisers would speed by on their way from meetings in town to Paddy's for evening drinks and leaving parties, where people who spent their days working on education or trade policy, on assisting the government in achieving economic growth, would regale newcomers with stories of their time in the field in Afghanistan or Somalia. And, looking for an internet connection in Monrovia, I would use the Royal Grand Hotel's restaurant lounge, alongside dozens of other expats who were there to discuss capacity building, Millennium Development

Goals and deliverables over £20 sushi. But what struck me most of all was not the differences between the two countries but the sameness of the international community I was seeing in both places, outside *and* inside the archives.

For centuries, Africa has drawn the attention of Westerners full of good intentions, people who want to come and help, and particularly people concerned about Africa's poverty, lack of economic development and uneven integration into the global economy.

The international economists, aid workers and development experts who were everywhere in Freetown in 2008 had their predecessors in the Washington Consensus reformers of the 1980s, who sought to increase African economic growth efficiently through the expansion of the private sector and business rather than the state. They had their predecessors in the 1950s technical experts sent by European empires and the United States to speed up economic development in the face of the growing threat of communism. They had their predecessors in the 1900s campaign led by E. D. Morel for government regulation of trade and labour practices in the Congo Free State. They had their predecessors in 1841, when Thomas Fowell Buxton sent a small flotilla from the UK to modern Nigeria to teach people how to farm. They had their predecessors in 1791, when the Sierra Leone Company's first officials arrived from the UK with their plan to use commerce to end the slave trade.

These generations of people setting out to try to help Africa's economic development were largely driven by a desire to do good, to improve the world. But they all started from the same premise: that African economies needed their help. Ignorant of African political economy, they believed that there was a set of universal economic laws which could be applied anywhere and that Africa's leaders were simply ignorant of these laws, or African cultures needed changing – 'improving' – so that the laws could be applied.

At the same time, these do-gooders often ignored what *was* probably a universal economic observation – that people respond to incentives. How they do so, the cultural framing of incentives and their unintended consequences are different, not only in Africa but in all kinds of historical and regional contexts. But many of these interventions sprang from the idea that, because of the warped incentives of slavery, which had created awful economic behaviours and relationships, Europeans would have to introduce proper incentives and create new cultures. To paraphrase the Nobel Prize-winning economist Douglass North, they would have to fix Africa's economies by giving them a new history.

There is an economic phrase that I think about a lot: *ceteris paribus*. It means 'other things being equal'. It is used in economics to show how economic theories can be applied universally. For example, *ceteris paribus* is applied to the Law of Demand, suggesting that the level of demand for a good will depend on its price. It ought to be the case that, other things being equal, the higher the price, the lower the demand. Other things are not always equal: there may not be cheaper alternatives, people might be taking fashion trends into account when considering their purchases, and not everyone will have access to the same information. But if we set those aside, the Law of Demand is true *ceteris paribus*. I think about *ceteris paribus* a lot because it shows a fundamental tenet at the heart of economic theories: the extent to which the discipline relies on assumptions. (I was horrible at spelling as a child and I remember sitting in middle school, intoning the mnemonic that 'to assume is to make an ass out of u and me'.) *Assuming* that everything is equal, this is how the economy ought to work.

But on what is the basis of that assumption of equality founded?

Repeatedly, in the case of economic interventions in Africa, it is assumed that all states have equal economic power within the world. It is assumed that they have the same incentives to regulate trade *and the same power to implement those regulations.* It is assumed that businesses have the same incentives to manage supply and demand *and the same power to respond to those changing forces.* It is assumed that individuals have needs and desires as consumers *and the same power to purchase or boycott.* If these assumptions hold true, then the economic principle being applied will be a success. And what is *not* assumed is the role of politics and culture and *power* in shaping African economies.

These Western assumptions – and their consequences for Africa – are the subject of this book.

◆ ◆ ◆

Over the past 200 or so years, despite their good intentions, the people who have intervened in Africa, introducing policies to tackle enslavement, poverty and underdevelopment, have repeatedly run into obstacles because of their fundamental misunderstanding of where African wealth came from, how slavery was connected to development, and how to balance wealth creation and economic growth with development for all.

Slavery was a system that was woven through many different aspects of the Atlantic economy by the end of the eighteenth century. Intervening in the slave trade was *not* a straightforward proposition, even if it was morally justified.

If, for instance, we wanted to eliminate the use of fossil fuels, there are many ideas floating around as to how we might do that. We might tax fossil fuel corporations out of existence, or incentivize people to switch away from petrol and diesel cars. Build nuclear plants. Reduce individual consumption of fossil fuels. Ban oil and gas exploration. The list could go on. And each of these would address the problem from a different perspective: is change most likely to come through individual behaviour, through corporations, or through national or international laws?

With something as embedded in the workings of the modern global economy as fossil fuels, it becomes apparent pretty quickly that 'banning fossil fuels' is far more complicated than the simple premise implies. Fossil fuel infrastructure is everywhere around us – cars, plastics, airplanes, heating our homes. Fossil fuel companies also employ millions of workers worldwide, people who rely on these companies for their living. And the fossil fuel corporations themselves have invested a lot of capital – often the money of pension funds or philanthropic endowments – in their future growth. And so to legally abolish fossil fuels would end the global system as we know it.

This isn't necessarily a problem. Some people do indeed want an end to the global system as we know it. But since they aren't a majority, effectively removing fossil fuels from the economy while keeping it ticking along at its current pace is the goal of most policymakers who are trying to do something about climate change. Can they make it worthwhile for consumers to switch to alternative sources of energy? How quickly, and with what levels of incentive? Can they find those employed in fossil fuels other jobs? And can they sustain asset growth through new investments in alternative energy sources?

When it came to the abolition of the slave trade and enslaved labour, similar questions should have been asked. But they weren't. And a major reason why they weren't asked is because many anti-slavery advocates (in, for example, the UK) associated slavery with the distant plantations of the West Indies or the US South: they didn't recognize the contributions slavery was making to their own economy. The abolitionists who campaigned against the consumption of sugar produced by enslaved labour saw the specific connection between the commodity they were eating and the slavery that was producing it, but failed to see how fundamentally slavery had changed the world economy.

Instead, policymakers, humanitarians and businesspeople tried to fix the wrongs of slavery without addressing how it had become wrapped up in all aspects of Atlantic Africa's external and internal systems. Although Britain and France compensated their own slaveholders (a partial recognition of the value of slavery to their own economies), slaveholders in Africa were not compensated, the argument being that the slave trade had brought death, destruction and corruption to Africa and had permanently scarred the continent in ways that could only be remedied by the intervention of guilty, but penitent, white people. And, crucially, the enslaved people themselves were never compensated, neither in the Americas nor in Africa.

When the Atlantic slave trade was legally abolished in the early nineteenth century, European political economists turned their attention to understanding the relationship between slavery and underdevelopment in Africa. Some posited that the slave trade had created a predatory elite in Africa who waged wars and raided their neighbours in search of captives to sell for income and for the 'gifts' that slave traders handed out. Another theory was that African people had become so dependent on the 'worthless' things that slave traders sold them that they had no choice but to continue. Most agreed that the economic incentives offered by the slave trade had distorted the economy away from 'productive' labour like agriculture and manufacturing.

Idealistic economists and humanitarians came to Africa equipped with ideas. Ideas about growth, about debt, about unemployment, about women's economic empowerment, about inflation, about industrialization, about trade, about inequality, about self-sufficiency and about economic governance. But their ideas about Africa's economies were based on assumptions that, other things being equal, African economies would work in the same way that European economies did. (Never mind that, in many cases, Europe's economies *didn't* work. Certainly not equally well for everyone.)

What happened next was part of a very slow process in which gradually, over a century and a bit, and especially between 1885 and 1960, Europeans gained political and economic control over almost all of the African continent. How that happened has been the subject of a vast amount of research and debate among historians. Most people probably have a vague idea that the slave trade and imperialism in Africa were linked in some way. And in a certain sense, that's correct. Both the slave trade and imperialism were extractive and exploitative economic relationships that did not benefit the majority of Africans and helped to create wealth for a large minority of Europeans.

But there was another process at work, which helps to explain why abolitionists, missionaries, philanthropists, humanitarians, development experts and international organizations have repeatedly failed.

There has been a persistent strand of thought in public life outside Africa that specific economic interventions – often based on misunderstandings of the universality of Western economic development, as well as misunderstandings about the role of slavery in the commercial, financial and industrial revolutions – were the magic bullet that would improve Africa's commerce, its labour, its fiscal governance, its approach to debt, its ability to achieve development and growth. These interventions were based on a belief that Africa is poor, backward and corrupt, for which people have variously blamed despotic slave traders, laziness, a lack of things to trade and a poor understanding of money and finance.

For just over two centuries, well-meaning people have been trying to right the horrific wrongs of the slave trade, creating a legacy of interventions in Africa that attempt to remedy the mistakes of previous generations. But they have had real – and often harmful – effects on the African economies themselves. The problem has been an assumption that the West's own understandings of how 'the economy' works were universal, rather than culturally formed.

In the 1820s, for instance, no one in Britain would have been advocating for getting women into the workplace as a crucial goal of modern economic development; in fact there were plenty of people arguing that women's agricultural roles in various African economies showed that those places were backward. In African agricultural economies where women did much of the planting and harvesting, European observers commented that this showed that women were not well treated, that African men took advantage of them, and that moving women *out* of the workforce and into the domestic sphere of home and family was the correct (European) path towards modernity. This assumption – that European ideas about the economy are universal, scientific and timeless – led to a sense of superiority about Western solutions.

◆ ◆ ◆

What I saw as the difference between Sierra Leone and Liberia in 2008 was a difference in control over policy. It was a small difference – both countries were full of development experts and aid workers, and both sat at the bottom of the global league tables on development indicators – but it was one that hinted at the role of power in undermining any value of assuming *ceteris paribus*.

Liberia's civil war was really several, spanning more than two decades and devastating the economy and population of both the capital and the countryside before spilling over into neighbouring Sierra Leone. There had been long-simmering resentments at the heart of Liberia's conflict, in part over the economic inequality between the descendants of the Black American settlers – who had held political power continuously from the colony's founding in the 1820s to a coup in 1980 – and the rest of the country's Indigenous population. Many Americo-Liberians had fled during the wars. But while Liberia's economy and society suffered enormously during the wars, its charismatic dictator, Charles Taylor, was liked by business and had the support of anti-communist leaders in the West. One of the consequences of this was that the Liberia of 2008 was well positioned to become a darling of development economics. Its new administration, headed by the former World Bank officer Ellen Johnson Sirleaf, had been trained abroad. Sirleaf herself issued a call for the diaspora's return, leading to my friend's presence back in Liberia (and ability to give me a lift to the airport) after years spent in the US during the war. The diaspora arrived with ideas of how an efficient and modern economy should work, shaped by their time in the US and in US educational institutions.

Meanwhile, Sierra Leone's civil war had been instigated in part by Charles Taylor's regime in neighbouring Liberia. It was a shorter war, begun, as many Sierra Leoneans believed, by outside actors rather than emerging from a sharp economic divide. This laid the foundations for a very different post-conflict reconstruction in Sierra Leone.

The difference that most struck me, as I stumblingly attempted to articulate in answer to my friend on the way to the airport, was how the two countries reacted to their unequal global economic power. Liberia's response demonstrated the leadership's knowledge that there is power in being perceived as a compliant and powerless economy, one where any manner of economic experimentation can be tried as long as it comes fully funded. Sierra Leone responded differently, seeking out its own commercial relationships with mineral companies, Chinese investors and aid organizations in what felt more like a somewhat chaotically regulated free market of development ideas, but one where Sierra Leone's politicians were doing the choosing, where they had created a situation in which they had (some) political power through their ability to veto.

This was a very schematic observation, and I couldn't tell you which was a better approach: the Ebola crisis of 2013–16 that hit both countries makes it difficult to have any long-term sense of whether one method worked better than the other. More importantly, this book argues that there isn't a way of measuring these things 'objectively'. Culture, power and history cannot be smoothed by *ceteris paribus*.

But what was interesting about these two different approaches to post-conflict reconstruction was the sense both countries' leaderships had of their powerlessness and the strategies they had for dealing with it. It was clear that *internal* politics, power, cultural assumptions and ideas about inequality, national wealth and development were just as important as external ones in shaping how people reacted to and created change. Where Sierra Leone's leadership began to feel well supported by robust political party machines, Liberia's leaders turned to the diaspora and aid agencies. As has rightly become a rallying cry, Africa is not a country. But neither is any one African country a unified entity. The internal class politics, cultural negotiations and power dynamics that shape policies have been continuously reshaped by historical events – events that often get ignored by well-meaning interventionists who think of the continent as a blank slate.

It is all well and good to say that countries should raise interest rates to deal with inflation. Or that too much national debt is bad. Or that a certain balance of trade is ideal. Or that too much or too little regulation stifles business growth. What is more important than saying these things is *who* is saying them, how well they understand the state about which they are speaking, and what power they have to do something about it. For the past 200-plus years, the people who have had the ability to intervene in Africa have largely been outside it, in the world's richest countries. And with the declaration of their good intentions comes a paternalist power: 'I am doing this for your own good because I know better.'

This book is a history of Western attitudes, and many of the historical sources it draws on do not specify the colonies or countries in Africa that they are writing about, or the sources are themselves making arguments about the continent as a whole, arguments that often missed the specificities of the economies they wanted to help and the specificities of their own economies. For instance, misconceived ideas about Africa's 'natural abundance' led nineteenth-century Europeans to argue that the continent should have been overflowing with agricultural surplus, if only Africans had been properly trained in modern agricultural techniques instead of incentivized to raid for enslaved captives. In Sierra Leone, resources and energy were poured into agricultural education, model farms, the introduction (and untimely death from disease) of oxen and horses. Arguments between European officials about whether cash crop production or agricultural self-sufficiency was the ultimate goal of all of these interventions led to policy flip-flopping. African leaders – who hoped to remain independent of European control by demonstrating their ability to manage their economies to European standards – didn't know whether to satisfy that requirement by planting sugar cane for export or planting rice to feed their populations.

Or what about corruption? Discomfort and annoyance about the role of payments to the officials in charge of the slave trade in Dahomey led novice nineteenth-century European merchants and businessmen to argue that they had to bribe African leaders to conduct their trade. Rather than understanding these payments as tariffs or trade taxes, which were redistributed through the political networks that upheld African polities, they categorized them as a form of corruption and worked to ban them. But, instead of improving the economy, this weakened the political power of their trading partners and destabilized their regimes, leading to the endemic warfare that European powers decried as undermining economic progress by creating instability and insecurity.

And private businesses trying to operate in Africa faced similar problems. Confusion over the terms of labour contracts and misunderstandings of the patterns of working life in South Africa led to frustration by European employers in colonial cities and mining towns, who were primed to think that slavery had made their workers lazy and undisciplined. They failed to understand that their workers were required for the harvest back at home, or that they had signed contracts based on the lunar, rather than the solar, calendar. This led to draconian policies including the introduction of passes for those workers to move around the country.

And repeatedly, the exploitation of Africa has been helped by the sly use of the language of humanitarianism by people with nefarious motives. The Scramble for Africa, the most notorious instance of rapacious European expansion in African history, was justified by the argument that European intervention was needed to finally end the slave trade and the use of enslaved labour on the continent.

To me, as a historian in Freetown and Monrovia in 2008, the problematic role of foreign workers' assumptions seemed clear: the diagnosis of the problems facing Sierra Leone and Liberia often came down to the priorities of the governments and institutions that the development experts and aid workers represented. Managing inflation and unemployment, ensuring collection of taxes, offering incentives for bringing industry into the country, the employment of women and the provision of education – all of these probably seem like universally good ideas. Maybe they even *are* universally good ideas. But they are definitely historically specific ideas about what the government's role in the economy is, who counts as part of the economy, and how the economy relates to society's goals.

I didn't say all of this to my friend that day – it wasn't a particularly long ride. But his question made me think. In the years since 2008, I have written books and articles about the economic and political consequences of the abolition of the slave trade and taught African history to students in several UK universities. In that time, I have been consistently surprised by how little is known outside of academia about the wealth of research done by economic anthropologists and historians of economic thought. Year in and year out, I encounter well-educated students who may have some vague notion of the slave trade and of imperialism in Africa, and who probably have a much clearer sense that Africa is a poor continent today. Despite many decades of excellent scholarship on the problematic assumptions of development economics, or on conceptions of wealth and poverty in specific African societies, this information has not always made its way out of the ivory tower.

One consequence of this has been the continuation of those same ideas that Africa is poor because it is 'traditional' and 'unchanging'. Another consequence has been the tendency to think that only specific types of imperial economic extraction were bad, and to be vigilant and wary of the exploitation of Africa while ignoring the other aspects of well-meaning economic experimentation and intervention that have equally been part of African countries' experiences of empire and neocolonialism.

When I discuss these ideas – with students, members of the public, friends and colleagues – they will often note that the West *meant well*. Do good intentions count for nothing in the history of interventions in Africa? Wasn't it clear that, on balance, empires had largely *tried* to do good – ending the slave trade, bringing education, bringing commerce, bringing railways and legal systems, building hospitals?

This book offers one reply: the road to hell is paved with good intentions.

CHAPTER 1

A KING WITH HOLEY STOCKINGS, OR MEASURING WEALTH

Seated at a table next to Naimbana, the King of the Temne, twenty-one-year-old Anna Maria Falconbridge observed her surroundings. Here she was, in Sierra Leone, West Africa, after an eighteen-day boat journey from England. She, her male English companions and the king were the only ones seated; the other women stood around the table, although they were queens according to Falconbridge. The table was laid with silverware. The king was dressed in a scarlet robe embroidered with gold. This was his third outfit change of the day, having previously worn a black velvet suit; before that, a purple embroidered coat, white satin waistcoat, breeches and embroidered stockings; and, on first meeting, a loose white frock and trousers. These clothes drew Anna Maria's attention because in the 1790s, when she was writing, clothing was not only a marker of status and wealth, it was also a significant investment. The pair of velvet breeches alone would have cost the equivalent of more than ten weeks' rent for a tradesman in London.[1]

But Anna Maria was noting these luxurious fashions out of a sense of irony. She was setting the scene for the friend she was writing to, trying to explain her experiences of West Africa, the culture shock and exoticism of her trip. She contrasted King Naimbana's obvious wealth in material goods with the fact that his stockings had holes in them and one person, whom she took to be a queen, wore neither shoes nor stockings. She also commented that the town comprised houses 'composed of thatch, wood, and clay, something resembling our poor cottages, in many parts of England'. Naimbana's large new house was made in the same style and from the same mud and thatch materials as the rest of the town, 'but much larger'. The queen was dressed 'in a dignified style' but 'was considered old' at forty-five. Tea and coffee were on offer, but sugar was currently unavailable. It is clear from her descriptions that Anna Maria was trying to place herself, to figure out whether to revere the King of the Temne or look down upon him and his court.

Anna Maria Falconbridge was not an average tourist. While travel accounts by European slave traders in Africa had been published since the sixteenth century, Anna Maria's was something new. She was part of a mission in 1791 to Sierra Leone to set up a trading company explicitly dedicated to the abolition of the slave trade. The Sierra Leone Company would trade with African merchants but would not accept enslaved captives in payment, in order to encourage diversification away from a dependence on slave-trading. The slave trade that Falconbridge's husband had come to West Africa to stop was both a moral and a commercial problem. Africa's economies were suspect from the outset of this first well-meaning intervention.

The Sierra Leone Company selected Alexander Falconbridge for the task of re-establishing communication with the Temne after an earlier plan to settle Black British colonists in the region fell apart. Anna Maria had married Alexander at the age of nineteen and sailed with him to West Africa.

It is somewhat remarkable that Anna Maria travelled with Alexander on this mission as their marriage seems already to have been on the rocks by the time they left Portsmouth – her letters make it clear that his drinking was a problem. But maybe she saw an opening to write a bestseller. Her observations of Sierra Leone were written in a style of travel writing that was very popular at the time, as letters to a friend back in Britain, subsequently published as a book.

Reading through her letters, we can see wealth and its corollary, poverty, expressed in different terms: material possessions, cleanliness, status and inequality, and natural abundance.

Natural resources featured prominently in Anna Maria's writing. The approach to Sierra Leone by boat saw 'richly wooded and beautifully ornamented' mountains rise from the sea. The palm 'is a valuable tree' for the oil and wine that it produced. Tasso Island in the Sierra Leone River was 'well wooded' and 'if cultivated would be a fruitful one'. Pineapples and lime trees were 'the spontaneous production of the country'.

These views of Africa's abundant natural resources, simply waiting to be exploited, were both part of a long tradition of writing about Africa and hinted at a new argument concerning the continent's wealth and how it could be developed.

◆ ◆ ◆

Only fifteen years before Anna Maria's trip, in 1776, the political economist and 'founder' of modern economic thought, Adam Smith, had published *The Wealth of Nations*, taking the anglophone world by storm. In it he questioned the logic of establishing new colonies, especially focusing on the Spanish and Portuguese conquest of the Americas in search of gold and silver: 'of all those expensive and uncertain projects, however, which bring bankruptcy upon the greater part of the people who engage in them, there is none, perhaps, more perfectly ruinous than the search after new silver and gold mines'.[2] In contrast, he saw the prosperous colonies as those engaged in agricultural production. Extraction alone wasn't true prosperity. But why?

Where the search for natural wealth – particularly gold – had animated the imaginations of medieval and early modern writers interested in Africa, by the end of the eighteenth century thinkers like Adam Smith and the French economists associated with the Enlightenment had reframed wealth as something that was *produced* by labour, and in particular, labour applied to productive land.

These writers were especially keen to contrast the success of a certain type of British and French settler with the declining Spanish Empire and its supposedly monopolistic control of commerce and production. Since the second quarter of the eighteenth century, both the French and the British had opened up a lot of their Atlantic trade, scaling back their monopolies and state-backed companies in favour of individual merchants and planters.

For centuries, the global marketplace was conceived as a zero-sum game: if I produce more than I consume, I win; but if I consume more than I produce, then I lose. This resulted in policies like mercantilism, the basic premise of which was that national wealth came about through a balance of trade that was export-oriented with restrictions on imports. It was a form of protectionism, in other words.

Mercantilism, though, was the enemy of the modern economy, according to Smith and his followers. Even though it was the system that had helped make many empires – and the people who ran them – fabulously wealthy, mercantilism's monopolistic economic growth came at the expense of consumers.

In the early British Empire, mercantilism and protectionist policies had largely been achieved by taking over new territories that had the potential to produce the resources and food needed to remain 'self-sufficient' while competing with other European empires in cornering certain re-export markets. If a British person spending money on French-produced sugar was a net loss to British national wealth, then Britain needed to ensure that it could grow its own sugar. But if both Britain and France produced sugar, then they would only grow wealthier if they could either find another market to sell it to – the new United States, maybe? – or if they could find another crop they could grow in their colonies and the other couldn't – something like cotton, perhaps.

At the heart of mercantilism was the idea that the national wealth was made up of the total aggregate wealth of all the people in the nation put together, minus whatever they spent outside the nation (which included the empire).

Mercantilist policies, Smith and his followers argued, had made *certain people* rich, but only through government subsidies and monopolies. The Royal African Company, for instance, had benefited the Duke of Chandos and King Charles II's brother, the Duke of York (who became James

II). It had made certain shareholders very wealthy. But it had been a failure as a commercial enterprise. By dissolving the monopoly and opening up free trade, many more people were able to have a go at the slave trade – investing in a one-off trading voyage or providing new services like insurance.

◆ ◆ ◆

Smith argued that there were several 'factors of production' that led to the incredible wealth in the British Caribbean: land, labour and capital. Later economists have argued that capitalism exists only where you have free markets in all of these factors. Smith's definition links these economic ideas with progress, modernity and superiority. But the free market in labour that made plantation production so wildly successful was really a free market in a commodity – enslaved labourers – not competition for wages among labourers. And, of course, the land that was so profitable had been stolen by European settlers from Indigenous people, rather than paid for at a fair market rate.

The rationale for the theft of this land, though, linked back to how Smith framed the productive forces. Land that wasn't being used productively – according to British ideas about productivity – was untapped potential. As people became increasingly aware of that potential, they really couldn't see the land as anything but a landscape of giant £ sterling signs.

This is how Anna Maria Falconbridge arrived in Sierra Leone, with a mindset that had already become widespread in the Atlantic world by the end of the eighteenth century: that land, labour and capital were first and foremost factors of production, rather than having other cultural, social or religious significance.

Historically, the Temne view of land was quite different to that held by Smith and his British contemporaries. Land was not owned individually but by the community. Strangers and outsiders to the community could effectively 'lease' land for use, but it could not be bought and sold as a piece of private property, used for collateral against debt or passed down as inheritance.

This misunderstanding about land was at the heart of the British mission that Anna Maria was accompanying: the first British settlers who had arrived in Temne territory believed that they had purchased land for their colony in perpetuity. The Temne, on the other hand, thought that they had lent the land to specific individuals. Naimbana pointed out that 'he had not a right to sell' the land on which the settlers had set up their homes, and explained that 'this is a great country, and belongs to many people'. He continued: 'I can live where I like; nay, can appropriate any uninhabited land within my dominions to what use I please,' but this right did not extend to the sale of land to strangers in perpetuity, which required 'the consent of my people, or rather the head man of every town'.

♦ ♦ ♦

While land could not be thought of as private wealth, for King Naimbana and his wives there were other ways of measuring wealth that operated below Falconbridge's radar. She commented on the number of Naimbana's wives, and explained that his town of twenty houses consisted entirely of the king's wives and what she described as servants. What she was observing, but did not necessarily notice, was the way that Smith's second factor of production (labour) operated in parts of the West African economy, a form of wealth based in the accumulation of dependent people.

The abundant, and from Falconbridge's perspective underexploited, land available to the Temne and other groups she encountered on her trip was contrasted with a rather sparse population. She occasionally came across small settlements of twenty to several hundred people as she travelled along the rivers around Sierra Leone. This ratio of land to people was in stark contrast to England, where there was a much denser population and land was, particularly after the Enclosure Acts beginning in the seventeenth century, relatively scarce. Enclosing formerly common lands as private property created a scarcity of land available for building on, for farming and for pasturage. And that scarcity was at the heart of land's high value in England. But in West Africa, and other places where the land-to-labour ratio was high, it was people who were scarce, and their labour was valued accordingly.

What Falconbridge and her compatriots failed to account for in their observations was what twentieth-century scholars came to call 'wealth in people', or, in other words, the value that slavery contributed beyond labour.[3] Yes, it was probably more economically efficient to pay a worker a one-off wage for a job than to feed and clothe an enslaved labourer outside the harvest season. But in the American colonies, the ostensible owners of enslaved people could hire out their labour, could use them for small capital improvements (fixing machinery, repairing fences), could borrow money on the basis of their value and, like money earning interest, could increase the size of their labour force through the birth of enslaved children. By turning people into property, slaveholders could do all the things we do with property.

In the context of King Naimbana's court, 'wealth in people' included dependent relatives, people in his debt and clients. In some ways, it would be easy to think of this as a type of power experienced in the modern workplace: if a person is near the top of the corporate ladder at a company, they have lots of people who report to them, and a measure of how far up that ladder they are is partially reflected in the number of people under them. Part of their skill in working up the ladder is doing favours, proving themselves to be effective in producing results for the people above as well as those below them. Ultimately, they then report to the CEO or the board. A board member can actually sit on multiple boards, giving them much more of this kind of power, or control over people.

The point of all that power accumulation in the modern office, though, is ultimately to be rewarded with a higher salary. The economic anthropologists Jane Guyer and Samuel Eno Belinga talk about this in the African context as being an issue of convertibility: exchanging wealth in people for wealth in things.[4]

What Falconbridge and later travel writers and colonial governors and merchants may have failed to realize was that wealth in things didn't always come *after* wealth in people in a lot of West African societies. Kings could use expensive things to buy followers, wives and enslaved people. Part of Naimbana's wealth was measured in his ability to distribute things to his followers. Getting material goods in exchange for trading rights, for instance, or for the lease of a piece of land to a European, was important because he could give them as presents to his followers, who would then be able to further pass them on to their followers. Returning to the modern corporate workplace, this would be like the head of equities in Dallas giving a managing director a pot of money for bonuses to award to her team as she saw fit.

In this economic system, it might seem perverse to get involved in the slave trade – selling people for things. And in a sense it was, particularly as the slave trade ramped up over the eighteenth century. People were already seen as a form of wealth, like land was in England, which made it easier for everyone involved in the exchange to think about trading people for money or goods as akin to trading money (or land) for money or goods. People became a form of commodified wealth. Those doing the trading were the middlemen, purchasing enslaved people from other middlemen traders further into the interior, who in turn had purchased them or possibly captured them. With the goods they received in trade they were then able to grow their wealth in people.

Anna Maria Falconbridge did not necessarily fully see this picture as she travelled around Sierra Leone. She did understand that a larger number of wives and 'servants' signified higher status in the villages she encountered. But she expected that power flowed in one direction: exchanging command of people for an accumulation of things. Wealth in things was more her preoccupation, or rather, trying to understand how expensive items fitted into a situation that she generally dismissed as one of poverty.

And, to a certain extent, there was a display of that more familiar form of wealth. Expensive clothes were one of the major items of consumer expenditure in the eighteenth century, and the fact that the king and his wives wore lots of them showed Falconbridge that they were definitely wealthier than others in the town. Even Adam Smith recognized – sort of – that there was some kind of relationship between things and people, though he found it perverse: 'an industrious and frugal' European peasant's accommodation 'exceeds that of many an African king, the absolute master of the lives and liberties' of his subjects. For Naimbana the expensive clothes were really there to command power and respect among the Europeans he met – who recognized and valued this form of wealth – while his 'real' wealth was in his followers and in his primacy over equal headmen of the surrounding villages. Naimbana had wealth in people.

Of course, there was an opportunity cost in the Atlantic trade that made wealth accumulation possible, since African traders were selling off people who, if the trader had the means to purchase them, could have become the trader's dependants. And as the Atlantic slave trade grew, this had a devastating impact on the ability of people like Naimbana to build wealth in people. No wonder, then, that Naimbana was willing to sit down with Anna Maria's husband and the colonists and renegotiate the terms of this new form of wealth: property rights in land.

Falconbridge's husband wanted Naimbana to sign away the rights to a piece of land in exchange for payment. But if he did that without securing the approval of the other headmen, and doing so through the payment of gifts, then he risked losing their trust and ultimately the social view of wealth that mattered to him.

In the passage of *The Wealth of Nations* where Smith describes the reason for British success in generating wealth from the Americas, his focus is on the market for wage labour, not enslaved labourers. Smith and other early political economists had a blind spot about the work done by enslaved people. Slavery, Smith thought, was a backward *social* institution rather than something that could be explained by economics. In fact, it wasn't until the work of Eric Williams, a scholar from Trinidad, in the 1940s that the economic value of enslaved labour to the early development of the industrial economy was really raised in a systematic way.[5] People campaigning against the slave trade and against the use of enslaved labourers on plantations in the United States, the Caribbean and South America actually argued that it was *more* expensive to use enslaved labour than wage labour because they saw it as belonging to an older, feudalistic version of society. And an important part of making that argument was pointing to the existence of slavery in ancient societies in Egypt, Greece and Rome, but also to its existence in 'backward' societies that had not progressed beyond it: in the Ottoman Empire and Africa. Essentially, they said, slavery cannot be part of the modern economy because Africa has slavery and Africa is not modern. But, in fact, the type of slave trade that Africa, Europe and the Americas were engaged in *was* innovative and modern, and was based on a misunderstanding about the role of slavery in African political economy.

And that misunderstanding proved deadly.

◆ ◆ ◆

The Atlantic slave trade was rooted in a commercial bargain that benefited people willing to engage in a dehumanizing traffic. As with a lot of morally dubious human activities, a set of cultural norms had arisen to regulate it over centuries, in Africa as well as in Europe. In ancient Rome, which formed the loose basis for many emerging ideas in the European Renaissance, enslavement was a result of warfare. Enslaved people were then sold around the Roman Empire, but could also buy their freedom, be granted freedom, or rise in the ranks of the military.

A similar form of enslavement existed throughout large parts of western Africa. The collapse of several large West African states in the fourteenth and fifteenth centuries accelerated enslavement as warring successor states made slaves of their enemies and took advantage of a new ready market in the Atlantic, willing to pay well for a growing number of captives.

The Portuguese and Dutch initially observed the slave trade within Africa and thought they had finally found a trade they could get involved with. They had been struggling to find a niche for their own products in Africa. African consumers didn't have any particular interest in what the Portuguese had to sell. The Portuguese wanted to buy African gold, but needed something to trade. They started buying enslaved people and selling them elsewhere along the coast for gold. Soon they began shipping them to the Americas as labourers.

The Portuguese assumed that the African traders were selling 'their countrymen' simply because they had the same skin colour. And that since some people did it, it must be legal. And that if it was legal, and yet so obviously odious, then Europeans shouldn't feel too bad about making money from selling people with obviously backward views of morality.

This was the misunderstanding that started it all. In the sixteenth and seventeenth centuries, there were numerous attempts by some African states to end their involvement in slave-trading. Slavery was legal in most African societies, just as it was across the world. But European traders understood the legality of enslavement within certain circumstances – capture in warfare, practising witchcraft – to mean that all forms of enslavement were legal. European traders interpreted the existence of enslaved people – some of whom had customary rights and could not be sold – as carte blanche for the enslavement of all Africans.

Those African political leaders who did attempt to explain these circumstances were ignored. For instance, a petition from the region of modern Angola in the seventeenth century tried to use Catholic doctrine to end the slave trade.[6] But it was feared that such local attempts to block slave-trading outright could lead to war with European monopoly companies. Leaders who opposed the slave trade found themselves replaced by European-backed coups that put regimes friendly to slave-trading in power. This was the case in eighteenth-century Ouidah (in modern Benin), where a reformist king was thwarted by the slave-trading merchant elite and their European allies. And crucial to this process was the repeated claim that because slavery was allowed in 'Africa', the Europeans were doing nothing wrong by taking advantage of the institution.

Over the course of the next 200 years, despite protests from some African states, the creation of new fortifications to protect against slave raiders and the repeated pushback from the enslaved themselves, European traders stuck to the line that the slave trade, which had become increasingly vital to the expansion of commercial agriculture on the plantations of the Americas, was OK because it was legal in Africa. The Catholic Church was the first – but not the last – to endorse the view that enslavement was actually *beneficial* to the enslaved because they were being taken out of the supposedly barbarous conditions of Africa and introduced to Christianity.

What began as the trafficking of around 500 people a year in the early 1500s grew to 80,000 a year by the end of the 1700s. The Atlantic slave traders didn't simply take advantage of the existing trade in order to export labour to plantations in the Caribbean, and North and South America; they made it into a new gold rush. Competition among the European empires over access to the wealth of the Americas drove the demand for enslaved labour, and a search to make every leg of the new global trade profitable to the different merchants involved. Cities grew up to conduct and direct the trade. New dynasties arose through their control of the wealth that paid for the captives. New institutions and adjacent industries emerged to assist in the financing, insuring and provisioning of ships involved in the 'Triangular Trade' between Europe, Africa and the Americas.

In Africa, new centres sprang up in Saint-Louis and Gorée, the islands off modern Guinea and along the Sierra Leone coast, around the forts at Elmina and the Gold Coast. Trade fuelled the emergence of Bonny and Old Calabar, and the continued role of the Kingdom of Kongo through Luanda and Cabinda. Bristol, London, Liverpool, Nantes, Bordeaux, Cadiz, Lisbon, Barcelona and Amsterdam all owed their growth to the expanding Atlantic trading system. The slave trade was literally building the wealth of the modern world. Both European slave traders and their African counterparts sought to maximize profits and increase their share. And in the second half of the eighteenth century they hit a goldmine.

◆ ◆ ◆

The year was 1780. There was a war raging in the British colonies in North America. This had dented Atlantic trade, but Britain still managed to export over £10,000 worth of goods to the unspecified destination of 'Africa'.

Most of these goods – including wheat flour, beer, cheese, woollen products and biscuits – were intended to provision the forts that had sprung up along the West African coast to house the British traders. These little homes away from home were separate, self-reliant expat communities.

Or at least, that was the idea.

At the fort at Cape Coast Castle, the English trader James Morgue recorded that in 1779 he had spent 324 ounces of gold's worth of trade goods on local purchases and services.[7] In the Gold Coast (modern Ghana) the eighteenth-century explosion of the slave trade had created a thriving local economy.

There had been trade with Europe in this part of Africa since Henry VIII sat on the throne of England. By 1653, Cape Coast Castle had been built by the Dutch West India Company and its African labour force. The English captured the fort in 1664. Over time the gold trade was replaced with the trade in enslaved people, and after 1712 the trade in enslaved people was deregulated by the British government. That deregulation meant that the slave trade was open to any British trader with the capital to participate. The castle, which had started as a national corporate position on the coast, transformed into a bustling urban centre with a dark and inhuman trade at its centre. But, like a lot of dark and inhuman commerce, many of the people benefiting from it were only seeing it in parts: facing the full picture would have – and did – raise objections.

Looking the other way was profitable, and that profit was building a powerful new economy. As early as 1750, the castle employed a great many local people. There were caboceers or 'headmen', linguists, messengers, warehouse-keepers, soldiers, cooks – as well as local merchants providing the meat and rice and oil and water that kept the castle fed and healthy (-ish) in between shipments from England. The English merchants married local women from the Fante and Asante ethnic groups. Their wives provided important commercial links to the trading networks that extended inland, and important connections to the political elites based away from these coastal outposts. The inheritances from their husbands could be shared with children, nephews, aunts and brothers who would invest them in new commercial frontiers.

What is the scale of the kinds of money that were created in these economies? The historian Ty M. Reese says that in 1750 the castle's linguist received payment of £70 annually; the warehouse-keeper received £27; and a soldier received £18. For comparison, a London labourer in the same decade might get something like £15 a year, if they worked continuously.[8]

The 'penyins' of Cape Coast – described by Reese as 'the elected head[s] who represented the family in local and regional affairs' – each received a flask of rum as a weekly payment for allowing the English traders to occupy the fort and undertake trade.[9]

These gifts and payments made an impact on the local economy. Leaders could build up a political constituency by distributing the wealth. More people – attracted to the coast by the potential for trade – meant more power.

African states had increasingly favourable terms of trade in the period – that is, they were able to get increasing amounts of English goods in exchange for the things they were exporting. In the period 1761–70, England brought home more wealth than it spent through world trade. But in the same period, it spent more than it got in Africa. Wealth was accumulating in these coastal places, even as it was being extracted from elsewhere. This was the status quo of the late-eighteenth-century slave trade, one that had been achieved over two centuries of negotiation.

In the second half of the eighteenth century, opening up the West African trade in enslaved people to competition had several effects: it raised the price paid for enslaved people on the coast, as European traders competed with each other for limited supplies; and it lowered the cost of purchasing enslaved people in the British and French American colonies (the traders were still restricted to their own nation's colonies). With the decrease in the cost of labour, sugar prices also fell, making it cheaper and easier to buy sugar in the home markets in Britain and France, and leading theorists like Smith and his French counterpart, Nicolas de Condorcet, to conclude that free trade was better for building the wealth of nations than monopolies, which only benefited the elite.

Free trade had, in fact, been the preference of the *sellers* of enslaved people in Africa. In ports like Ouidah, in the Kingdom of Dahomey (modern Benin), the throne held a monopoly – they were the only sellers of enslaved people. Because of this power they refused to sign exclusive trade agreements with any European buyers, preferring to use competition to drive up the price that European traders would pay for enslaved people on the coast.

The demand for enslaved people grew. Prices on the coast skyrocketed with all the competition among buyers. And all that income meant more public works, more development and more wealth in people. In Dahomey,

When any public work is to be done, such as the erection or repairs of royal buildings, the King summons his Coboceers and portions out the labour among them, paying their people for their trouble. Thus the work is performed with great dispatch. Besides such necessary disbursements, the King pays a considerable yearly tribute, in cowries and merchandise, to his formidable neighbour the King of Eyeo [Oyo]: part of which is defrayed from the contributions levied upon those states which are tributary to Dahomy. The residue of the royal treasure is, upon various occasions, distributed with a liberal hand among the Dahoman grandees, and even among the interior subjects, so that the receipts and expenditure are nearly equal; and the money which flows to the royal coffers, from the King's subjects and vassals, thus circulates again among the people.[10]

Enslaved people provided the labour to build these public works. They were also the exports that allowed governments in Africa to import capital in exchange.

With prices of enslaved people on the coast going up, slave traders encouraged *buyers* of enslaved people in the Caribbean and in North and South America to pay with credit. No money to buy the increasingly expensive people who would produce the sugar? No problem. Simply pay with the next season's harvest, the one those same enslaved people would produce. And why not keep a running tab with a merchant house in London or Bristol or Liverpool or Glasgow? Then you could buy other items on credit too. With increasing demand for sugar, prices were going up all the time. Credit was easy to pay back, and loans could be taken for larger amounts. And with these new credit mechanisms, investment and speculation became commonplace. The commercial finance revolution had begun.[11]

The conditions at Cape Coast Castle, then, were a dynamic response to the market conditions on the coast. It seemed obvious that there was money to be made from the increased demand for enslaved people, both in sales and also in the adjacent industries that grew up around enslavement. In other words, the market was pretty much working the way it should.

♦ ♦ ♦

When Anna Maria Falconbridge arrived in Africa in the midst of this boom period as the vanguard of an abolitionist, humanitarian movement, she and her shipmates were infused with Adam Smith's ideas of the relationship between the economy and government. And Africa seemed to provide them with a perfect case study of exactly how commerce had gone wrong: kings collecting bribes, barter instead of money, and a reliance on enslavement. Clearly, they thought, Africa had a trade problem. And so they set about trying to explain exactly how this problem had made Africa poor and backward.

The focus of these first campaigns against the African slave trade was commerce. The Sierra Leone Company hoped that providing a new avenue for commerce would draw African traders away from the slave trade and towards other trades in order to access the material goods that they had become used to receiving. The idea was that they could find *other* commodities to trade instead. After all, the trade from Africa had started with things like gold and ivory. Why not go back to that?

The problem was the Sierra Leone Company itself, according to Anna Maria Falconbridge. Despite their philanthropic credentials, she complained that they were apparently sending shoddy goods, or things that were of no use. And they were really reluctant to send what was in most demand – guns and alcohol – because they had moral qualms about it. Abolitionists worried that if they traded guns and alcohol, they would fuel predatory states that would then turn to slave-trading. They didn't trust the African traders or leaders they were negotiating with. They couldn't believe they wouldn't use their power in the wrong way.

The abolitionists thought that a bit of a stick to go with the carrot of their new trade would push things along in the right direction. In the midst of the Napoleonic Wars, the British government was more than willing to throw its military weight around. And so the British colonial government in

Sierra Leone set about signing treaties with as many African leaders as it could. The idea with the treaties was that there was some kind of enforcement mechanism: if the signatory failed to protect their people by banning the slave trade, then the British could intervene.

But, as the US discovered in the 1990s War on Drugs in Latin America, this approach isn't particularly effective, especially if there isn't much of a market for the other stuff you might sell instead. Making the slave trade illegal wiped out the value of enslaved people as commodities, at least in the Atlantic, legal trade. And since the growing demand for sugar in Europe had made the demand for enslaved labour so high, the prices of the enslaved people whom Africans had been selling at the end of the eighteenth century had been at a peak: no replacement commodity had so much buying power.

The abolitionists, then, also proposed buying land to set up new model farms to show Africans how to grow the commodities that were in demand at that point – especially sugar. And this is where they ran into the land and labour problem again. Yes, the land seemed to come pretty cheap (although with unexpected complications like those Alexander Falconbridge was trying to iron out), but the labour did not. The labour needed to produce the commodities in demand in the global market was simply diverted from the slave trade. And pretty soon the domestic price of enslaved people was back up again – something that pleased the people who had invested in wealth in people, but which meant that slavery itself was on the rise in Africa itself.

◆ ◆ ◆

Books like Anna Maria Falconbridge's became increasingly popular as people in Britain became more interested in Africa as a continent in need of their help. The slave trade was bad – both morally and, people like Smith and his followers argued, economically – and readers thought that this had created moral and economic underdevelopment, a lack of economic growth, little investment and a precarious existence for many people. In other words, poverty. But, just like the idea of wealth, poverty isn't actually a straightforward concept.

Despite Falconbridge's perceptive observations, she fell into a classic tourist trap of failing to reflect meaningfully on her own society. Yes, wealth in things was the basis on which she expected to be able to assess Temne society. But, as any Jane Austen fan could tell you, wealth in Britain at the time was *more* about wealth in people than Anna Maria was acknowledging.

The marriage market, for instance, was a pervasive economic institution in late-eighteenth-century England. It is easy to see how an advantageous marriage was about building up 'wealth' – in land, mostly, and the returns on that land. It is also possible to see how that wealth was used to accumulate people. It is notable that part of the calculation of wealth in a Jane Austen novel, for instance, was how many servants a family can have on a given annual income. In *Sense and Sensibility*, Marianne Dashwood says she needs to marry someone with £2,000 a year to maintain a household and ensure 'A proper establishment of servants'. In other words, money was for accumulating people, and not just in the British slave economy of the Caribbean.

As Falconbridge recorded in one letter to her friend, the Temne themselves understood how the British wealth-in-people economy worked. An adviser to Pa Bunkie of the Temne warned him that the sudden generosity of the British at Freetown was 'because they think your services will soon be requisite for them'. Having twelve months' experience of the settlement, the Temne adviser commented: 'do you know white men well enough, to be convinced they never give away their money without expecting it returned many fold?' But Pa Bunkie replied that he knew all about gift economies: 'I know they want something,' but he would take the gift anyway. 'I shall not consider the present by any means binding on me.' Only fifteen days earlier, King Naimbana had sent the colonists a 'remarkable fine ox' as a present. Wealth in things and wealth in money could be used to buy people's loyalty and their favours – monetary or otherwise.

Adam Smith might have rejected patronage as an outdated and irrational system of interpersonal relations, but in reality people were still a source of power, family networks mattered, and personal debts and a gifting economy were crucial to the economic development his own country was experiencing.

Take, for instance, links to the settler empire. The historians Andrew Thompson and Gary Magee looked at thousands of records of Post Office remittances – money sent to family back in Britain, like Western Union or (Transfer)Wise today. What they found was that family connections provided money for those who stayed home, and that they advertised investment opportunities in the colonies.[12]

And it only takes a few minutes in the papers of a merchant's archives from the late eighteenth century to see that having family in high places – the Colonial Office, Parliament, or a second cousin by marriage who was a lord – was held out as a lifeline in times of economic hardship. Jane Austen herself was part of the 'pseudo-gentry' who were related to landed gentry but who had to work for a living. Her fictional characters were more than aware of the importance of marriage in establishing – or dooming – the well-being of the wider family.

In fact, this would turn out to be a crucial lesson for Anna Maria Falconbridge. While she had ignored the advice of her relatives in marrying Alexander, the wedding can only have been an astute union for him. The couple were both from Bristol, and while Alexander had very publicly turned against the town's booming industry of slave-trading, Anna Maria's family, the Horwoods, were still involved – and profiting from it. While it was Alexander's relationship to the abolitionist Thomas Clarkson that made his career, it was Alexander's relationship to the slave-trading Horwood family that made his money.

In December 1793, in the midst of her second voyage, Anna Maria wrote to her friend that Alexander had died. But rather than continue on as an unattached widow, she remarried – to another Sierra Leone Company official – within a fortnight. Together they petitioned the Sierra Leone Company for money that was owed to Alexander from his service. But Anna Maria had made snide comments about the company's incompetence, and with her connections to the continuing slave trade their campaign was doomed. They never saw a penny.

Anna Maria Falconbridge was not setting out to write an economic text on Sierra Leone. But in her observations she made the kinds of classic assumptions and misunderstandings

that increasingly fed into a belief in an underdeveloped
and fundamentally different African economy. Instead of
recognizing the similarities in the complicated ways that
Temne and English societies exchanged wealth in people,
money, favours, things and land, she assumed that the king
with holey stockings lived in poverty.

CHAPTER 2

LEARNING TO BE FARMERS

Thomas Fowell Buxton had never been to Africa. In 1839, at fifty-three years old, he knew he was unlikely to go, although, in a letter a few years later, he expressed a wish to visit the Niger River. His career – as the MP responsible for the passage of the Slavery Abolition Act in 1833 – was entering a new phase.

As he sat down in his study in Norfolk to begin work on *The African Slave Trade and Its Remedy*, Buxton was sure that he knew where it had all gone wrong for Africa. Specifically, the slave trade had 'suppressed all other trade' and 'direct discouragement is thrown upon agriculture'. Agriculture, he felt, was the key to solving Africa's problems.[1]

Buxton saw evidence of this need everywhere when he read about Africa. And he read a lot. Once he'd committed to a cause, he would sink his teeth in, staying up late into the night, working and planning. It was this dedication that had led him to victory in the fight to abolish enslaved labour in the West Indies in 1833, or so his future son-in-law thought: 'he spared no pains to achieve his purpose'.[2] His wife worried that he needed respite from all his other responsibilities so that he could focus on this plan for Africa.

Despite the abolition of the slave trade in 1808, and despite the abolition of enslaved labour in British colonies in 1833 (which came into effect the year before he sat down to write), it was clear to him that slavery was still a problem for Africa. And since he felt it was not Britain's fault any longer, he turned to look at what other causes there might be.

What he came up with were descriptions from travellers' accounts of 'negro ferocity' and 'barbarous' slave-dealing chiefs who neglected their people and hoarded wealth. Page after page of the book he was writing was filled with second- and third-hand accounts of gruesome tortures and inhumane treatment of enslaved people by cruel leaders. But what struck him most of all in these accounts were the descriptions of the state of agriculture.

Cultivation of the land is only possible through the security of property, he reasoned, and the slave-raiding that was encouraged by the chiefs who were growing rich from the illegal slave trade was making everyone less secure.

In an area protected by the English, however, he noted that people felt safer and 'betook themselves to cultivating the land, and every available piece of ground was under tillage'. Drawing on the work of travel writers, missionaries and merchants, he painted a picture of fertile Africa, a place both remarkably productive and deeply insecure and neglected. Somewhere, he thought, that could benefit from a bit of agricultural education.

◆　◆　◆

Thomas Fowell Buxton was an unlikely character to be promoting the benefits of agriculture. 'Elephant' Buxton may have been six foot four inches tall, but he was by all accounts a gentle and scholarly man, more at home in a parliamentary debate than in the fields. Born in Essex to a family with some vaguely aristocratic connections, he had moved to Ireland in the belief that he might be due to inherit some land. When that didn't materialize, he stayed in Dublin for university. This hope of a landed inheritance was pretty much the closest that he ever got to agriculture in his life prior to setting pen to paper on his plan for Africa.

Instead of farming he went into business in London, at the brewer's where his uncle was a partner. He lived in London with his wife, the prominent Quaker Hannah Gurney. The two had been childhood friends, and their marriage when he was just twenty-one secured his place in the elite after his Irish prospects didn't pan out. In London they lived, rent-free, in the house set aside as a perk for the director of the Truman, Hanbury and (after he was made a partner in 1811) Buxton Brewery.

But Buxton wasn't satisfied with just being a partner in a successful business. He was in awe of his wife's religious principles. In a letter to Hannah before they married, he wrote: 'I have read in our Bible with the greatest interest and I think I may tell thee I hope with some benefit . . . I must tell thee my love that I believe I may say that I never felt so earnest a desire to correct my faults and to devote myself heartily to endeavouring to improve myself in those things which . . . will contribute to our mutual happiness.'[3] He was drawn to prison reform and other progressive campaigns alongside his business interests. The philanthropies he was involved with were local concerns. His brewery was based in Spitalfields, and Buxton was interested in education and poor relief for those in the area, including out-of-work silk weavers.

Thomas Fowell Buxton, then, was a man of conscience and principle. He associated with the major reformers of the day and was never shy about his convictions. But he was also a man of business.

In 1812, he was travelling when he sent Hannah a note outlining his growing concern that business and charity were not always compatible. Staying with a brewer and his family in Berwick, Buxton wrote to Hannah that he felt 'like Satan admitted unto Paradise, meditating the ruin of this poor woman and her family who perfectly unconscious of any danger treat me with every kindness and attention'. If he had been able to be the master of his own fate, he wrote, 'As far as I am concerned, I would certainly rather endure any loss than distress them. But on the other hand were I to be guided by my feeling and not my reasons, am I acting for myself. Am I not sent to be paid by my partners in confidence that I will do justice to their interests?'[4] The tension between his obligations to humanity and his desire to create efficient economic outcomes was something that would occupy him for the rest of his life.

◆ ◆ ◆

Although Buxton had been involved in charitable works since early in his marriage to Hannah, he first gained fame as an activist when he gave a speech at the Mansion House in 1816 in support of the out-of-work Spitalfields silk weavers. The campaign for the weavers raised £43,000, in part as a result of his activism. William Wilberforce took notice. Buxton's philanthropic star was on the rise.

But what exactly did Buxton hope to do for the silk weavers and workers of London? He wrote about some of his broader plans, and implemented them where he could. In his own brewery, for instance, Buxton encouraged his labourers to learn to read and write. Not entirely sure that the carrot of additional skills was enough, he offered the stick of firing anyone who couldn't read and write after six weeks. He also helped to establish a school for workers' children, subsidizing the fees – though not entirely. The school charged a penny a week in an effort to get parents to value the education they were paying for.

With these philanthropic methods, Buxton took the rationale of business and applied it to improvement: workers needed a mixture of incentives and disincentives to perform labour efficiently. He was in good company in advocating these kinds of approaches in the 1810s and 1820s. But it was about getting the balance right between carrot and stick. And when it came to the Spitalfields weavers, he feared that an earlier generation of workers who had pushed through wage protections had spoiled the industry for the current generation.

The Spitalfields silk weavers had been the beneficiaries of a consumer boom in the eighteenth century. The end of sumptuary laws restricting how people dressed meant that now anyone could buy silk, if they could afford it. Prices for domestically produced silk were high. Rising incomes and the lower cost of living facilitated by global trade, as well as the out migration of many workers to new colonies in the Americas, gave tradesmen an initial boost in their incomes. There was increasing demand for their services and there were fewer people to do the work, particularly with the protection of guilds and with the introduction of tariffs on the import of foreign cloths in the 1690s and 1700s. The Calico Acts of 1700 and 1721 were supposed to protect the domestic textile industry from competition generated by Indian and French imports.

But as the economic historian Robert Allen has shown, the initially large profits to capital investment in domestic industry slowed down with internal competition by the end of the eighteenth century. This was good for consumers – with more competition, the prices went down – but bad for workers. Managers turned increasingly to mechanization and (as the economic historian Jane Humphries adds) child labour to cut costs, increase productivity and keep their profits high.[5]

In the case of the Spitalfields silk weavers, this started to happen in the late eighteenth century. The Spitalfields silk weavers were at the forefront of direct action to try to protect wages in the eighteenth century. Their (often violent) activism in the 1760s and 1770s had resulted in the Spitalfields Acts. After decades of struggle, the weavers had a wage settlement that ostensibly protected them. But there wasn't consensus about whether this was a good thing or not.

For the weavers who were employed, their wages were finally secured. But others found work hard to come by because the smaller shops that would have employed them couldn't afford the minimum wage. And for the shops that decided not to apply the minimum, there were alternative labour markets in the North. They could simply move to where the wages were cheaper.

Various commentators on political economy argued that consumers were being swindled by overpaid workers. Bernard Mandeville, whose famous *The Fable of the Bees* was an early moralist tract on the beneficial role of consumers in spurring economic development, wrote: 'Everybody knows that there is a vast number of Journeyman Weavers . . . who if by four Days Labour in a Week they can maintain themselves, will hardly be persuaded to work the fifth.'[6]

This was where the debate was when Thomas Fowell Buxton got involved in the 1810s. He wanted to improve the workers' conditions, and thought that if the minimum wage was lowered more weavers could be employed again. He also agreed that the workers would be able to afford more in their own lives if the standard of living was improved by reducing tariffs on a wide variety of goods. Making food cheaper, for instance, would allow the workers a higher quality of life without needing to cut into the (apparently) slim margins of the employers.

In the meantime, Buxton raised money and awareness to support the weavers and invested in education as a re-skilling exercise to help the next generation to get better, skilled work. Never mind that silk-weaving had been a skilled occupation: the labour force needed to be flexible and responsive in order to be efficient. And he made the decision, as director of the brewery, to shift to steam power from manual labour.

◆ ◆ ◆

For early-nineteenth-century political economists, discovering the value of a basic unit of labour was fundamental because it informed the bare minimum that labour needed to receive of the price of a good. In other words, how low could prices go and what effect would this have on standards of living?

Adam Smith, for instance, had an argument about how things were priced. His 'labour theory of value' ended up being circular because the prices that consumers paid always had to factor in the price of the labour that the consumer had to perform to get the money to buy the product in the first place. But where did slavery fit in to that? If enslaved people were providing their labour 'for free', then the goods they were producing could be a lot cheaper than if self-employed farmers were producing them and needed to pay themselves.

David Ricardo, the British political economist who sought to refine Smith's theories, wanted the labour theory of value to 'determine the value of the commodity independently of variations in wages'.[7] Ricardo's theory – comparative advantage – explained why trade allowed wealth to accumulate in different societies. Comparative advantage was the idea that countries sold each other the goods that they had a comparative – but not necessarily absolute – advantage in producing. The classic textbook example of Ricardo's theory is about Portuguese–English trade. Portugal could produce its own cloth as well as its own wine. England produced cloth. But by specializing and engaging in free trade with each other, both countries could make and consume more cloth and more wine. The economic historian Thea Don-Siemion once explained this to me in the clearest analogy: if you need to wash dishes *and* cut the grass, and your five-year-old daughter offers to help, giving her the task of washing the dishes increases efficiency and free time to play together when you've both finished your chores, even though you have an absolute advantage in both washing dishes and cutting the grass. So, even if both the West Indies and India produced sugar, India would still end up importing West Indian sugar because the West Indies had a comparative advantage in sugar production because of the efficiency of its enslaved labour.

But political economists were also worried that there were distortions at work. By the nineteenth century, they were concerned that Poor Laws interfered with supply and demand, distorting wages and prices as a result. Across the expanding empire, including in Britain itself, workhouses, Vagrancy Laws and Poor Laws were developed piecemeal from the early seventeenth century, with different local initiatives and national laws to replace the role of the Church in providing alms and account for the increase in wage-dependent workers.

By the late 1820s and early 1830s, at the same time that British lawmakers were debating the abolition of slavery in British Caribbean plantations, they were also considering the reform of the Poor Laws. In both cases, a question sat at the heart of the reforms: who was *really* paying for the cost of labour? How could the government make sure that taxpayers weren't subsidizing their own consumption?

◆ ◆ ◆

In Africa, the resettlement – in places like Sierra Leone, South Africa or Kenya – of African people enslaved into Atlantic captivity created a new urgency to these questions. Refugee policy was virtually non-existent. Government officials, naval officers and missionaries were making it up on the spot.

After 1808, there was a great deal of pride among the British and Americans for their role in the abolition of the Atlantic slave trade. When the French abolished their slave trade after 1815, these countries each believed their interventions were humanitarian and demonstrated the moral superiority of their national projects in Africa. And the welfare of the Liberated Africans whom they 'rescued' from the slave trade was important to them.

But it cost money. The Liberated African Department had charged British taxpayers something like £240,000 between 1818 and 1825, which sounds like a lot, but was only about 0.05 per cent of the annual UK budget, or about sixty pence per person per year – the same as six loaves of bread. So it wasn't particularly onerous, but it was something that people were aware they were paying for. This mostly engendered a sense of national pride, but conservative pro-slavery West India lobbyists responded to increasing attacks on taxpayer subsidies for slaveowners coming from the liberal anti-slavery press by demanding a government investigation into the aid being sent to Sierra Leone.

A Parliamentary Commission of Inquiry was sent out to Sierra Leone in 1825. And in 1827 the commissioners – James Rowan and Henry Wellington – submitted their report to Parliament. They wanted to know, what were Liberated Africans getting for all that money?

The answer was actually not all that much. More than half of the money had been spent on buildings for the Liberated African Department and paying colonial officials.

Administrators' salaries ate up a big chunk. And what was left?

The 'usual clothing given to liberated Africans on their first arrival' consisted of a check shirt, trousers and braces/suspenders, a nightgown for the men and boys, and a gown, petticoat and chemise for the women. But the Liberated African Department official the commissioners interviewed also said that 'much, however, depends on the kind of clothing and the quantity in store'. These refugees from enslavement were also given pots for cooking, tin dishes, spoons, drinking pots, kettles or wooden pails, and 'each male adult also receives a bill hook, a cutlass and a hoe'. In addition, the new settlers received rations of palm oil and rice, as well as some meat, and the commissioners reported that it had become the practice of the government to provide food rations for Liberated Africans 'for at least twelve months *after their dismissal from public employ*' – their emphasis.[8]

The commissioners were very concerned about the rampant spending. Even more, they were concerned that the effect of the free availability of land and the generous allowances were keeping Liberated Africans in a state of happy contentment. The commissioners had interviewed several of the Liberated Africans and had found that 'it is a matter of perfect indifference' to them what their productivity was. 'He can tell that he has eaten one part of his produce, planted another part, and sold the remainder; but by no means the proportions in either gross or in detail,' they complained. And they were concerned that this state of existence would continue 'as long as he can have, free of expense, any extent of land he pleases, and can change it as often as it becomes unproductive'.[9]

If that sounded like an ideal scenario for the Liberated Africans, Rowan and Wellington, the authors of the report, knew that the men reading the report in Parliament would recognize this as a problem. With no method for accounting for the rate of improvement or what might have caused a crop failure, how could these farmers work out their plan for the future? How could the government know what could be taxed? Without knowing the baseline of subsistence, how could anyone work out what was profit?

How did colonial governments in Africa try to work out the minimum subsistence? They experimented with buying and distributing the rations directly. They experimented with outsourcing to non-governmental organizations – to missionaries. In the case of the 1827 ration, they experimented with a cash payment so that Liberated Africans would be responsible for finding their own food and the government wouldn't have to deal with fluctuating food prices.

And they turned to their prison population. Year after year they experimented with what prisoners could live on. In an 1890 government Blue Book of annual statistics, the colonial government in Sierra Leone recorded that a full ration consisted of one and a half pounds of fufu, one pound of rice, two ounces of beef, a quarter-pound of salt, an eighth of a gallon of palm oil and one ounce of green okra. When African prisoners misbehaved they were given half-rations or, in extreme cases, the 'low' ration of three-quarters of a pound of fufu, half a pound of rice, a quarter-ounce of salt and water. The Blue Books often noted that the 'low' ration was not enough to keep the prisoner alive for very long.

The government was providing a form of subsistence-level welfare for the refugees it was resettling and for its prison populations, at least for a short time. But they didn't want to spend so much that they incentivized the wrong kinds of behaviour in Africa or, with the Poor Laws, in Britain.

The implications of this experimentation became clear to businesses as returns on capital investments in the early boom days of any particular business began to decline: how much could a business owner squeeze out of a labour force? What, above and beyond 'subsistence', was profit to the workers?

Knowing the answers to these questions would allow economists to work out things like growth rates. It would allow business owners to account for profits, to figure out the extraction amount and the value added. In other words, quite a lot of the theoretical underpinning of political economy rested on knowing what 'subsistence' looked like.

Adam Smith was concerned that if supply and demand were not allowed to flow naturally, people might consume too much. Or, to put it more bluntly, the *wrong* people might consume too much. In Africa, colonial officials in the first half of the nineteenth century worried that the people they were giving government rations to were not incentivized to work. But equally, observers on other parts of the coast complained about the 'laziness' of the people they met, pointing to the natural abundance of agriculture as leading to stagnation and a lack of work ethic – the same language they used when observing the working poor in Britain's countryside, or the weavers enjoying 'Saint Monday' off from work after an enjoyable weekend.

It became the pressing preoccupation of political economists to work out what contribution the price of labour made to the price of things, and what contribution the price of food made to the price of labour. Was there a way to keep wages down by keeping food prices down? Was there a way to avoid a price–wage spiral, driving up costs to employers? Buxton was particularly interested in this question because he saw that increased costs to employers meant lay-offs, and lay-offs meant more need for philanthropy.

◆ ◆ ◆

As Buxton gained a reputation as a philanthropist, he had his second shot at politics. In 1818, he joined Parliament as MP for Weymouth and Melcombe Regis. He was involved with prison reform, both in Britain and in the colonies. And he brought his increasing interest in overseas philanthropic campaigns with him.

He didn't forget the weavers of Spitalfields, though. In 1823, when the manufacturers brought a petition to Parliament seeking a repeal of the Spitalfields Acts – the ones that protected weavers' wages – Buxton weighed in. The parliamentary record notes that 'Mr. F. Buxton gave the petition his decided support, from a conviction that a compliance with its prayer would tend to better the condition of all connected with the trade, and of none more than the workmen.'[10]

It's hard not to think he may have been influenced not only by his own position as a factory director but also as a member of the new 'Alliance Marine Assurance Company'. This insurance company sold policies 'against the Perils and

Dangers of the Seas and all other Marine Risks', as well as lending money associated with ship repairs and improvements. The petition to remove the Spitalfields Acts – the petition that Buxton endorsed – pointed out that there was enormous room for the growth of the industry as a result of Britain's ability to import raw silk from its colonies in India. Imports of Indian raw silk had grown from 100,000 pounds in 1770 to 1 million pounds in 1820. The logic was staring them in the face: 'access to an unlimited supply of silk from its eastern possessions, an indefinite command over capital and machinery, and artisans whose skill and industry cannot be surpassed' would lead to Britain overtaking France as the world's largest silk manufacturer, if only the government would get out of the way and let wages fall to their 'natural' rate.

The father of comparative advantage was the first to endorse the petitioners in Parliament. David Ricardo noted with 'astonishment' that the Spitalfields Acts 'were not merely an interference with the freedom of trade, but they cramped the freedom of labour itself'. Trade, labour and capital needed to be 'free' to allow the economy to grow.

And this was Buxton's burning conviction in 1839, after a successful career in Parliament, leading the campaign to abolish slavery in the British Empire and compensate Britain's slaveowners for their trouble. As he set pen to paper to write *The African Slave Trade and Its Remedy*, he believed that a good economy was the natural result of good morals. Opening Africa up to commercial investment, agricultural production and the use of free labour would remove the incentives to trade in slaves, would undermine the despotic rulers who took advantage of their citizens, and would lift the continent out of poverty. Having laid out the failures of the abolition of the slave trade to actually stop slavery – slave-trading had dipped down to around 40,000 after 1808, but in 1837 over 103,000 people were trafficked across the Atlantic – Buxton set to work on his solution. He asked: 'Has Africa that latent wealth, and those unexplored resources, which would, if they were fully developed, more than compensate for the loss of the traffic in man?'

But why the emphasis on *agriculture* by a keen industrialist? Why didn't Buxton look at his own success in introducing steam power to the Truman Brewery and think, 'Aha! What West Africa needs is mechanization!'?

He opens the second chapter of his book with two quotations. The second, from the Black founder of the British anti-slavery movement, Gustavus Vassa (now mostly known by his pre-enslavement name, Olaudah Equiano): 'The commercial intercourse of Africa opens an inexhaustible source of wealth to the manufacturing interests of Great Britain.' It was Africa's consumers that most interested Europe's exporters.

Buxton sensed a market for British manufactures. And his vision of economic development was Africa as a vast consumer market. But 'this country [*sic*], which ought to be amongst the chief of our customers, takes from us only to the value of £312,938 of our manufactures'. This was only 7 per cent of what Britain sold to Asia, and only 2 per cent of what Britain sold to America.

What Buxton was perhaps only willing to hint at was that this was a *new* situation. Prior to the abolition of the slave trade, the growth in British imports into Africa was on a par with other world regions beyond the colonies – Africa was 'second only to the American colonies' as an importer of British wrought iron.[11] Cotton check cloth exports to western Africa grew twelve times between 1750 and 1769, when the slave trade was expanding rapidly. When it came to some industries, like arms, Africa had been the major market for British exports during the eighteenth century, representing nearly 50 per cent of the buyers for these specific goods.

In order to catch up, it was clear that Africa needed something new to trade – something other than enslaved people – for those consumer goods that Britain wanted to sell to it. Buxton assumed (from his reading rather than his on-the-ground experience) that African soil was particularly fertile, and so replacing the slave trade with 'the cultivation of her soil' was the obvious solution, not least because it suggested good, honest work; the kind of work that built up habits of forethought and industriousness that he felt Africans lacked as a result of the insecurity of the slave trade. Africa was filled with 'immense tracts of land of the most fertile character, which only require the hand of industry and commercial enterprise to turn them into inexhaustible mines of wealth'. Page after page described the vast wealth of Africa just waiting to be tapped by industrious labour. What were those labourers waiting for?

Property rights. That was the solution Buxton proposed. He argued that 'little more is necessary than to provide security, and convey a sense of security'. And who better to provide that than the might and power of the Royal Navy?

♦ ♦ ♦

Buxton wanted to do more than write a book about his ideas. He wanted action. And so he set out to convince his former colleagues in Parliament to back a plan. The British government would send an expedition up the Niger River to set up a model farm. The farm would produce cotton for export in order to demonstrate to the local residents that they could trade with Britain for the kinds of consumer goods that would make them 'civilized'.

Buxton approached Lord John Russell, an ally in the fight against slavery who still sat in Parliament. Russell became his spokesman in negotiations with the government, meeting with the Prime Minister, Lord Melbourne, and with the Foreign Secretary, Lord Palmerston. Buxton was anxious that the plan be put into action sooner rather than later – he worried that the momentum he had built with the abolition campaign was waning and people were losing interest. Luckily for him, the stars aligned. When Buxton met with Russell in September 1839 the government was supportive, speaking 'in the highest terms of the Buxtonian plan'.[12]

Specifically, Buxton's plan had proposed sending steam boats up the Niger to negotiate new treaties requiring the 'abandonment and absolute prohibition of the Slave Trade' as well as to set up new British bases along the way, for trading British goods for any legitimately produced raw materials. He set up a new organization to push his plans forward, the Society for the Extinction of the Slave Trade and for the Civilization of Africa.

But the real momentum arrived at the start of June 1840, when the society met in Exeter Hall in London. Approximately 4,000 people attended, including Robert Peel, who was then the leader of the opposition in Parliament, and Queen Victoria's husband, Prince Albert, who chaired the meeting.

Buxton argued that the real genius of this plan was that it would help both British workers and Africans: 'Great Britain wants raw material, and markets for her manufactured goods. Africa wants manufactured goods, and a market for her raw material.'[13]

The expedition was approved by Parliament, which set aside £60,000 for building and equipping new steamships, hiring the expeditionary team and purchasing seeds and other goods for the model farm that would be set up along the Niger.

But despite his best efforts, Buxton's plan hit snags. First, the government didn't want to build the boats. They offered to hire them instead. So the society raised the funds to build the boats themselves. Buxton told Russell, 'If you will not buy, we will hire them to you and make money by it.'[14]

After much delay and debate about when to leave for the coast, and what and whom to bring, three little steamer boats manned by a mixed crew of British officers, Sierra Leonean emissaries and skilled Kru sailors from the Liberian coast finally headed up the Niger on 19 August 1841.

The captain of the expedition, Henry Dundas Trotter, wrote a report at the end of August detailing what it had achieved so far. He ended his report with an important note about the first leader – Obi Ossai – with whom they had signed a new treaty. 'We consider it a fact worthy of remark', he wrote, 'that the substance of Obi's frequent interruptions was, that if he abolished the Slave Trade, his people must have some occupation by which to obtain subsistence.' In other words, the people whom Obi Ossai was representing relied on trade. Obi Ossai 'wished plenty of ships to be sent to trade with him'. Trotter and the other British negotiators 'endeavoured to impress upon his mind that trade can only be expected to flow in as the natural effect of demand and supply'. Obi Ossai, 'himself the chief merchant of his territory', found it difficult 'to conceive that, to a sovereign so powerful as he believes our gracious Queen to be, there can be any difficulty in sending as many ships as she pleases'.[15]

Captain Trotter understood supply and demand. He assumed that Obi Ossai didn't. But Obi was, in fact, directly explaining to Trotter the consequences that he knew a lack of demand for his country's produce would cause to the supply of world goods to his people. What good was an alliance with Queen Victoria if she couldn't provide a steady flow of goods? What good was this treaty if it hurt the standard of living of Obi Ossai's people? Ensuring access to global goods was a leader's job.

As the expedition made its way upriver they signed more treaties, purchased some land and planted Mr Carr, the representative from the 'Model Farm Society', at the new area designated for the model teaching farm at the confluence of the Niger and Benue Rivers. But the members of the expedition also began to get sick.

By the end of October – six months after setting out from Britain – the mission was effectively over. Captain Trotter wrote to Russell that 'River Fever' had decimated his crew. The model farm was left with one steamship and the rest returned to the coast, and then back to England. The model farm was abandoned shortly thereafter.

◆ ◆ ◆

At the same time that Buxton was setting out his ill-fated plan for the abolition of enslaved labour in British possessions, another person was thinking about economic development and the problem of the slave trade. Four hundred and fifty miles to the north of the model farm that Buxton's mission established, Mohammed Bello had been making similar plans for agricultural expansion.

Born five years after Thomas Fowell Buxton, in 1791, Bello was the son of the founder of what would become known as the Sokoto Caliphate. From the age of just twenty-six, Bello ruled over a vast territory stretching from modern Burkina Faso to Chad to northern Cameroon, and a population of anywhere between 10 and 20 million people.

Mohammed Bello had to juggle different economic constituencies. The merchants were powerful and rich. 'The caliphate needed the merchants to supply luxury imports, horses, and firearms for the achievement of their core vision of economic independence and prosperity for their people,' the historian Mohamed Salau writes. And 'the merchants primarily wanted the security of a state which could defend their vital interests, which included slave trading'.[16] But the public had supported the establishment of Bello's father's revolutionary government in 1804 because they had a shared loathing of the enslavement of citizens by the previous government. The trick, for Bello, would be to keep the merchants happy while finding new sources of tax income and new markets. He faced the same problem as Obi Ossai: how to replace the slave trade with a different way of paying for the imports that had become part of the modern life of his subjects. If the slave trade had provided the state with income to sustain a certain quality of life for its population, leaders would need to think carefully about how to manage a transition away from the slave trade in order not to lose those economic advantages.

Bello's response to the pressure from the merchants was to set up frontier colonies, populated largely by enslaved people, but he also incentivized immigrant groups with tax exemptions, free seeds and the protection of the state against bandits. They were then set to work producing commodities which could be sold by the merchants in exchange for the goods that they wanted to import into Sokoto.

The foundation of the Sokoto economy was agriculture. Specifically, independent household farms – in other contexts, their proprietors would be called 'yeomen', but in the literature on Africa, they are typically referred to as 'peasant farmers' or 'subsistence farmers'. But the foundation of its export economy was cotton and cotton manufactures. And crucial to the production of that cotton was enslaved labour.

Bello, like a lot of other leaders in slave trade economies, realized that he would need to pivot carefully away from the slave trade without necessarily abandoning enslaved labour, otherwise he risked losing the support of the aristocratic elites who had benefited from the slave trade. Like the British government itself, which abolished the slave trade thirty-one years before the abolition of enslaved labour took effect, Sokoto would attempt to replace the commercial gains of the slave trade with the commercial gains of slave-based agricultural production – at the continued expense of enslaved people.

Thomas Fowell Buxton made a throwaway point a few pages into his book on the economic situation in Africa. 'The chiefs along the Gambia,' he said, 'are now regretting the slaves whom they have formerly sold, as they find that their labour would be a source of greater wealth than the price received for their persons.'[17] The MP responsible for the success of the abolition of enslaved labour in the British Empire didn't object to the repurposing of enslaved people away from the slave trade into what came to be called 'domestic slavery'. And the expansion of 'domestic slavery' had the same impact on the Sokoto economy as it had had on the British Empire: rapid economic development, urbanization, the development of adjacent industries, a growing population and increased wealth for a landowning – and slave-owning – elite.

Over the period from the establishment of Mohammed Bello's government until the arrival of the Niger Expedition, cotton production had increased. In fact, the German visitor Heinrich Barth commented on his visit to Sokoto in the 1850s: 'I was astonished at the great quantity of cotton which was brought into the market.'[18]

Bello died shortly before the Niger Expedition arrived at the edges of his empire. Buxton had promoted the idea of a model farm at the confluence of the Benue and the Niger because it would enable trade with the Sokoto emirates to the north. The expedition, in fact, was intended to travel all the way to Rabba, the port where the British were allowed to trade with Sokoto per an agreement made during the British explorer Hugh Clapperton's 1823 visit to Sokoto. Sokoto had, understandably, wanted to keep Britain at the edge, confined to trading at a specific port. Bello's representatives to Clapperton had specifically refused anything that looked like territorial acquisition or the establishment of new settlements.

When the Niger Expedition turned back, they left the model farm on territory purchased from Sokoto's southerly neighbours with one small steamship and the support of the African sailors who had joined the expedition at Sierra Leone, the Gold Coast and at the mouth of the Niger. The model farm had been equipped with cotton seeds sent with the expedition. The planting and harvesting would rely on the expertise of the Liberian sub-manager, Ralph Moore, who, the historian C. C. Ifemesia notes, 'had learned cotton cultivation on the banks of the Mississippi', where he had been enslaved before he was freed and sent to Liberia by the American Colonization Society.[19] Despite Moore's best attempts with the British-provided seeds, they were eventually able to produce some cotton plants only by using African cotton that they bought from their northern neighbours in Sokoto.

And their neighbours weren't just producing raw cotton either. One traveller noted that the Sokoto city of Kano 'clothes more than half the population' of the region. The historian Mohammad Salau estimates that 'some fifty thousand dyers were engaged at some fifteen thousand dye pits in the Kano area alone by the end of the nineteenth century'.[20] The Manchester of West Africa. What the Niger Expedition found when they arrived in Africa was very different to what they had read in Thomas Fowell Buxton's books. Rather than a chaotic, war-torn countryside, with no industry to speak of, they found cotton plantations and prolific cloth production.

The Niger Expedition's Captain Henry Dundas Trotter brought back samples of Sokoto cotton which he donated to the British Museum: cotton thread, cotton cloths, cotton bags. He brought back silk cocoons, raw silk thread samples and silk headbands. The silk weavers of Spitalfields might have needed Buxton's charity, but the silk weavers of the Niger did not.

◆ ◆ ◆

Sokoto's slave-based cotton production thrived. And while imports of cheap British textiles grew in the second half of the nineteenth century as a result of a boom in the new coastal palm oil trade, they never really replaced the higher-quality, Sokoto-made cloths in regional markets.

It turned out that Sokoto could do large-scale agricultural production just fine, in a model that had suited the British – plantation production fuelling urbanization and industrial growth – without the well-meaning interventions of Thomas Fowell Buxton. But the development model that worked for both Britain and Sokoto was one based on enslaved labour.

Just up the Niger from the model farm, the Emirate of Bida was beginning a new type of plantation development. Usman Zaki, whom Captain Trotter tried and failed to visit in Rabba, had begun the development of *tungazi* – described by different sources as 'slave villages' or 'plantations' – which grew from fifty at the time of the Niger Expedition to 744 by 1873, largely under the leadership of Zaki's successor, and with the enslavement of large numbers of captives from the region to the south of Bida. And by the end of the nineteenth century Britain was in a position to do something about that.[21]

In July 1890, at the Brussels Conference, Britain argued that finally ending the slave trade and enslaved labour in Africa was the duty of the European powers that had signed the 1885 Berlin Agreement to divide up Africa among themselves. The Brussels Act bound signatories to 'put an end to the Negro Slave Trade by land as well as by sea, and to improve the moral and material conditions of existence of the native races'.

The person who would see to it that Sokoto ended slavery was not Buxton but Frederick Lugard. Lugard was a product of the British Empire, born in India in 1858 to a British Army chaplain and his wife, the daughter of landed gentry. By the time he arrived in Nigeria he had served in the army in the Second Anglo-Afghan War (1878–80), the Sudan campaign (1884–5), the Third Anglo-Burmese War (1885) and the Karonga War (1887–9), and had established the British administration in Uganda.

In 1894, 'the Sultan of Sokoto expressly recognised the Royal Niger Company' in a trade treaty. But only a few years later, in 1901, Lugard sent a messenger to the sultan explaining that the Royal Niger Company had since been taken over by the government and therefore that the treaty was now with the British Government.[22] This was poorly received. Mr Alfred Emmott, the MP representing Oldham in Lancashire, the heart of Britain's cotton textile industry, was concerned on behalf of Lancashire 'and other industrial centres trading with West Africa' that 'nothing of a hostile or unfriendly nature to Sokoto or Kano are intended'.[23] Despite reassurances, Lugard proceeded with a military campaign that destroyed Sokoto and incorporated the territory into British Nigeria.

Lugard justified the conquest of Sokoto, writing that 'the advocates of conciliation at any price who protest against military operations in Northern Nigeria' – people like Mr

Emmott and the Lancashire cotton lobby – 'appear to forget that their nation has assumed before God and the civilised world the responsibility of maintaining peace and good order'. Lugard saw his role as 'one of prevention of the daily bloodshed which has already denuded this country of probably half its population'. Lugard was made High Commissioner of the Protectorate of Northern Nigeria.

Ironically, Lugard later regretted his conquest of Sokoto. By 1922 he had published one of the most famous tracts in British colonial history, *The Dual Mandate in British Tropical Africa*. This book argued that in order to promote economic development, Britain needed to restore the authority of local elites. While he had come riding in as a saviour of the enslaved people living and working on Sokoto's plantations, he eventually realized that Sokoto's economic power had derived from the exploitation of these people. And while not exactly supporting a return to slavery, he articulated the fundamental problem of British economic intervention in Africa: who was it for?

Lugard came back to the agriculture question and repeated Buxton's belief that 'the problem of labour education is how to make greater use of the labour supply'. And, completing his 180-degree turn on the Sokoto Caliphate, Lugard proposed 'a scheme of colonisation by immigration from congested districts' to 'offer every inducement for cotton-growing' – the same model originally implemented by Mohammed Bello and the same group of aristocrats who originally benefited from Bello's plans.[24]

◆ ◆ ◆

In 1842, Thomas Fowell Buxton spent several frantic months trying to rescue the reputation of the Niger Expedition. He met with his old allies, wrote to friends, tried to get copies of *The African Slave Trade and Its Remedy* circulated far and wide. But it was not to be. The expedition already had critics – both free traders who worried that the government might interfere with their profit margins, and British workers who balked at £100,000 (the final cost) being thrown down the Niger. But few had objected on the basis that, actually, Africa's agricultural sector was doing just fine, thank you very much.

The project failed for any number of reasons – bad timing, disease, lack of personnel. All of these would be taken into account when the British tried again half a century later. But the real failure would stay the same because the 'remedy' that Buxton proposed solved a problem that didn't exist. The area around the Niger had plenty of commercial agriculture and it had an impressive amount of economic development. It also had stark economic inequality, and its development – like Britain's – relied on enslaved labour. But when Lugard arrived to 'civilize' and improve the region in 1901 he found that his plans for economic development replicated the exact policies that were already in place.

CHAPTER 3

GETTING PEOPLE BACK TO WORK

'No one wants to work any more' is a refrain that might sound familiar to our modern ears. But it would have also been familiar in 1846. A settler in South Africa wrote in that year that he was frustrated by the workers he had hired to his farm. He had expected that if he contracted someone to work 'for a specified time' and 'at a given rate of money wages', he had 'a right to the services of those persons, until the time expires'. It became increasingly clear, with the abolition of the slave trade, that the problem of the African economies, as far as Europeans were concerned, was one of labour.[1]

Missionaries who came to Africa to preach and convert also arrived with a sense of their role in economic development. They hoped to help Africans learn to be industrious workers after the slave trade had destroyed their productive economies. They wrote helpful dictionaries to get employers and employees speaking the same language. They set up missionary schools to train the next generation of workers. And they were frustrated by economic realities at every turn.

As slavery gradually came to an end in the Americas between the 1830s and 1860s (finally ending in Brazil in 1888), political economists in Europe began to fret about how to incentivize formerly enslaved workers. Many moderate abolitionists had argued that the economic case for ending slavery was that enslaved labour was more expensive than free workers. Enslaved people were 'idle' for parts of the year and had to be supported in childhood, sickness and old age, while free labourers could just be paid a market rate for the labour they were performing for their employer. It was a bit of a shock when this didn't turn out to be true. Enslaved labour was much cheaper.

Unsurprisingly, people preferred to work for themselves rather than for demanding and capricious bosses. To lure them back into working for someone else would have required higher wages than employers were willing to pay. But rather than being accepted as a bald economic fact, 'no one wants to work any more' was dressed up as a moral failure. British thinkers Thomas Carlyle and John Stuart Mill debated whether or not African workers were inherently lazy.[2] British and French colonial administrators justified the use of compulsory labour in Africa by arguing that African workers were idle or unwilling to work for low wages. Understanding, predicting and correctly pricing labour productivity became an important part of models for governing and 'improving' Africa.

♦ ♦ ♦

In Chapter 1 we encountered the arguments about the ratio between land and labour. Part of this model was related to the idea that in a subsistence economy there is no incentive for waged labour: everyone has land and can make do with what they produce themselves. What you need in order to catalyse wage labour is debt or scarcity. This was what the agrarian historian of Europe Folke Dovring noticed when he pointed out that in Russia, whenever serfs started to improve their standard of living above subsistence, landlords responded by raising rents to capture that extra income.

But in places where there had been slavery, the abundance of land and scarcity of labour – which had induced the economic 'need' for slavery in order to make an extractive profit in the first place – meant that there was no natural land scarcity as an incentive. Of course, land monopolization by a small elite of planters could serve the same function, but this could also backfire into just owning an unproductive asset if migration away from that land was possible. Low land costs could lead to high labour costs. This specific relationship between the prices for land and labour later came to be known as the Nieboer–Domar hypothesis after the Dutch ethnographer and the MIT economist who later refined the idea, but it was first articulated by Edward Gibbon Wakefield in 1849.

Wakefield – a British political economist who rabidly supported colonization, particularly in Australia and New Zealand – was a strange guy. He wanted desperately to be rich, something that his middle-class job as a civil servant didn't provide. So he eloped with an heiress. When she died and he didn't get the full value of her estate, he tried to kidnap another underage heiress.

Remember back to Anna Maria Falconbridge and the concept of wealth in people? How it wasn't as cut and dry as 'Europe: wealth in land; Africa: wealth in people'? Our man Wakefield was trying to improve his status by snatching girls of high status. He was attempting to access wealth in status and wealth in things through the people he was attaching to himself.

Fortunately for the heiress, his plan was foiled and he spent the next few years in jail. During this time he penned essays in support of colonization. He believed that sending British workers to colonize other places was a necessary safety valve for a dangerously overpopulated, and therefore underpaid, British workforce. After leaving prison for his kidnapping attempt, Wakefield travelled around the settler empire and ultimately became an MP in New Zealand, where he continued to promote the immigration of new settlers.

Others had also noticed what Wakefield articulated. Wakefield's writing was regarded as an important contribution to political economy by the famous philosopher and India Office specialist John Stuart Mill. One South African settler reported that while land was not particularly expensive, 'English servants obtain a rate of wages slightly higher than they could in England' and he encouraged 'domestic servants, and young, active out-door labourers' as well as 'a good many female servants, such as cooks, housekeepers, and nurses' to emigrate.[3] High wages were what made colonization attractive to the 60 million or so Europeans who left the continent in the nineteenth century.

Labour shortages can lead to a variety of outcomes. As Herman Nieboer and Evsey Domar would go on to suggest, the land–labour ratio is neither a necessary nor a sufficient condition for slavery's emergence in a particular place or time.[4] European colonists hoped for one of those outcomes: high wages. Other outcomes in other places and times included the cultural removal of particular forms of labour from the marketplace. Household labour in a lot of contexts is unpaid simply because the weight of the cost would collapse the market-based consumer economy. Childcare provided through the marketplace also suffers this problem. And in other contexts, labour shortages can incentivize wealthy and powerful people into forms of coercion and the enslavement of labour.

Another set of scholars working much more recently used a vast data set to understand living standards across a number of British colonies in Africa during this period. Marlous van Waijenburg and Ewout Frankema worked with a set of annual sources created by the colonial administrators. These so-called 'Blue Books' were pro forma administrative tools, meant to allow the Colonial Office to track economic development across the empire. They consist of a whole range of categories, including wages. And it was wages that these scholars used to try to understand where African workers fitted in the global standard of living. They created a consumer price index made up of a standardized basket of goods that reflected the bare-bones minimum that workers could survive on so they could determine the real wages of unskilled urban male workers from 1880 to 1965. What they found would not have surprised anyone attempting to recruit labour in Africa at the time. They found that wages were 'well above subsistence level, rose significantly over time, and were, in some places, considerably higher than in major Asian cities'.[5] What their research confirms is the argument that Wakefield made: abundant land and scarce labour made it expensive to pay workers in Africa.

◆ ◆ ◆

For white settlers in South Africa, faced with the high wage demands of workers who didn't really need their employment offers, stricter and more violent ways of coercing labour by taking away access to land seemed like a good solution.

But beyond the practical economic basis for high wages there were more surprising problems at work in shaping the argument about 'laziness' and wage labour in colonial Africa. The South African farmer at the start of this chapter sets out a problem that the historian Keletso Atkins examines in her book (with possibly the best title in the history of publishing) *The Moon Is Dead! Give Us Our Money!*. The problem, as Atkins lays it out, is that there were different and competing understandings of time at the heart of the contract, and this led to conflict which fed into and supported the stereotype of 'lazy' African men. In isiZulu the *inyanga* was a lunar month of twenty-eight days. In English and in Afrikaans the month or *maand* was between twenty-eight and thirty-one days. And so, in 1855, a frustrated missionary noted that employees would turn up before the end of the month to demand their wages because 'they cannot understand there being more than 28 days in a month. It is impossible to make them believe there are 31.'[6] As in so many other cases, this was a misunderstanding of the economic context. In South Africa, where industrialists and farmers were exasperated with their workers giving up before the end of the month, they neglected to realize that contracts for 'a month' would mean different things to workers operating on the lunar calendar and employers using a solar calendar.

In sugar plantations in Natal, South Africa, meanwhile, managers complained that they could not get workers who would put in the hours needed to process the sugar cane during harvest time. Zulu workers were used to labouring from an hour after sunrise to an hour before sunset, but 'it is difficult either to induce or compel [them] to work either before or after'. This created a problem for sugar production, since it needed continuous labour during the winter months, when the Zulu work day would be about eight and a half hours (as opposed to the summer's twelve hours). But again, this wasn't really a problem of discipline or laziness. It was a problem with the introduction of a particular commodity that had been developed for global markets in conditions of enslaved labour, where workers were compelled by force to work all night. Free workers would not compete with that.

Worse, the methods adopted by employers to try to enforce time discipline just ended up chasing labour out of the market. People understandably preferred to work for themselves rather than for managers who beat them for not adhering to European notions of time. But were these really even 'European' notions of time, or just the employers' imposition?

In a classic article on time and its relationship to industrialization in Britain, the historian E. P. Thompson gives some ethnographic examples drawn from anthropologists in Africa and the Pacific in the mid-twentieth century to show that modern notions of 'time' are imposed on older ways of counting and measuring the passage of time. In one example, an anthropologist explains that daily time is measured among the Nuer in Sudan as organized by the succession of daily agricultural tasks.[7] And, as the title of Atkins's book suggests, when the 'moon is dead' (i.e. the month is over), South African labourers expected payment for the time they thought they had agreed to work – regardless of the arbitrary number of days in their employers' month.

But notions of time were sticky, and not just in Africa. Thompson explains that in the early twentieth century another ethnographer visited the Aran Islands, off the coast of Galway, Ireland, and 'when I tell them what o'clock it is by my watch they are not satisfied, and ask how long is left them before the twilight'.

Of course, how labour is valued has as much to do with place as time. Conventions about how that time is divided up are remarkably persistent. The hour has come to dominate most work in post-industrial economies, while monthly calculations are reserved for salaried employees. The minimum wage in Canada varies by province and ranges between Can$11.81 and Can$16 per hour. And in Britain the minimum wage is based on four age sets, ranging from £6.40 for under-eighteens per hour to £11.44 for those over twenty-three. But in other places the month has continued to be the measure of a labour contract. The minimum wage in Angola is measured by months – the equivalent of US$61 per month – and is paid thirteen times a year. Guinea-Bissau legislates the equivalent of US$30 a month plus a bag of rice. And in South Africa in the second half of the nineteenth century the day rate was in competition with the monthly rate, with neither measure of time quite matching what the two parties to the contract meant.

◆　◆　◆

Embedded in the designation of a 'pre-industrial' understanding of time is a value judgement that suggests that some ways of understanding 'time' are better than others and that pre-industrial 'time' was primitive and backward. And in both formulations, the implication is that modern industrial time has been related to the take-off of Western economies. The idea of the 'Protestant work ethic' is tied to religion for a reason: the relationship between money and time is linked through morality.

Although Catholic missionaries had been going to Africa for centuries alongside the Portuguese colonial officials operating in Angola, it was only with the abolition movement that new, independent Protestant missions began to arrive in large numbers: the Church Missionary Society, the Basel (Switzerland) Mission, German Moravian missionaries, the London Missionary Society, the Baptist Missionaries, the Wesleyan Missionary Society, the multi-denominational American Board of Commissioners for Foreign Missions. From the get-go, these comprised individuals who were deeply ambivalent about Europe's role in Africa. They felt a strong sense of guilt and responsibility for the slave trade. They felt obliged to help the victims of the trade because they saw their own governments as responsible, in part, for the degraded state of Africa. And they weren't wrong about that.

But they came to do more than preach the Gospel. They wanted to teach the Protestant work ethic too. In 1885, in Anne Isabella Thackeray Ritchie's novel *Mrs Dymond*, the proverb 'Give a man a fish and he will eat for a day, teach a man to fish and you will feed him for life' appeared in print for the first time. Ritchie, the author of the fish proverb, was not an economist. Her novel, serialized in *The Cornhill Magazine*, was unlikely to have been the first place the phrase had appeared – it is taken for granted in the dialogue, suggesting it was in wider circulation. And just like the phrase, the author's views and her audience were broadly representative of the popular middle-class ideas of the economy in circulation at the time of the Scramble for Africa.

Ritchie was the daughter of William Makepeace Thackeray, the famous author of *Vanity Fair* and a one-time Liberal candidate for Parliament. Her family were steeped in connections to the empire – India, in particular, but also the abolition movement. Her brother-in-law and editor at *The Cornhill Magazine* was Leslie Stephen, who was the son of the anti-slavery activist James Stephen. James Stephen had been crucial in drafting the 1833 Slavery Abolition Bill in his role as Colonial Secretary. He then went on to become the Regius Professor of History at Cambridge and to hold Thomas Malthus's economics chair at the East India Company College. Leslie Stephen's mother was Jane Catherine Venn, daughter of the founder of the Church Missionary Society. These humanitarians saw Britain's mission in the world as bringing economic and moral education that would enable other people to become like they were. The emergence of the fishing proverb into popular fiction was a good reflection of this group's view of their mission in the world. This wasn't exactly high intellectual economic thought, but it was widespread and influential.

The author Mary Kingsley, for instance, carried the spirit of Anne Ritchie's proverb with her on her first trip to West Africa in 1893, at the age of thirty-one. After a second trip in 1895 she published two books – *Travels in West Africa* (1897) and *West African Studies* (1899) – which were popular and made her a regular on the speaking circuit in Britain.

Mary Kingsley was a product of the industrial age. European economists had worked out the best, most efficient ways to organize a society, and it was Europe's responsibility to bring this knowledge to Africans. Technical improvement and training for the modern economy, though, was not about preparing African workers for the knowledge economy or the division of labour celebrated in Smith. It was about fulfilling the promise of David Ricardo's 'comparative advantage'. The Africans who participated in missionary education were supposed to understand that they were on a *gradual path* to improvement, but that they shouldn't expect to run before they could walk. Kingsley and other observers saw the emergence of Ghanaian lawyers and Nigerian bishops and Liberian statesmen and Sierra Leonean intellectuals as odd when so many of their compatriots were still living 'backward' lives. Since it was intervention from outside the continent that had created this inequality, it was probably outsiders' responsibility to fix it too. Missionary education was all well and good, but was it *practical*? As Kingsley complained, 'Alas! None of the missions save the Roman Catholic teach the thing that it is most important' they should learn: 'namely, improved methods of agriculture, and plantation work'.

But why was this inequality a problem in Africa when similar rates of inequality existed in Britain? The spread of industrialization and the improved standard of living that cheaper consumer goods brought with it had created a new problem for political economists to explain and solve: who was going to do the work within the modern economy? Unskilled labour was fast being outsourced to other regions of the world, but there were not enough people to fulfil the demand for semi-skilled labour that remained. Meanwhile, there were people living in poverty and underemployment despite the demand for semi-skilled work. The rise of technical schools was a policy solution targeting these problems.

This might all sound familiar: coding academies aimed at inner-city schools, pressure for universities to focus on producing STEM graduates, concern that 'people' are getting useless degrees in gender studies or literature. In the late nineteenth and early twentieth centuries, policymakers worried that there were too many people with rudimentary missionary education (literacy, numeracy, but also philosophy and ethics and argumentation) and not enough people with an education in modern agricultural techniques or machine repair. In Britain, this coincided with increased concern that many of the skilled and competent men who made up the lower-middle classes were departing – as Wakefield had advised – for places like Australia, Canada, South Africa and the US, where they would have more opportunity to farm their own land or run their own businesses, rather than working for factory bosses or as skilled farm labourers in Britain.

But these particular concerns about education were also tied up with the challenges of social mobility created by economic improvement. It was one thing for the son of an earl to study theology and become a bishop. But if the son of a wealthy entrepreneur did so, was that disrupting the social order? Social mobility implied improvement, but unless social rules were put into place to keep everyone within their class then economic improvement for the working class could mean social decline for the upper class.

Mary Kingsley took these domestic debates about the standard of living and class identity with her and saw West Africa through these eyes. While certain levels of wealth and accumulation were unseemly to Kingsley, she believed that the goal of the civilizing mission should be to bring different classes into parity with their British counterparts. In other words, economic intervention should improve the quality of life, but shouldn't disrupt class systems. Economic improvement was different from social mobility.

And so while Europeans were encouraged to move to Africa in search of high wages, Africans were taught to expect low wages. The economic historian Pim de Zwart carried out research showing that in South Africa between 1835 and 1910 the standard of living for white residents increased while it stagnated for Black and coloured people. Skilled jobs were reserved for white people, unskilled labour for Black and coloured people.[8]

◆ ◆ ◆

Missionaries were not blind to these developments. They were involved in pointing out the callous and overly arbitrary forms of labour violence by unscrupulous European merchants.

At the Berlin Conference that initiated the Scramble for Africa in 1885, King Leopold II of Belgium had proposed a 'Free State' along the Congo River. The other colonial powers had gone along with it for a few different reasons. This new territory promised continued access for their own firms because it would operate on the principles of free trade. It would also cool tensions between France and Britain, which had been rising across the 1870s as they competed for new territorial acquisitions and exclusive trading rights. Leopold's intervention was welcomed as a means of preserving free access to the Congo and all that it promised, while diplomatically dealing with the Anglo-French rivalry.

Leopold also went on to host the Brussels Conference in 1890, discussed in the previous chapter, which set out a new campaign against the Central African slave trade. It justified colonial expansion on the basis of finally ending the slave trade and improving the 'moral and material conditions' of African peoples.

Missionaries arrived in Congo to ensure that 'moral' improvement accompanied the material improvement that they believed trade would bring. They soon became concerned about what they witnessed on the ground. The draconian policies of the European rubber companies revealed the exploitative nature of European colonization. It turned out that the abundant wild rubber growing across Central Africa was particularly labour-intensive to extract. This made it more expensive and less productive than Asian plantation-grown rubber. Leopold decided to establish a *Force Publique* to drive up labour efficiency through threats of inhumane treatment of the Congolese population. They tortured, maimed and killed Congolese men, women and children in pursuit of rubber.[9]

Missionaries were at the forefront of documenting and publicizing the atrocities taking place. The major objections to King Leopold's rule in the Congo Free State at the turn of the century, though, focused on the *quality* of the Europeans involved rather than the ultimate project they were all engaged in. It was generally agreed that part of the moral and material uplift of the colonial project was helping Africans to 'understand' rational economic behaviour. Profits were obviously the point of colonialism. It was just that usually there was another point as well: the improvement of Africa and the development of its economy. Notably, very little objection was raised to other forced-labour projects across Africa.

The argument against Leopold's rule in Congo was not framed as an anti-imperial crusade. Instead, many people – from the Black American missionary Reverend William Shepherd, to the Irish soldier Roger Casement, to the English shipping clerk E. D. Morel – sought to remove Leopold's power and place it in the hands of the Belgian government. But they did not stop there; they went further, seeking to reform imperial governance and use the tools of transnational imperial cooperation to restrain the greedy impulse of rampant capitalism. Imperial power didn't need to be abandoned, they argued, it just needed to be focused on improvement rather than exploitation. And while missionaries were crucial to ending Leopold's reign of terror, the outcome – handing the Congo Free State over to Belgian governance – promised little improvement for Congo's people. But for the campaigners against Leopold's rule this was the best possible outcome. The Belgian state could now make Congo a profitable investment rather than purely asset-stripping it.

♦ ♦ ♦

Missionaries, then, consistently saw their role as moderating European commercial excesses. They took that role seriously. In South Africa, they provided the dictionaries that translated from isiZulu into English and Afrikaans, signalling the importance that the *morality* of time use would take on. Employers and employees were often at odds because of these dictionaries. A British South African settler wrote in 1848 of the missionaries that 'every one must appreciate the good intentions of the really conscientious members of the mission', but objected to their presence on mission stations set up near settler farms, since servants, 'discontented or hopelessly lazy', had a tendency to leave employment for 'the nearest station, where he can indulge in the greatest luxury'.[10]

The missionary dictionaries had more functions than simply translating words and concepts. Missionaries were also trying to instil an industrious Christian work ethic in the Africans who spent time at their mission schools and Sunday schools. The missionaries also wanted to forewarn any European heading out to Africa with a dream of colonial riches – land is so much cheaper than in Europe! – that there was a corollary: labour was not.

Missionaries ended up advising the route to 'labour discipline' that had played out in industrializing Europe over the course of the seventeenth and eighteenth centuries. Land should be made private; labourers should be encouraged into employment through high rents, consumer debts and taxes, which would teach them the value of money and therefore of time. Missionaries in South Africa wanted their converts to 'feel the propriety and necessity of forming habits of industry and frugality'. In East Africa, at a missionary station set up for people fleeing enslavement, the head of the Church Missionary Society complained that those who were going to work for other Europeans were learning bad habits and the colony as a whole should promote the standards of work discipline (including whipping) used by the missionaries. In Sierra Leone, the Church Missionary Society Temne vocabulary also reported that *Yóna* (*yo*) was the term for work. In various examples of how this phrase might be used there is a glimpse of the European view of Freetown's economy in the nineteenth century. The author gave the example of '*yor mapant*' ('pretend to do work'), a phrase it might be useful for an employer to be able to accuse a worker of.[11]

But there were other visions for the moral relationship between money and time. In Algeria, North Africa, the sociologist Pierre Bourdieu's mid-twentieth-century observations that 'Haste is seen as a lack of decorum combined with diabolical ambition' and that a clock is known as 'the devil's mill' suggest morality at work in trying to *enforce* or create the appropriate behaviours within society.[12]

While European missionaries in Africa were suggesting that there was only one modern approach to hard work, there are plenty of still-active English proverbs that hint at a different perspective. The old proverbs 'Haste makes waste' or 'A stitch in time saves nine' do not, for instance, suggest that you should go home and take a nap. They suggest care and attention to detail, but also that such slow, careful attention will save you time in the long run. While there was plenty of moralizing in the new economic logic of money and time, there were – in Europe and across Africa – coexisting moralities cautioning against the pursuit of wealth and miserly overwork. Charles Dickens's *A Christmas Carol*, for instance, was first published in 1843 and by the end of 1844 had already been printed in thirteen editions. Dickens's Scrooge is the quintessential miser, who has turned the virtue of hard work into a vice by refusing to allow his employees time off for a holiday he didn't want to celebrate.

◆ ◆ ◆

In South Africa, where Zulu morality dictated that no work was done after nightfall, and that the day without a moon was the sacred day when no work was done, South African labourers found themselves in trouble with the Christian missionaries for working on the Sabbath. They ultimately faced a strictly imposed curfew at night to prevent domestic servants from leaving the houses where they were working to take on extra night work in the port. Their hustle for more income made European employers wary: if workers had more than one source of income, if they were working hard on the side, then they might earn enough to set themselves up in business. They might not *need* to work for European employers any more, even with increasing restrictions on land ownership. It was, after all, hard work *for someone else* that the missionaries were trying to teach.

But while Europe's Christian missionaries tried to solve the labour problem with a particular view of the relationship between time and money, the Islamic Mourides in Senegal were inventing their own development solutions, which attempted to solve several problems at once.

The eastern region of Senegal (referred to by the French colonialists as 'Western Sudan') had been the site of political upheavals since the late eighteenth century, when revolutionary leaders had attempted to set up new states governed by the laws of Islam. Across the nineteenth century, the coastal regions, which traded with and were ultimately annexed by the British and the French, had been in a tense relationship with the more secular kingdoms in the continent's interior and the Islamic states beyond that often led to outbreaks of war. It was in this context that the Mouride Sufi movement was started by Shaykh Amadou Bamba (1853–1927) in 1883. Among other things, the religious order promoted peanut agricultural exports. Students of the brotherhood devoted themselves to a spiritual guide, learning from him and doing unpaid agricultural labour on his behalf for ten years, after which they received a share of the brotherhood's land. And it was startlingly successful in absorbing labourers, educating them in both Islam and in agriculture, and in transforming Senegal's economy.

The Mouride brotherhood absorbed labour, built training into their model, but also delivered upward mobility to its adherents in ways that European models never managed. And that promise of upward mobility made the brotherhood enormously politically popular. Just one photo of Bamba exists. He is swathed in white, with only his eyes and nose showing. The image, taken in 1913, can be found graffitied on walls across Senegal today. The French, who started off *very* sceptical of Bamba – exiling him for most of his life – eventually came round to his way of doing things when they realized what a successful model his brotherhood had turned out to be. Did they learn anything from this? Of course not. They continued to think their experts had all the answers about economic growth.

In British colonies, similar transformations of cash crop agriculture had been driven by the African producers rather than by British innovation. Sierra Leone's merchants had fanned out across the West African coast, setting up trading partnerships in Gambia, the Gold Coast, Nigeria and the Cameroons. Competition between Senegalese traders and Sierra Leonean traders for the groundnut crops grown on the upper reaches of the Rio Nunez in modern Guinea drove prices up, and agriculturalists responded to the increased demand. By the 1870s, the price for groundnuts had climbed to new heights and Sierra Leone's and Senegal's Black mercantile population were able to start investing their returns in other capital projects, secure credit and, possibly most importantly, send their children to school and university. A whole generation of Black lawmakers, doctors, ministers and schoolteachers had emerged as second-generation wealth made their social advance possible.

But this growth was built on a shaky foundation. The slave trade had been abolished, which left international traders with little collateral to claim. While Buxton's idea had been the establishment of property rights, and while it was clear that agriculture was taking off, land was still not really something that could function as collateral for itinerant European traders with no local rights. A South African settler wrote in the 1840s, for instance, that the low value of land had 'lately rendered it almost impossible to raise money on land at all'.[13]

When new agricultural commodity trades finally picked up in the 1860s, replacing the slave trade as a source of African export income, new investors piled in. International traders were getting high prices for palm oil from West Africa, for Senegalese peanut products, and for cotton from Egypt and Nigeria – particularly after the outbreak of the American

Civil War. But the price boom was short-lived. The export merchants, who had financed growth with debt in the boom years, found themselves in financial hardship when commodity prices contracted in the Long Depression that began in 1873.

When the economy crashed, as it did in 1873, European trading firms found that they had very little recourse for recovering their loans in Africa.[14] They called on their European governments to bail them out, and those governments turned to their old standby, treaties – in particular, treaties giving European companies the right to another form of collateral to ensure that their debts could be recovered: land. What had previously been an abundant resource could now be restricted. The Europeans began their land grab.

◆ ◆ ◆

One problem facing new colonial governments was the relationship between getting cheap-wage workers and improving subsistence conditions. In the decades immediately following the partition of the continent and the divvying up of land after the Berlin Conference in 1885, it was fairly straightforward to generate low-wage work through the introduction of taxes and vagrancy laws. The historian Frederick Cooper describes this as 'small islands of wage labour, dependent on the poverty' of the surrounding areas.[15] The push of young men into a migrant labour force to work in cities, mines and on white people's farms made it 'theoretically possible for employers to pay workers less than the true social cost of their subsistence', leaving it to 'the unpaid labour of women . . . to subsidize the raising of children and care of the elderly'. This was the dream workforce that the missionaries had tried to create.

Direct taxation of the newly occupied territories was the immediate priority for arriving administrators, who were directed from London that there was 'no hope of development, unless we retain the power and practice of direct taxation'.[16] But the instability of West and Central Africa during the nineteenth century had been the result of the shift from the indirect trade taxation that had characterized the slave trade to more direct taxation of the population as the slave trade waned. Across the region, people had felt exploited by this and had chosen to migrate to other places, or to follow revolutionary leaders. The wars that resulted created the instability that had allowed European colonizers to play enemies off against each other as they seized control of the continent. But as European states came to govern these same people, they soon realized that governance and economic development are expensive.

The European approach to taxation in colonial Africa reflected European ideas about value. Land was valuable in Britain, where it was scarce. And so the European states tried to implement a flat-rate 'hut tax' to raise revenue for the state on the basis of landed property. In Sierra Leone, the first hut tax, implemented at the start of 1898, was supposed to be ten shillings for a house that had four or more rooms and five shillings for a house with three or fewer rooms. That was abandoned for the flat rate of five shillings by the end of 1898.[17]

The shift from valuing labour to valuing land would take some time. In the meantime, it would be necessary for the colonial state to rely on the pre-existing measure of wealth in African society: people.

The colonial state turned to labour tax. And it had the unlikely support of a coalition of people. Labour tax was an old story. Called *corvée* in the French Empire, these taxes had been a feature of feudalism that extended back at least to pharaonic Egypt – it's how (we now know) the pyramids were constructed. People within a state received the benefit of the protection of that state in exchange for the contribution of in-kind taxes (agricultural produce) and a certain number of days of labour per year.

The availability of cheap workers through the labour tax system made rapid infrastructure development suddenly possible. Unlike African leaders, who were liable to coups or democratic ousting if they suddenly raised taxes, the Europeans were able to command labour using the threat of overwhelming violence. And overwhelming violence was everywhere in the first three decades of colonial rule, in part because of the incentives laid out in the Berlin Conference in 1885. The delegates who met in Berlin between November 1884 and February 1885 may have drawn lines on maps to indicate the territories they would be colonizing – largely in order to prevent the European states from going to war against each other – but in principle they had to demonstrate 'effective occupation' of the territory, or it would be subject to rival claims. Effective occupation could be demonstrated by having a 'frontier force', by white settlement, by the effective collection of taxes or by the construction of roads, railways and other signs of permanent infrastructure investment of the kind associated with governments.

For the territories that had not been a long-standing part of the global economy – those beyond the range of the port cities along the African continent's coasts, for instance – demonstrating European effective occupation was difficult. French Equatorial Africa was a notorious example; Anglo-Egyptian Sudan another. In both of these colonies military occupation, rather than civil administration, indicated both the resistance of local people to the imposition of foreign rule and the resources needed to enforce that rule. Civil administration was supposed to be largely self-sufficient through taxation. Military occupation could draw on the more generous budgets allocated to the army.

In Nigeria, the spread of a cash economy in the 1870s and 1880s meant that labour taxes were a less reliable source of unpaid workers for large infrastructure projects. In 1915, the House Rule Ordinance – which made it possible for the government to get labourers from local chiefs for public works and government service – was scrapped.[18] Instead, the state relied increasingly on prison labour. The scholars Belinda Archibong and Nonso Obikili were the first to systematically measure the value of unpaid prison labour in British colonial Africa. They estimated that the net value of prison labour on average across the first half of the twentieth century was £195,260 per year, with the share of prison labour in colonial public works expenditure making up an average of 101 per cent of the total.[19]

But they weren't the first to try to figure out the savings that the government made by using convict – as opposed to free – labour for public works. Because of the need to finance the colony through internal taxation, the governors themselves were always rationalizing their choices to the Colonial Office. The Governor of Northern Nigeria wrote that 'The value (calculated at 2/3 of the market rate) of prisoners' labour in connection with public works, which would otherwise have had to be paid for in cash was 3,878 pounds.'[20] The prisoners were 'hired out' to different government departments for a fee, which was paid to the Prison Department in a system that gave a market value to the labour, but purely for internal accounting purposes. The fee that the Public Works Department paid the Prison Department was something like 60 to 80 per cent below the market rate for wages.[21]

This was not a system that was limited to Africa. Although slavery had been formally ended in the United States at the end of the Civil War in 1865, the 'Reconstruction Amendments' to the US Constitution – the ones that designated the formerly enslaved as citizens and protected their rights – also included a clause that allowed for unpaid prison labour. The implementation of 'black codes' criminalized behaviours including 'vagrancy' and the breach of labour contracts with penalties that resulted in the imprisonment of large numbers of formerly enslaved people. But with insufficient prison infrastructure, states turned to 'convict leasing' as a means of feeding and housing prisons, and later to the use of chain gangs for the construction of state infrastructure. Scholars have drawn the obvious parallels to enslavement itself, but the more contemporary parallel was to the system of forced-labour recruitment being used in the concessions and by colonial governments.[22]

In colonial Africa, the European states used labour taxes to supplement cash taxes or taxes in kind. The workers contributed a month (though whether that was a lunar month or a solar month was, as we have seen, up for debate) per year to building railways, roads, ports, prisons and other public works as directed by European colonial officials.

The British state in Uganda used forced labour to build roads from Entebbe to Lake Albert, a road towards Jinja and permanent government offices in district capitals. The use of enslaved labour was an ongoing problem for many states – colonial and independent alike. The proponents of indirect rule were particularly concerned about the impact of the abolition of slavery on their local partners in colonial government. Frederick Lugard had done nothing to abolish slavery when he arrived in Uganda in 1890. His feeling had been that it wasn't a good idea for British rule to 'overturn at once the customs and traditions and institutions of a country to which we have freshly come'. He also felt that retaining slavery had 'definite advantages in the prevention of idleness, and the enforcing of respect for rank, which alone enables the government of a semi-savage country to be carried on'.[23] In fact, when a group of Baganda leaders decided to abolish slavery in 1893, the British representative who received their emancipation declaration commented that 'it is perhaps only a pretext to avoid work on roads, etc, by pleading as excuse no slaves'.[24]

All the European powers relied on forced labour to undertake the development projects that were intended to improve the efficiency of commerce. Forced labour was accepted as a form of taxation and built the entire modern infrastructure of the colonies. In Uganda, the 'kasanvu' system was introduced in the early twentieth century by the governor as a way to ensure a constant supply of available labour. In this system, all men were liable to one month of labour for the state or private European employers. Although they were paid for this labour, they were also responsible for paying a tax which exactly and conveniently equalled the rate that they were paid.

The Commissioner and Governor of Uganda from 1905 to 1909, Henry Hesketh Bell, reported back to the Colonial Office on the colony's ability to do road work 'at almost no cost to the government'.[25] The cost came in the form of paying Baganda agents to collect taxes and ensure that 'the roads are kept in proper order' and to keep 'the European officers acquainted with all important occurrences among the natives, and report[ing] all serious offences'.[26] Twenty-eight of these agents were paid by the British for this work, at different rates reflecting their hierarchy: 'four are of the first class and receive 40 rupees (£2 13s. 4d.) per month; eight are of the second class, receiving 20 rupees; and 16 of the third class, receiving 10 rupees a month'. The salary was actually an innovation, replacing 'the percentage which they previously received upon their collections of hut-tax' as an incentive to ensure that they collected enough.

As with the slave trade, the economic incentives offered by the new system attracted new people to power and influence. The imperial system, like all economic, social and political systems, worked because it had benefits for its stakeholders, and those stakeholders had the power to keep the system in place.

But empire was not democratic, and it was not intended to benefit the majority in any more than a 'trickle-down' way. Abolitionists, liberal economists and missionaries promoted the idea that, while labour conditions in colonized parts of the world were not great, by virtue of new links to the global economy the standard of living there would begin to improve, even as the standard of living in the European countries also improved through access to new resources extracted from those colonies.

These little nudges towards 'civilization' and economic development were supposed to be done on the cheap. The whole project rested on the basis of mobilizing latent economic potential, *not* on matching governance with an outlay of resources, which only happened where European capital was involved. Empires would bail out George Goldie's Royal Niger Company or use forced labour to assist Cecil Rhodes's mining ventures in southern Africa. But they would assiduously pursue what was termed the 'revenue imperative' for local populations. That is, the colonies were supposed to pay for their own development.

◆ ◆ ◆

The Congo–Océan Railway was one of the most chilling examples of the state's use of forced labour as a means of rapidly and cheaply developing economic infrastructure. Built across French Equatorial Africa (the modern Republic of Congo) between 1922 and 1934, the work was overseen by the Société de Construction des Batignolles, a French civil engineering firm originally founded in 1846 (and trading today as Spie Batignolles SA). More than 14,000 workers died during the railway's construction.[27] These were nearly all people who had been effectively trafficked from other parts of

Africa, and they protested against the horrific conditions. The African intermediaries whose cooperation had made foreign governance by a handful of Frenchmen possible balked at supporting the French over their own local constituents. The resulting Kongo-Wara rebellion (1928–31) against French conscription ultimately saved Congolese lives. But that victory came at enormous cost to those men who were brought instead as conscripted labour to the French Congo from areas in Chad and the Central African Republic.

The rationale behind the construction of this deadly railway was the desire by concessionary firms that had bought the right to land within the French territory to transport rubber, palm oil, ivory and lumber from their private concessions up the Congo River from Brazzaville to the Atlantic Ocean port of Pointe-Noire. The concessionary system has been called 'colonization on the cheap' by the author of a recent book on the Congo–Océan Railway, J. P. Daughton.[28] In parts of Africa like Nigeria or Uganda, where the colonial state was able to graft itself onto existing systems of revenue collection, the drive to self-sufficiency in tax income was fairly quick, even if it wasn't painless. But in parts of Africa like Namibia (governed as German South West Africa until the First World War) or French Equatorial Africa there was little existing tax base to tap into, and few obvious assets to strip for profit. Instead, concessionary companies were an answer. These functioned something like a tax farm: companies purchased the right to govern a particular territory as a monopoly. African traders and cultivators could *only* buy from and sell to the concession company, and only one concession company was allowed in a given territory. Each concession company then paid an annual rent to the government and, in the case of French Equatorial Africa, a 15 per cent royalty on any profits. In other words, the state outsourced revenue-raising.

In the case of French Congo concessionaries, while the concessions were vast, the profitability was limited by infrastructure. The impassable rapids between Brazzaville and the ocean meant that only an overland route was possible, but it would take an enormous feat of manpower. The French government had so far even failed to put in place reliable telegraph wires, let alone undertake the construction of over 300 miles of rail that would require tunnelling through mountains, building bridges over steep ravines and navigating thick forest. Luckily for the concessionaries, the French had refused to sign the International Labour Organization agreement that would have restricted their use of conscript labour.

The French metropolitan government authorized a loan of 21 million francs in 1909 to pay for roads, railways, communications, hospitals and other administrative buildings. By 1921, as one observer noted, 'the loan of twenty-one million had been exhausted, with very little to show for the expenditure'. A second loan was issued in 1914, for 171 million francs, all of which were restricted to the construction of the railway. The 'labour problem' that faced all white employers looking for cheap workers in Africa reared its head. And the government responded by restricting the number of forced labourers who could work for concessionary companies and attaching them to the railway project instead, at a rate of one franc a day, with an additional ration and lodging cost of 1.8 francs per man per day. Even assuming that these were paid, this would net the company building the railway a guaranteed profit of 20 per cent above costs because paying for the labour force was left to the colonial state.[29]

◆ ◆ ◆

Congo–Océan was a particularly egregious example of this wider phenomenon of forced labour. But it's hard to see how any form of labour taxes and forced labour could be seen as very well intentioned. Who could possibly suggest that this was a good thing?

Well, lots of people actually.

Frederick Lamport Barnard, a naval lieutenant who wrote *A Three Years' Cruize in the Mozambique Channel* about his time in an anti-slave trade patrol in the mid-nineteenth century, commented on the French hiring of enslaved labourers. The negotiated contract between the French at the Île de Bourbon and the Iman of Zanzibar permitted 'slaves to be hired, provided the price of their freedom is paid, and that they are willing to go for a certain number of years'.[30] It was Barnard's hope that this arrangement would see the African's condition 'considerably improved, as he may eventually return to his own country with a sum of money and a trade, and perhaps this may be one of the best means of commencing civilisation in Africa – without which the slave trade never can be put down, with all England's sacrifice of life and treasure'.

The argument that the slave trade could only be suppressed by 'civilization' and that 'civilization' would only be possible through the hiring of enslaved labourers might seem circular. But it was widely shared. As the Colonial Secretary responsible for assigning the contract for the Congo–Océan Railway project argued, 'in the name of humanity's right to life, colonization, agent of civilization, will take charge of development'.[31] Economic development itself was the thing that would allow Africans to be free. All they had to do was allow colonization to happen, and everything would be well.

There was clearly a belief held among colonizing powers that labour in Africa was improperly incentivized. This case had been building since the end of British slavery. It was the argument that said Africans didn't have proper labour discipline; they needed missionaries to teach them the morality of hard work; they needed to be taxed in order to drive them into work; they needed to be coerced into providing the labour for modern infrastructure development. And this was the dominant argument of the day.

In a sense, this was the turn-of-the-century 'nudge' economy speaking. Political economists thought that to incentivize behaviour, governments and employers only needed to make small adjustments in the relationship between people, money, work and property. By telling people that under the new colonial government they would have to pay taxes and that they had two options for paying them – in a month of unpaid labour for the state, or in work for wages offered by European companies, settlers and governments – the colonizers believed they had created a labour force where previously there had been, in their eyes, a kind of complacency, a status quo that seemed obviously backward because it hadn't resulted in railways and concert halls and in an efficient global consumer market.

♦ ♦ ♦

Faced with the possibilities of helping to get a post-slavery economy off the ground, missionaries descended on Africa with advice about how to become better workers. They learned local languages and translated concepts in order to provide helpful advice about thrift, timeliness and industriousness. They hoped to build a model workforce, drawing on lessons from Europe's industrial transition. But in their well-meaning paternalism they took their own particular views of African workers – that they *should* work for someone else, that laziness was an inherent trait – and applied a very partial understanding of the kinds of incentive structures that had created the conditions for poorly compensated wage labour in industrial Europe. They thought that Africans needed to learn about time and about discipline and hard work. Faced with the challenge of development on the cheap, colonial governments made the same decisions. Labour was too expensive. People needed proper, industrial education and the right incentives. They needed to be forced to work.

But it wasn't that people didn't want to work. It was that, given the choice to work for themselves, on their own land, or for someone else indefinitely, who would choose the latter?

CHAPTER 4

MONEY PROBLEMS

In 1883, Richard Burton arrived in the Gold Coast. It had been nearly twenty years since his previous visit, as British Consul for West Africa. Burton had published four books about his time travelling around the region, and the major takeaway was that he did not like it. So why did the sixty-two-year-old Burton hop on a boat bound for the Gold Coast two decades later?

The clue is in the colony's name: he went in search of gold.

In *To the Gold Coast for Gold*, Burton's 1883 two-volume travel book, he calls out his readers as fools for not having taken advantage of the abundance of the Gold Coast. '[H]alf the washings are wasted . . . not a company has been formed, not a surveyor has been sent out?'[1] The gold is practically there for the taking – 'Africa will one day equal half-a-dozen Californias' – just come and grab it.

The Pall Mall Gazette reviewed Burton's work fairly harshly, pointing out that 'the great difficulty' with African mining 'is the labour question', which would have to be solved by the remedy of 'coolie immigration'. However, the main point of the book – that 'there is still gold in abundance on the Gold

Coast' – was repeated by the *Gazette*, which was really the purpose of Burton's public relations stunt.[2]

Burton's expedition to the Gold Coast had been financed by James Irvine, a Liverpool palm oil merchant and philanthropist who operated at least six gold-mining companies.[3] There were no good intentions in Burton's expedition. Mining is definitely an exploitative practice. The labour conditions were terrible. The mining was environmentally destructive. The gold and other mineral rushes led by speculators like Cecil Rhodes were notorious for their violence and depravity.

Burton's speculative mining venture turned out to be a pyramid scheme, and this makes me smile because Burton got a little comeuppance from the Africans to whom he was so often claiming to be intellectually superior. But it also marks an interesting moment because of what was happening with British interventions in African money supply at the same time.

◆ ◆ ◆

Richard Francis Burton's first impressions of West Africa were not positive. After a peripatetic youth in Europe and an exciting career in the British Indian Army, he had made a name for himself as a travel writer and explorer – travelling to Mecca in disguise and searching for the source of the Nile. But he had recently married back in Britain. In order to provide a steadier and more respectable stream of income than his earlier adventures, he took a government posting in West Africa. He was in a foul mood because he had to leave behind his new wife. As a determined free spirit, he resented working for the government. He particularly hated the abolitionists and missionaries he found everywhere in West Africa. And as someone who revelled in difference and the exotic, he was not a fan of the Black lawyers and doctors, churchmen and teachers who made their homes in the Victorian cityscapes of Freetown and Lagos.

Burton's consulate was located on the island of Fernando Po, about thirty miles from the coast of modern Cameroon. The island had briefly served as a new site for processing Liberated Africans rescued from the slave trade by the Royal Navy, when Freetown was temporarily out of fashion in the 1820s. Some of these Liberated Africans remained, alongside several missionary groups and settlers trying to make commodity agricultural production into a viable way of life. Burton despised the whole place and thought that British 'civilisation, commerce, and Christianity' were corrupting Africa.

During that first visit to the Gold Coast, Burton wrote a chapter in his *Wanderings in West Africa* dedicated to 'Gold in Africa'.[4] It explained the processes of finding gold and extracting it, but he quoted the seventeenth-century Dutch traveller and merchant Willem Bosman to point out the inefficiency of African methods of extraction. His lament was that, since Europeans would never be able to control the land in Africa, there would never be occasion to 'produce much richer treasures than the negroes obtain from it'.

Burton and the other Europeans interested in gold were frustrated by the apparently haphazard and casual approach to prospecting in West Africa. In Kongkadu, part of the Kingdom of Asante in modern Ghana, after the harvest, Bosman reported, women would do some gold-washing, but 'for years in the same spot' without searching for the origin of the gold and therefore getting it all at once. Never mind that the 'get-it-all-at-once' approach to mining silver was exactly what caused inflation in Europe in the seventeenth century. Slow and steady accumulation of gold was much more suited to the rate of economic growth in Asante.

Away from the Gold Coast, towards the interior of West Africa where Richard Burton was reporting from the gold fields, the Asante government had historically maintained control over the currency through a few mechanisms. Since the Gold Coast had been a source of gold for Europe, Africa and the Middle East since antiquity, the Asante government controlled all the gold through the equivalent of a central mint. Any gold nuggets found within Asante or brought into Asante had to be turned in at the royal mint, where they were pounded into gold dust, which was the medium of exchange. In the neighbouring Kingdom of Dahomey, Burton complained in 1864 that when Spanish gold doubloons were used to pay for slaves 'the monarch monopolises all the gold'. In other words, the Asante government's management of the currency was pretty effective.

Burton concluded his chapter on 'Gold in Africa' with a quotation from 'Mr Wilson', who had written in an account of western Africa: 'these mines should be worked just as they are' because 'the world is not suffering for want of gold, and the comparative small quantities that are brought to the sea-coast keep the people in continual intercourse with civilised men, and ultimately, no doubt, will be the means of introducing civilisation and Christianity among them'.

Burton completely disagreed. He wrote that it was a 'vain hope' that Africans would be improved 'by European intercourse' and thought it was 'regrettable that active measures for exploration and exploitation' were not put into place. Luckily for Burton, this opportunity opened up a decade later.

◆ ◆ ◆

In their ongoing pursuit of free trade, the British government had authorized the purchase from the Dutch of their territories on the Gold Coast in 1872. This expanded the British presence on the Gold Coast, but it also brought British attitudes about tariffs into direct conflict with the Asante Kingdom. For the centuries that the Dutch had occupied the Gold Coast they had always paid rent to the Asante, as a form of annual tax. But the British refused to pay it. The two sides went to war in 1874. When the combined British forces – which included the coastal Fante and a West Indies regiment – defeated the Asante in 1875 they implemented free trade, abolished slavery in the kingdom and set out to see what they had won.

In 1877, shortly after the violent conquest of the Asante Kingdom, James Irvine paid two agents to search for gold in the northern regions of the Gold Coast colony. The agents had apparently bought the leases to a number of well-known mines along the Ankobra River for £40,000, but failed to follow Richard Burton's advice to go to the source. Irvine then created a series of companies and issued shares in them, and had himself bought out of the leases for £75,000 of investors' money.

So where does Burton fit in to this scheme? Irvine hired him in 1881 to keep investors interested in his companies and the potential riches they might mine in the Gold Coast. Irvine also appointed Burton to the board of directors of one of his mining ventures and paid him in shares. Burton had stumbled, it seemed, onto both a literal and a figurative gold mine.

◆ ◆ ◆

When the British and their Fante allies defeated the Asante Kingdom in 1875, gold dust ceased to be the money of the kingdom. What took place next has been described by economic historians and anthropologists as a 'currency transition': a shift from pre-colonial currency to one 'enhanced by colonial policies such as the creation of currency boards, the demonetization of indigenous currencies, the introduction of taxes to be paid in cash, and wage labour'.[5]

Britain had gone onto the gold standard gradually from the beginning of the eighteenth century. This was an important measure to try to combat the credit crises that resulted from the merchant banking Bills of Exchange which had proliferated in the early nineteenth century. Tying the paper money in circulation to the metal money held by the government gave Britain measures to control the amount of currency in circulation and, in theory, the amount of credit, since banks were legally responsible for converting currency into gold and could not print money beyond their reserves. The circulation of more paper money was linked to the problem of inflation, and in an economy driven by the desire to keep both wages and the cost of living down – to maximize the profitability of capital investments – inflation was worrying.

Britain was practically alone in the gold standard until the mid-nineteenth century, when the sudden discovery of gold in California and Australia pushed France and the United States, which had used both gold and silver, onto gold. I had to read four different explanations of why this happened to understand it, so you'd better believe I'm going to share that with you now. Basically, the ratio between gold and silver was fixed in these two bimetallic economies. In the US, legally, the price of sixteen ounces of silver was equal to the price of one ounce of gold. But since the market priced the underlying commodities (silver and gold) at 15.5 to 1, anyone who could afford to buy one ounce of gold would take that to the mint in exchange for sixteen ounces of silver (the legal exchange value), sell the silver and make the difference as profit. If enough people did this, then the mint would be out of silver and only have gold.

Why does this level of detail matter? Because gold and silver were operating as both currency and commodity, and they each had two different prices as a result.

Which takes us back to the West African coast, where Richard Burton was being rude about African intellect and shilling for James Irvine.

The abolitionists were not fans of commodity currencies because they thought that it was demeaning for enslaved Africans to be sold for stuff. They thought commodity currencies were a primitive, unsophisticated and inefficient form of barter. To a lot of anti-slavery activists reading about 'bartering' on the African coast the system looked opaque, backward and irrational. African people selling other African people for 'mere baubles and trinkets', or what the historian Philip Curtin termed the myth of 'guns and gewgaws', understandably looked like a terrible tragedy rather than something they wanted to understand.[6] The anti-slavery activists thought it was obvious that the African sellers of enslaved people were undervaluing enslaved people since they themselves did not value the various goods – the beads, alcohol and cloths, the low-quality guns – that they were being exchanged for. This appeared to be a barter economy in which Africans were systematically, for centuries, getting a really bad deal.

The classic textbook explanation of barter and the emergence of modern money, drawing on Smith, starts with the idea that a baker who wanted some meat would have to wait until the butcher wanted some bread to make an exchange. This is inefficient, and Smith writes that it 'must frequently have been very much clogged' as a system. Money, then, exists to smooth this system and represents an innovation in the division of labour that signals the onset of civilization (civilization being synonymous with the division of labour that makes the job of the 'Enlightenment political economist who doesn't have to bake his own bread' possible).

It is clear that there were standard conversion rates, which indicate that the African economies *were* monetized, but that, like most commodity markets, prices changed as a result of supply and demand. Traders who showed up on the coast one year to sell alcohol, for instance, might find that it was 'not much in demand', and as a result they had to either sell more of it in exchange for the thing they were trying to buy (because it wasn't valuable) or switch to another commodity. Traders who arrived at the same time as other ships would also receive a lower price for their goods. Competition changed the value of what they had to sell and changed the prices of the things they were trying to buy.

The key point is that the selling and the buying took place simultaneously, with the conversion price of the commodities on both sides of the trade subject to change. Trade on the coast was *not* like buying something at the supermarket; it was like standing in the trading pit of the Chicago Mercantile Exchange. A commodity trader trying to sell oil and buy gold has to pay attention to the price (supply/demand) of both commodities. They are both priced in pounds or dollars, but those prices are changing to reflect supply and demand and they are changing relative to each other.

John Matthews, a Royal Navy lieutenant who wrote of his travels in Sierra Leone in the 1780s, explained the money system along the coast this way: 'From Senegal to Cape Mount the name of the nominal value given to goods is called bars, from which it is denominated the bar trade; from Cape Mount to Cape Palmas they are called pieces, and therefore the piece trade; from Cape Palmas all along the Gold Coast to Whydah, they are termed Ackeys; from thence to Benin Pawns; and from Benin to Bonny, New and Old Calabar, Camaroons, and Gaboon, Coppers.'[7]

In the Gold Coast, an ounce of gold was equivalent to the denomination sixteen ackies (each weighing one-sixteenth of an ounce, or 1.8 grams of gold). But if you weren't trading gold the trade could look like this one, recorded by the Royal African Company: '3 perpetuanas and three sheets (both types of cloth) = 1 ounce and two ackies = 9 chests of corn'. For comparison, that would look like three barrels of Brent Crude Oil = US$123.21 = 1.94 grams of gold. In both cases there is still a monetary value at the heart of the trade, even if traders don't trade into the monetary denomination first.

Early-nineteenth-century Europeans thought that 'modern' states had systems of exchange that used monetary currency, but Africa did not. If there was a 'propensity' for all people to barter, as Smith would have it, then what would make modern states and modern economies different was the civilized rise of monetization. In the imagined modern economy of the early nineteenth century, everything for sale would have a cash value and goods, or as in the last chapter, time, would all be measured through cash equivalence.

But this ideal of monetization ignored the widespread existence of non-monetized exchange in supposedly modern European economies. Namely, it ignored the existence of both gift economies and credit economies as coexisting features of even fully monetized economies. Typically, gift economies and credit economies are treated separately by anthropologists and economists. But really they're not all that different. If a friend invites you over for dinner, they have given you a gift of hospitality. You probably brought a bottle of wine or some flowers or dessert. But that isn't supposed to be the cash equivalent of the dinner. And if you tried to pay for your meal in cash on your way out of the door, you probably wouldn't be friends for much longer. You *are*, however, socially in their debt: you will probably need to invite them over for dinner soon, and then they will bring a box of chocolates.

In West African coastal exchange there was a further reason to rely on commodities rather than currencies. It was a credit system. African traders took goods from European traders on credit and a promise of repayment. They then went into the markets away from the coast and exchanged the European goods for the items that were in demand on the coast – whether that was ivory, palm oil or enslaved people. This time delay allowed African traders to test the goods in the market and ensure they were of good quality and worth what they were expecting. If they weren't worth what the Europeans had said they were, then the African merchant could return to the European trader with fewer enslaved people or commodities in exchange; or they could just never return with the repayment and end the relationship.

Cross-cultural trade demanded convertible currency mechanisms and a means of guaranteeing authenticity. The value of goods was calculated based on the ability of the traders to determine authenticity and the known demand for the good elsewhere. This helped to develop mechanisms of trust and accountability. Credit and debt are foundational to economic exchange because they allow time into the equation. In a close-knit community, maybe the baker is happy to keep providing bread to the butcher daily, while at the same time keeping account of what meat he is owed at some point in the future. He knows and trusts the butcher, and so he is happy to keep track of that himself and believes that when he shows up at the butcher's one day to ask for some meat, the debt will be honoured. In longer-distance trade, other forms of credit assurance need to enter the picture as well: trading collateral, guarantees, futures options on commodities, letters of introduction, even hostages. Think about all the times you've needed to pay a deposit on a flat, or towards a car: this is a form of guarantee. For African merchants involved in the Atlantic trade with Europeans, and for Europeans trading with African merchants, debts were a form of wealth that were yet to be realized.

◆ ◆ ◆

The historian Marion Johnson did groundbreaking work in the 1970s to try to undo the stereotype that African trade was not monetized before colonial governments introduced currency. She specifically researched cowries – a form of small shell imported into West African markets from East Africa and the Indian Ocean. In her research, she demonstrated that cowries were not a form of 'primitive money' but were 'a sophisticated form of currency capable of adaptation to the particular needs of West African trade'. Cowries were useful as currency since they couldn't be counterfeited. They also couldn't be devalued in the way that metallic currencies could, by 'shaving' pieces of gold or silver off the coin or adulterating the metal content. Adding cowries to the exchange rate, in 1823: 16,000 cowries = sixteen ackies = one ounce of gold = £2.[8]

Cowries were a good currency because they were rare, they were durable, and they couldn't be fraudulently imitated. Cowries, in other words, functioned a lot like gold: they were used for religious purposes, like the gold owned by the Catholic Church in medieval Europe; they were 'mined' relatively cheaply; their price fluctuated on the market. At the end of the eighteenth century, a ton of cowries – around 800,000 shells – cost up to £80.

Individual cowries were never worth very much. Their value changed over time, decreasing especially rapidly in the second half of the nineteenth century as their supply grew. But pennies aren't worth much either and they are still useful to an economy. An economy that can support a lot of small change – so-called fractional money – implies that monetization is widespread because low-value goods can be paid for with low-value cash or coins. You wouldn't want to try to run a shop with only pennies; but a shop that only used £100 notes would also be very inefficient. If you run a shop that still uses cash in the post-COVID-19 world you will need a float – a mix of different coins and notes so that you can make change. And if I get £20 from the bank but want to give my kids their £1 allowance, then I need to break that £20 into, ideally, twenty £1 coins so I can have the right amount for weekly allowances for a couple of months (in reality, and to their chagrin, I tend to give them credit in the imaginary bank). In the case of trade, it is important to have small-value money so that you can make change and pay people.

In the nineteenth century, fractional money below the value of a British penny was useful in an economy that had less growth than Britain. As one scholar explained, for consumers along the West African coast, 'a British penny was worth about 125 cowries and . . . a person's food supply for a whole day cost perhaps eighty cowries'; a single banana cost five cowries, or 'one twenty-fifth of a penny'.[9]

◆ ◆ ◆

Could European traders arbitrage this system? Absolutely. They took advantage of the fact that they were able to source glass beads or cowries relatively cheaply; European merchants also attempted to make cheaper versions of expensive Indian cloths in order to try to cut their costs and increase their profit margins. Finding an edge was the name of the game, and as a result British wholesale traders on the ground in places like Lagos resisted the shift from trading-pit-style exchange as long as they could, even as political economists back in

Britain argued that monetization was part of the package of civilization that the empire was bringing to the world. The British government was pushing against Britain's traders because they thought that monetization would improve West Africa's economies by making them more rational and their international trade easier.

It is important to remember, though, that the monetary systems in operation in Europe, the United States, Latin America and European settler colonies were far from the stable and rational systems that were being contrasted with African 'barter'. Throughout the first half of the nineteenth century, foreign trade around the world was most often conducted using bills of exchange – effectively like an I.O.U. that could be exchanged at a particular merchant or banking house, or could be exchanged again (often at a reduced rate to its face value). Even national currencies switched on and off the silver standard throughout the century. In the US, prior to the National Banking Act of 1863, banks issued their own currencies, backed by little more than trust at certain points. The impact of this private issue of currency was that a dollar didn't actually always equal a dollar: if the bank issuing it was far away, or was unknown to the recipient, it could be worth less than if the bank was in the same town as the transaction, or had a good reputation.[10]

In other words, the imagined vast difference between African currencies and other currencies was just that: imagined. It was based on the idea that because the currency was a commodity (cowrie shells) it was not real money – as though gold and silver were not also commodities. Observing someone buying a banana with five cowrie shells was seen as a nonsensical barter exchange.

But this wasn't a harmless assumption. It was one coloured by a sense of superiority and lack of knowledge. By 1817, the British felt they had just 'fixed' their own monetary system and they wanted to help other people to understand how backward their views of money were. Having faced down their own problem with wildly unregulated currency, Britain felt particularly well placed to advise other economies.

Between 1644 and 1672, 12,700 small-currency tokens were privately issued by firms in 1,700 different towns in England in order to enable small transactions. The economic historians Thomas Sargent and François Velde have called this 'the big problem of small change'.[11] They describe how, at the same time as all these token small coins were circulating, the gold 'guinea' coin was tracking the gold market rather than having a fixed value. So in 1695, for instance, guineas were accepted as payment for taxes at the market rate for gold of twenty-nine shillings. In other words, the gold of the guinea coin was still functioning as a commodity, valued at the point of sale on the market rather than as a symbolic unit of account. The British guinea was not all that different from the West African 'ounce'.

At the end of the seventeenth century the British government had attempted to solve both the problem of small change and the existence of a market-value gold coin by fixing the relationship between the shilling and the guinea at twenty-one shillings. But by the 1770s private firms were once again issuing token coins, this time as fractions of a stable gold money that did not change value with its commodity price. It still wasn't until 1816, with the Coinage Act, that gold was made the standard of value, and in 1817 private coinage was made illegal. It took twenty years in practice for private tokens to be phased out. Even once they were, the coins retained their old denominations: pounds, shillings and pence, in units that remained stubbornly undecimalized until 1971.

Converting between different mediums of exchange was a standard practice in international commerce and travel in the eighteenth and nineteenth centuries. But the idea that one system for converting made more sense or was the 'rational' approach lay behind the British interventions in African money systems. Colonial administrators and merchants argued that having African and European money systems use the same ideas of convertibility and units of account would take some of the mystery and confusion out of the process for traders – and inadvertently reduce the power of African merchants in the bargaining process. But at the heart of these changes was a belief that British policymakers and businessmen had solved this problem and that bringing their solution to the 'backward' world of African 'barter' economies would monetize them and improve the efficiency of trade, regardless of any evidence to the contrary.

◆ ◆ ◆

By the 1860s and 1870s humanitarians had new worries about Africa's economies: they were concerned that the cheap goods – made cheaper by the Industrial Revolution – which had replaced the imported luxury cloths and manufactured goods into Africa were a sign of Africa's growing poverty. Instead of global trade bringing African consumers high-quality goods that they wouldn't otherwise have access to, traders were accused of dumping cheap imports on the coast, undervaluing the commodities (palm oil, rubber, peanuts) that they were getting in exchange and then selling them on international markets for many times the price they were paying.

And if commodities are money, then does a glut of cheap commodities signal rampant inflation?

Cowries were small change. For a booming economy, doing a lot of transactions in small change can start to be unwieldly. Was there an alternative, higher-value currency, something equivalent to a £100 note? This depended on the local economy, but could range from cattle to cloth to gold Spanish coins to, crucially, people: essentially, mobile, indivisible assets with a known monetary value. The economic historian Jan Hogendorn says that in Northern Nigeria enslaved people functioned as high-value currencies. When the Royal Niger Company reported back to the British government in 1899 on how trade worked in the Sokoto Caliphate, their representative, founder George Goldie, said that cowries were not used for making very large payments: 'slaves were the means of large payments . . . in the north'.[12]

The abolition of the slave trade and attempts to abolish enslavement in African colonies had the same effect as abolishing the £100 note. And as the nineteenth century came to a close, the enclosure of lands within the newly designated colonies had a similarly detrimental impact on cattle wealth.

With the abolition of slavery spreading with British and French rule, though, the value of enslaved people as investments began to decline. Property rights in people were unevenly replaced by property rights in land. Any asset's value lies at least partially in what people will pay for it in the future. And with a shrinking market for enslaved people there was less demand, which meant that prices started to decline. Wealthy people began to diversify their investments into other assets.

High-value luxury commodities like Indian cloths and guns were an option as they also functioned as larger forms of currency. The declining value of these commodities as industrial processes replaced artisanal production also contributed to inflation. While an Indian cotton textile may have been an expensive commodity in the eighteenth century, British factory-made cloths were worth a lot less, meaning that more of them were needed to buy the goods Africans were selling. And with more cloths in circulation, they were worth less in internal markets too. As commodities, this was a good thing: more people could afford cloths than ever before. As a currency, it was more problematic.

From the 1860s, the number of cowries circulating in West Africa began to increase rapidly. Cowries were brought by traders returning from the Indian Ocean – particularly the Maldives. Originally this trade was also regulated by the state, just like gold was in Asante. Portuguese merchants, for instance, were given a licence by their king to bring 500 quintals of cowries for the São Tomé trade. But with deregulation in favour of free trade, any merchant could bring in cowries. And with the boom in palm oil trading from the mid-nineteenth century, more cowries were needed every year. The governors on the Gold Coast estimated that in the peak palm oil years in the second half of the nineteenth century, 150 tons of cowries (120 million cowries) were coming into the colony annually.[13]

More Europeans became interested in African commerce and needed to get their hands on cowries to make trades. They also needed them to pay wage labourers in their employ. As cowries came into demand further in the interior, with more markets joining the cowrie currency zone and becoming integrated into the Atlantic economy, the price of cowries went up in the European markets. It took more European money to buy a ton of cowries.

Traders are always looking for an edge in any hyper-competitive commodity market. Searching for cowries in the Maldives, one merchant stopped off in Zanzibar and found a different variety of the shell. These turned out to be acceptable to some African palm oil merchants back in Lagos, and eventually they came to replace the older – and increasingly scarce – Maldive cowries. The new, larger Zanzibar cowries were calculated at the rate of a ton equalling three gallons of palm oil to one silver dollar, and over 14 billion cowries were imported into West Africa between 1851 and 1869. Like a newly discovered gold or silver vein, this shift was a boon to traders such as the Hamburg firm of O'Swald, which managed to monopolize the Zanzibar cowrie trade in the early years.

But this wasn't a swindle or a scam. The African merchants weren't being duped by cunning Europeans. From the perspective of the African governments overseeing trade, there were advantages to the new bulky Zanzibar cowries. The King of Dahomey, Gezo, declined to transition to metal coins because they could be easily counterfeited, and when assessing the wealth of his kingdom's merchants, 'the very bulk of cowries made it impossible to conceal accumulated wealth' and avoid taxation.[14]

In Dahomey, the cowrie currency was regulated by the state. Archibald Dalzel, who lived in Ouidah before becoming the Governor of Cape Coast Castle, published a history of the kingdom. In it he wrote that 'The well-known shells called cowries, which come from the *Maldiva* islands, are the currency of the country, where one thousand are reckoned equal to half a crown. These circulate in the country, loose; but all disbursements from the King's house are made in branches of strung cowries, containing two thousand each, deducting one fortieth part, as a perquisite to the King's women for piercing and stringing them.'[15] This taxation was a way of taking cowries out of circulation, managing inflation and contributing to government revenue.

Although the Zanzibar cowries were significantly cheaper than Maldive cowries in the early transition years, they also were worth less in the West African market. One reason for this was that they were larger and therefore harder to transport inland for trade. If small coins are convenient because they can be used for small purchases, they are also convenient because they can be carried easily. The same was true of the Maldive cowries, which were transported together in convenient forty-cowrie strings and could be worn around the neck. The larger Zanzibar cowries were bulkier, and the cost of carrying them inland was considerable. Prices were going up along the coast because of a combination of increased trade, more integration into a cash economy and the rise of waged labour (in place of enslaved labour), all of which contributed to rapidly increasing demand. This made carrying around these larger cowries unwieldly. Inflation wasn't a problem – it was a signal of a booming economy – but the specific money medium wasn't fit for purpose.

Imagine if a loaf of bread cost 50p when you were young and now, as a result of year-on-year growth and normal

Consumer Price Index inflation, it costs £3. You can just switch from carrying a 50p piece (or more accurately, fifty pennies) to three £1 coins. The problem in West Africa in the 1860s wasn't that the price had gone up but that people were having to lug around 300 pennies to pay for bread. Burton, in fact, provided the evidence that prices were going up. He was surprised to find, on a trip to Dahomey, that a snack he bought had increased from three cowries to twelve in six years. But wages were also going up. Prostitutes were charging four times as much as they had previously – eighty cowries instead of twenty. What was needed wasn't necessarily deflationary measures but the issuance of new, easier-to-manage currencies at the same rate of exchange.

Life in a highly monetized economy with a widespread low-denomination currency does not itself signal poverty, even if the purchasing power of another country's money is significantly higher. What it might suggest is that the country does not rely heavily on imports for basic needs. This was, in fact, the opposite of what nineteenth-century humanitarians thought: that African economies had become too dependent on imports and the 'easy' and 'corrupting' option of stealing people to sell into slavery rather than being productive and 'industrious' as farmers and manufacturers.

◆ ◆ ◆

What was happening in the cowrie currency zone was pretty much the exact opposite of the gold standard problem plaguing Europe and America in this period. Before the gold standard was introduced, banks had issued their own paper money at a rate that made the money supply grow faster than the supply of gold. This had caused economic crises every few years when people went to reclaim their gold during a downturn and were met with blank stares by bank tellers who simply didn't have the gold reserves to pay out. The state-backed gold standard introduced strict controls on this and could prevent some crises, but it also caused deflation by stifling growth. The global supply of gold simply did not grow as rapidly as the economy. Paper money and credit allowed the economy to boom, as money supply could keep pace with people's ambitions. Tying the economy to gold kept it reined in and based in manageable multiples of what was actually available. Economists thought about the problem of how to maintain the gold standard while facilitating growth, and the obvious answer was to find more gold.

The silver and gold rushes of the first age of imperialism in the fifteenth and sixteenth centuries had transformed Europe's economies and its economic relationships with the rest of the world. The ability to pay for foreign luxury goods – tea, silk, Indian calicos – in silver had dramatically reoriented global trade and caused the first wave of capitalist expansion in the sixteenth century. But it had also caused inflation, particularly in the Spanish and Portuguese empires that controlled the silver mines. In the British narrative, this Iberian inflation led to a kind of Decline of Rome level of excess that accounted for plucky England defeat of the Spanish Armada and ultimate victory in the nineteenth century as Britain became the world's largest commercial empire.

But even Britain's growth was starting to slow by the second half of the nineteenth century. Like all good capitalist enterprises, the early easy growth had slowed and there were two choices about what to do next: continue to expand or find new markets. Empire allowed it to do both at the same time.

The transition away from the use of specie money in Europe – gold thalers and doubloons, silver dollars – coincided with the new gold standard and with the cowrie crisis in West Africa, and also with a new way of thinking about money and value. By the 1870s, the orthodoxy of the labour theory of value was being called into question by a new generation of economic thinkers. Adam Smith had proposed that the cost of a good was determined by the cost of the labour that went into producing it. But what if prices weren't set by the cost of labour but by how much people were willing to pay for the good? In 1871, the economist William Stanley Jevons suggested that people's desires 'are minutely registered in the price lists of the markets'.[16]

This new idea of value fitted with the cultural mood. Richard Francis Burton was at the cutting edge of a movement that believed in 'cultural relativism'. Although Burton was not much of a humanitarian, he was pretty astute about the relationship between Christian missionaries and their superior attitudes. Burton regularly called out the extreme cultural confidence that Britain had about its own way of seeing the world. He was more than happy to mock Victorian values, including attitudes to political economy, religion, humanitarianism and the civilizing mission. He recognized that the work discipline promoted by missionaries was not fit for purpose and didn't take into account local cultures or economic understandings. He believed that all was not equal, but he also didn't *want* it all to be equal: he valued exoticism, was a proponent of the ideology of the 'noble savage' and, as its corollary, thought that some races were 'better' than others because they were more authentic. In essence, he wasn't a particular fan of the homogenizing effects of globalizing commerce.

The early-nineteenth-century British interventions in West Africa had been premised on the universalist ideas that were popular in that age: all men were created equal; man was perfectible; all were Brothers and Sisters in Christ. Burton didn't buy it. Having spent years playing dress-up in India and Arabia, he was convinced that different cultures created fundamentally different people. Everyone was not actually an aspiring Englishman, including Burton himself, who chafed at the strictures of Victorian life. Burton's romantic idea of cultural relativism was beginning to infuse a wide variety of approaches to anthropology, politics and economics as a new generation travelled to Africa and were disappointed to find successful businessmen and women who could speak their language, dressed in the same clothes and thought about political economy in the same ways. Burton and other romantic imperialists wanted either victims to save, or exotic cities to discover. They wanted otherness.

It probably wasn't a coincidence that this shift from a fixed idea of value to a more culturally and socially influenced one was happening as other economies were beginning to catch up with Britain's lead, and were doing it in their own ways – Germany and the United States in particular. And it was the US economist Irving Fisher who took the idea that price and value were influenced by more than supply and demand to its logical conclusion: most people suffered from what he termed a 'money illusion'.[17] The money illusion was, he argued, the widespread belief that your money's inherent value stays the same while prices change. So if you buy a loaf of bread for £1 this year, and £1.50 next year, your brain tells you that bread has got more expensive rather than that your money's value has decreased.

The thing is, this is kind of rational. Since the beginning of modern globalization in the fifteenth century, the tendency towards inflation has been met with periodic crashes, with a more efficient allocation of supply to meet demand in ways that drive prices down, with government regulation and with technological improvements that reduce the cost of production. So while 'bread gets more expensive', a basic Kindle costs much less in real terms than it did ten years ago.

◆ ◆ ◆

In West Africa, import and export prices had been changing since the era of the slave trade. In a famous article published in 1992 the historian Robin Law demonstrated that there was probably some inflation in the Kingdom of Dahomey, an argument that contradicted the assumptions of the time that strong West African states like Dahomey operated a type of pre-capitalist command economy alien to Europe.[18] In fact, Robin Law shows that the international exchange value of cowries changed at several notable points, reflecting the adjustment of the Dahomey government to market conditions. European and US ship captains on the coast wrote back to their trading partners in Rhode Island or London or Nantes complaining that they weren't getting a very good price for their trade goods because of competition from other traders.

Food prices went up and the cost of imported goods went down, with five gallons of palm oil buying 4,000 cowries in January 1727, while in January 1726 the same amount of palm oil would only buy 3,400 cowries. A century and a half later, Burton blamed his own experience of a price rise on the wars that were diverting labour from agriculture.

While the international exchange rate fluctuated over the nineteenth century, by the 1870s inflation had started to cause problems in West African cowrie currency markets precisely because people began to resist payment in cowries as they devalued so quickly. The general consensus on the coast, explained by Burton and other observers, was that this wasn't a money supply problem but a demand problem: there was too much demand for the goods that could be bought with cowries. The multiplicity of acceptable currencies in the West African market should have meant that this wasn't a problem for economic growth. As with bimetallism, trade should have just shifted to a more acceptable money.

Earlier in the nineteenth century, cowrie currency floated alongside silver and gold coins. By the second half of the century, as European trading partners were phasing out their own use of gold and silver in favour of paper money backed by the gold standard, these other silver and gold coins became rarer, increasing their value relative to cowries at just the time when the new, less valuable cowries entered the market.

Some coins were already in circulation in West Africa, in particular the Spanish silver dollar, which was exchangeable for pounds sterling at the official rate of four shillings two pence. But because silver was getting cheaper in Britain in the 1870s, traders could buy silver dollars there for only three shillings and six pence, take them to West Africa and exchange them for a profit (perfect arbitrage). However, the British colonial government was then taking silver back to the British market when it collected taxes in the colonies. And so the British colonial government stopped accepting Spanish silver dollars, a move that immediately destroyed the value of numerous large firms who held their assets in these high-value coins.

The sudden demonetization of Spanish dollars in West Africa and the inflation of cowries were not Africa-specific monetary problems in this period. The Coinage Act of 1873 had also eliminated the silver dollar in the US. But this had been unpopular, particularly among farmers facing a decline in the prices of their goods, who argued that economic growth was at risk of being hampered by the gold standard in Britain and the United States. This was famously pointed out by the populist politician William Jennings Bryan. His 1896 'Cross of Gold' speech argued that the gold standard was keeping the US economy from fully rebounding after the Panic and subsequent Long Depression of 1873, and that going back to a bimetallic monetary system would inject the economy with cash, which would then boost spending and improve the lot of farmers and other producers.

In the West African case, I wanted to know who felt the impact of this inflation. If deflation hurt everyday farmers in the US, whom did inflation hurt in the cowrie zone of West Africa?

So I went and asked the economic historian Tony Hopkins, who has written extensively about the African merchants of Lagos in this period. Hopkins is also the author of *An Economic History of West Africa*, the gold-standard (ha!) text on the economic changes affecting West Africa in this period.[19] And he was clear: 'The real losers were big men who held stocks of cowries as wealth and found that they could not exchange them for goods or silver coin without taking a loss.' As with inflation everywhere, the people who would lose out were those with a large amount of savings, investors and creditors.

◆ ◆ ◆

Money, of course – even the gold standard – is based to some degree on trust. Trust that the market value of gold will remain stable. Trust that the coin has the correct amount of gold in it. Trust that the gold backing the token or paper money will be there when you want it. Trust that money can be converted into something with value to the recipient. Fundamentally, money can be anything as long as you trust that it will have the same value in the future.

But sometimes money has *more* value in the future. A savings account or an investment can see money grow. And the economic growth that was linked to discovery – of new mines, of new land, of new technologies – was a particular kind of trust that had the potential to generate money from nothing. The assumption that investment was a way of making money was a really novel – and kind of crazy – idea. But it kept happening: some lucky person would invest in a shipping venture, or in a new mining company, or in a plot of land that turned out to have gold in it, and soon they were splashed on the society pages. Of course, it was a gamble – everyone in Victorian Britain knew the risks of winding up in the debtors' prison. And in the late 1870s it may have seemed as if some of that early and exciting period of huge risk and huge reward was coming to a close. The possibility of making money, fabulous amounts of money, from a tiny investment, though, was still out there, and Africa seemed like the last frontier. And it was this hope that Burton capitalized on with his stock-pumping for the Guinea Coast Mining Company.

Eighteen new mining companies were listed on the London and Paris stock exchanges in 1881 and 1882, and buying and selling land concessions became a hot market for a year or two. Between 1880 and 1904, £43 million was invested in 476 gold exploration companies involved in West Africa. Burton, incentivized by his share ownership, was more than happy to sing the praises of the Gold Coast in Britain's national newspapers. He knew exactly which anxieties to play into as well, citing the rising fortunes of the US economy: 'I take courage by observing that the Gold Coast, which threatens to oust California from her present prominence, is deemed worthy of Yankee jealousy.'

But the board of directors of the Guinea Coast Mining Company, which included Burton, were skimming off the top of the company, even as it became increasingly clear that the mines weren't going to pay out. The concessions it had bought were old and unprofitable. The company's only value lay in its rising stock price, rather than in any actual gold. Returns on investment came purely through new stock purchases. The company's secretary committed suicide in 1883, terrified by the knowledge of the pyramid scheme he had enabled. But the buzz around the publication of Burton's *To the Gold Coast for Gold* helped Irvine to keep the news from shareholders and potential new investors for two more years.

When the company was liquidated in 1885, Burton was among those who lost everything they had invested. He had placed trust in Irvine, but also in his own underestimation of African capabilities. He assumed that the supposedly inefficient methods used by the African gold washers would be easy to improve on and would generate immediate returns. All it would take was efficient labour power and the allocation of British capital.

♦ ♦ ♦

Richard Burton believed that people could be understood by the culture they inhabited: to understand people you had to embed yourself in their way of life. While this view of the world contained progressive elements, it was also kind of a cop-out. If West African merchants wanted cowries, Burton and the cultural relativists held, it was probably because of their deep cultural attachment to cowries rather than because of any economic ideas that could be compared to the kinds of thinking taking place in Britain. Burton was only the first in a long succession of interventionists who thought that his predecessors had made the wrong call. He disparaged the coastal African elites who had made European trade work for them, favouring instead the 'authentic' Africans who lived away from the coast. He assumed that these non-coastal Africans were worthy of respect because they hadn't been corrupted by trade or capitalism. He couldn't recognize a rational economic system even when one bit him on the nose.

And so, even though West Africa was experiencing a very similar dilemma to Britain – how to regulate monetary policy to best deal with economic growth – the solutions that British progressive economists turned to ignored these parallels.

Indigenous currencies were ultimately withdrawn from circulation. Old metallic-based currencies 'were eventually paid for in state currency at respectable prices, and cowries were not'.[20] When slavery was abolished in African economies, slaveholders were rarely paid compensation (in contrast to their European counterparts, who were paid for the slaves they were freeing). This had the effect of wiping out an asset class and creating a shock to the economy.[21] In contrast, the Indigenous currency swap did at least provide compensation. But the withdrawal of Indigenous currencies still had the effect of wiping out capital for one part of the population: men were compensated while women, who were the small-scale, local traders working with cowries, were not.

Falling back on assumptions about value and commodity currencies rather than thinking critically about the relationship between money mediums, the new British colonial government intervened unhelpfully in the currency problems that its increased trade was facilitating.

Where the value of money came from was an important question of the age. The shifting idea that value was not determined by the cost of labour but by the perceived value to the consumer had the potential to transform British understandings of African economics. But it didn't.

CHAPTER 5

UNEQUAL DEVELOPMENT

T. R. Batten, known to his friends as Reg, set out for Nigeria in 1927. He was twenty-three and enthusiastic about the possibilities of improving the lives of Africans. According to a friend, he had been 'inspired to undertake a career in African education by a missionary' when he was an undergraduate.[1]

Batten became a prolific writer in the field of education. Throughout the 1930s he published handbooks for teaching history and geography in Nigeria, which were translated into Hausa, as well as a set of textbooks called *Tropical Africa in World History*, intended to explain Africa's role in the world to his students in Nigeria. He also wrote a history textbook, *Africa Past and Present*. His goal, according to his friend the Reverend Dr George Lovell, was 'helping people to establish their *own* historical world-views and to think constructively and act creatively with proper respect to them'.[2]

Batten celebrated the old forms of community in Africa. He was a 'romantic', like Richard Burton or Mary Kingsley. Batten was part of a new generation that included the theorist of indirect rule Margery Perham, an influential writer on African affairs in the 1930s and 1940s. They arrived in

Africa in the period after the First World War and were a bit disillusioned with modernity. While Batten was in Nigeria and later in Uganda to promote education on a British model, he was also interested in preserving the things he identified as good about the African social, political and economic system that had existed prior to the arrival of Europeans.

In this regard Batten's view aligned with Frederick Lugard's. Batten arrived not long after the publication of Lugard's *The Dual Mandate in British Tropical Africa*. In Nigeria, he found the 'dual mandate' in operation through a system of colonial rule that emphasized both economic development and 'indirect rule' through 'tribal' structures. Lugard apparently even wished he could rebrand indirect rule as 'cooperative rule', a term that would make its way into Batten's thinking.[3]

Lugard's view of education was intended to 'replace the tribal authority', weakened by the colonial system, with another foundation for 'moral and intellectual truth' which would allow the 'tribal community to thrive in a changing setting'.[4] The high death toll of the First World War made it harder to staff the colonial services, and the high cost of the war weakened the finances of European capitals, making self-sufficient empire even more important. The colonial labour whistle-blower and Harvard professor Raymond Buell noted in 1928 that in French Equatorial Africa, 'the number of functionaries in the territory in 1923 was only three hundred and ninety-five in comparison with four hundred and ninety-five in 1914 – a reduction of about 20 per cent'.[5]

Understaffed and under-resourced colonial governments did what they could to balance out European companies' economic extraction with some level of development. But they also worried about the effects of development on the character of the colonies. The problem facing the colonial administration was how to accelerate economic development – the construction of railways, roads, telegraph lines, electricity – while not causing complete societal collapse. In the early years of Britain's governance in East Africa the concept of *maendeleo* – development – was already becoming popular among Swahili speakers.[6] Economic development wasn't a bad idea – plenty of African people had embraced it in the nineteenth century, including in Nigeria, only to be dismissed by people like Burton for getting above their station.[7]

But even if economic development was popular, it wasn't really something that either Africans or Europeans could do without a huge amount of access to capital. Lugard's response was a system of indirect rule that left some authority with the 'Native Administration', while centralizing other aspects of governance. As Margery Perham, one of its staunchest advocates, wrote, 'under indirect rule native institutions are incorporated into a single system of government and subjected to the continuous guidance, supervision, and stimulus of European officers'.[8] This had the practical result that the colonial state could operate on very small budgets. But while it solved the issue of too-rapid social change, it didn't solve what Batten thought was a more pressing problem: the corrupting influence of the powerful African leaders (chiefs) and the weakness of the masses who required British help.

Despite Batten's embrace of a romantic notion of the importance of tribal community, he also believed that 'the scope and nature of Africa's social and economic problems' was an undeniable truth.[9] But, unlike some conservatives, the progressive, romantic Batten didn't believe that Africans were destined to be perpetually behind Europeans. For Batten, education about Africa's underdevelopment was vital.

Batten's idea rested on two premises: a universalistic understanding of what 'economic development' entailed, and a particular idea about the kinds of government that were able to achieve it. Batten's hard work and influence were recognized by his superiors. In 1943, he became Vice-Principal of Makerere College in Uganda.

◆ ◆ ◆

At the end of the First World War, the victorious governments in Britain, France, Italy, Belgium and the United States set out to decide what to do with the German, Austro-Hungarian and Ottoman empires. Following a logic that the aggressor nations should pay for the war, the Treaty of Versailles set out a plan for dismantling these empires. But the US, led by Woodrow Wilson, was wary of being part of a process that simply handed over the territories of the vanquished to the victorious European powers. Although Wilson was an arch-racist, he was that curious combination which the historian Jay Sexton has identified in American political life: imperialist but not colonialist. That is to say, Wilson was happy to impose ideas he thought were universal onto other people – by force if necessary – but found authoritarian colonial rule distasteful.

Wilson's 'Fourteen Points,' which included pleas for free and equal trade, were largely intended for a European, rather than an African, audience. His preference for autonomy and self-rule among minority populations had been aimed at places in Europe like Alsace and Armenia which had been under the rule of the German, Austro-Hungarian and Ottoman empires. His speeches in favour of self-determination were not aimed at the African colonies of these empires. Nevertheless, his mention of 'autonomy' and his views in support of 'proper development' spread like wildfire through the colonized world. Together, these contributed to the emergence of a new debate between colonizers and colonized about what colonial rule was for, *whom* it was for and how to assess its effectiveness.

The League of Nations, set up as a response to Wilson's Fourteen Points, would oversee the administration of the former German and Ottoman territories by the war's victors. In Africa that meant new rulers for Tanganyika, the Cameroons, Togo, Ruanda-Urundi and South West Africa. These African 'mandates' were designated 'Class B' mandates (with the exception of South West Africa, which was a 'Class C' mandate). Mandates were placed over territories where the people were deemed unable 'to stand by themselves under the strenuous conditions of the modern world'.[10] Their 'trustees' would be responsible for the gradual development of these societies in preparation for eventual self-rule . . . at some undefined point in the future.

People like Batten, who joined the imperial project after these changes were implemented, were motivated by the idea of using the empire for good. They were concerned with distinguishing their own version of colonialism as a 'programme for colonial freedom' in opposition to the 'doctrine of racial supremacy' that was emerging in German imperial claims in the 1930s.[11] Batten was not alone in his worries about the effect on Africa of changing land distribution and labour practices. According to the historian Aaron Windel, encounters between rural Africa and 'the world economy' led many interwar experts to believe that 'African society was in flux, and it was up to experts to slow the change and to reconstruct society in ways that enlisted and strengthened community'.[12] This view of Africa drew on the work of many economists and social reformers working in Britain on 'the social question'. Batten was not alone. I've picked him because he serves as a typical representative of a large group. Plenty of others were also drawn to the work of moral economists like R. H. Tawney, who conceived of the economic problem as stemming from a 'question of *moral relationships*'.[13]

♦ ♦ ♦

In 1947, Oxford University Press published Batten's new textbook *Problems of African Development*.[14] In it Batten enumerated the many problems: 'From whichever angle we view the factors which at the present hinder African progress – the misuse of land, the inefficiency of labour, the poor organization of production and marketing, the prevalence of disease, the lack of education, or the difficulty of promoting sound political development', the author thought it was obvious that there were two clear causes: 'the poverty of most of rural Africa and the lack of adequate education'.[15] Specifically, he was concerned that the people clamouring for independence from European colonial rule only represented a small minority of the population who would dominate the majority and exploit them.

Batten argued that there were four things necessary 'before *any* dependent people can accept the responsibility of full self-government without disaster to themselves':

1) 'Sufficient economic development . . . which [is] now generally accepted as essential for the well-being of the modern state'
2) 'A satisfactory scheme of education for the masses which will enable every member of the future national community to play his part in controlling the destinies of his country'
3) 'Higher education of an adequate number of the most intelligent members of African communities'
4) 'Somehow forming a nation out of the bewildering agglomeration of tribes and clans which at present lack even a common language'.[16]

The tone of *Problems of African Development* would strike any reader now as high-imperial. Batten's defence of the colonial system, his condescension towards Africans and his belief in the superiority of British institutions are so obviously imperialist that it's hard to imagine how he considered himself a progressive. But he did. He was committed to a career in education. He wanted to go out and make a difference in the world. He wrote a textbook about the place of Africa in world history. He arrived back in Britain and taught at the Institute of Education in London, advancing ideas of 'community development' and advocating a non-directive approach that took community needs into account.

But, like a lot of the people we've met in this book so far, he thought that it was *his* job to make Africa perfect before it could be self-governing. And he thought this because he was worried that, if the colonial powers withdrew, greed and exploitation would befall Africa. He was invoking the intellectual inheritance of the abolitionists, who saw the slave trade as a perfect example of this problem in action. And he echoed people like Richard Francis Burton, who thought that contact with European culture had corrupted Africa. For Batten, self-rule would be impossible because democracy was impossible where economic power was so unevenly distributed.

Specifically, Batten cited 'Abyssinia and Liberia, tropical Africa's two independent countries' as being poor examples of self-governance 'precisely because the conditions outlined [above] were never fulfilled'. And what did that lead to? Batten didn't hold back: 'slavery existed in Abyssinia at the time of the Italian conquest, and something very akin to slavery was quite recently not uncommon in Liberia'.[17]

◆ ◆ ◆

If economic progress was measured by wealth, then the slave trade had generated a lot of economic progress. But that wealth was so obviously for 'the few' rather than 'the many'. As Batten wrote: 'the preoccupation of Europeans and Asians with this trade not only did positive harm, but also delayed for several hundred years any possibility that good might arise from the contact of Africans with people of more advanced races'.[18]

Batten was worried for the uneducated masses. His solution was in no way objectionable: 'education is needed to enable them to reach a common basis of shared values and interests so that they can co-operate effectively for their common good, while retaining and adapting purely local values and interests which do not conflict with the conception of the larger territorial community'.[19]

This idea that African elites could not be trusted was a commonly held belief since the first anti-slavery governors arrived in Sierra Leone. The slave trade and poor governance were linked in the minds of the abolitionists who pressed for naval intervention on the African coast. Malachy Postlethwayt, an advocate for the Royal African Company slave monopoly, was hardly an abolitionist. But he argued in the mid-eighteenth century that deregulation of the trade 'will ever spirit up wars and hostilities among the negro-princes and chiefs for the sake of making captives of each other for sale'. This argument had traction and abolitionists made a case for intervention in the economies of the region by building an image of Africa as violent, war-torn and chaotic as a result of the slave trade. The political economist Thomas Malthus, most famous for his theories about population, commented that 'the state of Africa, as I have described it, is exactly such as we should expect in a country where the capture of men was considered as a more advantageous employment than agriculture or manufactures'.[20] African states were assumed to be preying on their subjects or were inept in defending them from other predatory states.

Humanitarians had always seen part of their role as protecting African victims from African bullies. In 1928, Raymond

Buell published a two-volume bombshell book entitled *The Native Problem in Africa* based on research conducted between 1925 and 1926. The book was a methodical narrative of the development of each of the colonies and independent states in Africa, particularly focused on political economy in each territory. It was intended primarily as an argument for some form of indirect rule, aligning him with Frederick Lugard, Margery Perham and other 1920s progressive colonialists. As Buell wrote in 1928, 'It was one thing to conquer native tyrants and to keep out scheming European powers. But it was quite another matter to organize an administration which would not only be financially self-supporting but which would open this part of Africa to trade, and would advance the welfare of the native population.'[21] If the goal of colonial rule was, as plenty of people had been arguing for decades, economic improvement, then it was worth a systematic study of how that economic improvement was progressing. The book's biggest impact, though, was in raising concerns over labour practices in various parts of Africa.

At the same time that the French were forcing hundreds of thousands of African conscripts to build the Congo–Océan Railway, the independent Black Republic of Liberia had seen an opportunity to retain its economic independence by selling the right to hire Liberian labour for plantations and public works projects in Equatorial Guinea and Sao Tomé. But the Liberian government was not overly watchful of the hiring practices, and soon the League of Nations was receiving complaints of kidnapping and slavery.

Claims made in Buell's book were central to these allegations. *The Native Problem in Africa* was scathing about the Liberian government's approach to the question of Indigenous land and labour, sceptical of Liberia's financial governance, and uneasy about the United States' emerging role as the financer of European colonial development projects in Africa. The Liberian administration was responsible for having made the decision to allow labour recruitment for a fee and without much oversight at all. But in this way the Liberian state was not too different from the other colonial regimes. For Liberia, as much as for France or Britain, labour was a type of 'capital' the government could theoretically mobilize to facilitate development without raising foreign loans of the type that had, for example, caused Egypt to be put into financial receivership in 1879, kicking off the start of the Scramble for Africa. The tax base for Liberia's government had long been customs taxes, but in the government's attempt to demonstrate 'effective occupation' – the basic requirement to be considered the government of a territory in Africa after the Berlin Conference of 1885 – it had implemented a series of land and hut taxes and devolved the collection of these to officials based in municipalities. Buell reported that this system was rife with abuse and only a small percentage of the assessed value of property ever made its way to the central government coffers.[22]

Liberia also used forced labour for large-scale development projects like building roads and clearing land in order to establish its effective occupation of the territory it claimed. It risked losing that territory to the British or French on their borders if it could not show that it was making progress towards the economic development of the hinterland. From the end of the First World War, a chief was 'held responsible for the clearing of a road through his district, under the direction of the District Commissioner'. Within the context of Buell's general scepticism of Liberia's government, he noted that 'This work is done by wholesale requisitions of unpaid labour . . . in many cases natives have been obliged to work on the roads for four and six months out of the year.'[23] The Commissioner-General and the major commanding the Frontier Force were each 'entitled to thirty-two couriers, while a district commissioner and a Paramount Chief may each have sixteen'. Importantly, Buell noted, 'these porters receive no pay'.

While French Equatorial Africa was being carved into different land concessions, Liberia was selling labour concessions. An 1897 concession gave a German firm recruiting rights for six years. In 1903, the Liberian legislature sold recruitment rights for US$250 dollars per licence, and a fee of US$5 per recruit. There were further incentives to participate in the system at a local level. A new regime agreed in 1914 between Liberia and Spain ostensibly offered more labour protections. When Buell was writing, however, 'each recruiter in Liberia is paid five dollars for each boy, a system which several years ago at least encouraged compulsion. In some counties native commissioners engaged in recruiting, sharing the profit with the chiefs.'[24]

As with other colonial and settler states, Liberia's ruling elite, though Black, were seen to be passing on the benefits of development largely to their own class. Inequality was not only extremely obvious but was even partially the point: raising up the standard of living of a small elite helped to demonstrate the potential that Black people had to become rich and successful under capitalism. Liberia was an exemplar of the kind of 'racial neutrality' that progressive advocates of the civilizing mission admired.

But while some Liberians were benefiting from the sale of indentured labourers to Fernando Po, others were suffering from a lack of labour supply for their plantations within Liberia. And Liberia's apparent lack of ability to combine infrastructure development, sound fiscal strategies, effective occupation of the land *and* wise and just rule over the 'native' population was not used to cast light on the wider problems of the framing of economic development for all governments operating in Africa in the period. Rather, Liberia was used by critics to argue *in favour* of the protective benefits of European rule to those who might be exploited by Africans if they were not overseen by imperial humanitarianism.

◆ ◆ ◆

In the context of Uganda, where Batten was based at Makerere College, the historical linguist Rhiannon Stephens argues that 'to be rich was to have many people', as well as 'many animals, many belongings'.[25] In fact, Stephens identifies an important set of phrases that highlight Ugandans' ability to regulate the economy for themselves. She points out that Lunyole speakers had a verb, *ohuyaaya*, meaning 'greedily grab food at a communal meal', and *omuhombe*, which offered 'a criticism of those who were very wealthy because they scraped up every last piece of food for themselves, rather than leaving some for others to consume'.[26]

There was, then, plenty of pre-existing Ugandan moral and cultural infrastructure for regulating wealth, for ensuring distribution of wealth and for economic growth. Wealth itself wasn't problematic, but it was clear that there were structures in place for dealing with wealth that was perceived as deriving from exploitation. Stephens uses the story of a wealthy and powerful man called Okadaro, who sold grain to starving people during a period of famine. But since he had a grain surplus because of the labour of the very people he was charging for the grain, they destroyed his home 'in order to get "their" food'.[27]

These pre-existing checks on the greedy use of power were upturned by the imposition of indirect rule, which created a new bureaucratic class whose interest in wealth and power was aligned with the colonial government rather than with their people. In the case of Uganda, 'chiefs' were created as a brand-new official position in the region of Teso. At first, the 'Baganda men who were appointed as tax collection agents in Teso were remunerated with 10 percent of the tax that they collected, while the chiefs of those areas received 5 percent'. But after Ugandans issued complaints to the British about the collection agents, the Baganda were fired and 'the Iteso colonial chiefs received 10 percent of the taxes they collected. As had been the case with the Baganda men they replaced, the goal was to incentivize chiefs to collect as much tax as possible.'[28]

The invention of these chieftaincies gave the British the power to select people with minimal community ties. The chiefs' supposed neutrality also strengthened the British in their sense of their work as promoting justice and economic advancement. They chose people who had been victims of the previous regime. There was the case of R. N. J. Madaba, who ultimately became county chief of North Bugisu in Uganda after a tumultuous life as an enslaved child on the East African coast. He was freed when slavery was abolished in Kenya in 1907, and Madaba worked his way through British education and the ranks of the British native administration. This really was a case of education providing the pathway to wealth, but the idea of wealth had changed along the way. Wealth became about the opportunities to accumulate money and power through serving those above, collecting taxes for them and implementing their policies rather than an opportunity to distribute money and power through serving those below. And Uganda's residents remained sceptical as a result. The chief minister of Buganda in the 1920s, for instance, was suspected of having originally been a slave and was therefore disqualified in the people's eyes from holding office.[29]

♦ ♦ ♦

Batten warned in 1947 that 'The economic influences of the last fifty years have weakened communal ties, and have encouraged among many of the people a strong individualism and a materialistic outlook on life. The present demand for education is primarily due to its cash value and to the prestige it gives to the individual.'[30] But in fact that emphasis on private property had been a recent victory in the fight against forced labour. When concerns were finally raised in Parliament about the continuation of forced labour in 1922, the system was ended and a new law established that 'peasant cultivators of land in Buganda were guaranteed security of tenure and their rents to Ganda landlords frozen at what became progressively nominal levels'.[31]

While the previous arguments justifying colonial rule had emphasized the need for private property as a protection against exploitation and a means of countering slavery, Batten saw the liberal ideology behind these ideas of property as undermining the valuable historical communities that had existed before colonial rule. Private property was associated with inequality and exploitation. A somewhat rose-tinted story was told about many of the 'untouched' areas of East Africa as having been examples of harmonious, if primitive, communalism of the kind that anthropologists believed had existed in the European past, before the rise of industrial urbanization. Although progressive rather than fascist, these two approaches both saw modernity as having deeply problematic aspects that could have been avoided with proper attention to the preservation of traditional authority. For these people, the goal of British colonial policy should be to advance economic development while always balancing and tempering its speed and impact on society. Margery Perham argued that in Africa it was 'not too late' to prevent 'the disintegrating impact of western penetration'.[32]

◆ ◆ ◆

By the 1930s, the process of incentivizing wage labour and urbanization in Africa had been so successfully implemented that the International Labour Organization and the League of Nations began to worry about workers' health across Africa. As people moved away from subsistence agriculture, colonial administrators were concerned that food production would decline. Scientific advances in the study of nutrition led to a revision in governments' understanding of populations' dietary needs. The old measure of prison rations in terms of food groups – starch, meat, vegetables, fat – was reconsidered in line with an understanding of the role of nutrients as well as the importance of 'protective' foods like eggs, green vegetables and liver.[33] In particular, the need for these different nutrients would require countries to draw on their empires, and the empires to draw on the home countries. The International Labour Organization and League of Nations were influenced by a team of scientists and economists who promoted what amounted to 'a return to international comparative advantage', according to one scholar: 'the peasant would devote more of his land to fodder crops, or vegetables and fruit, would increase his cows and hens, and grow rather less wheat or sugar beet. As such a reorientation proceeded . . . imports of the great agricultural staples could be purchased with manufactured exports.'[34]

The relationship between the agricultural sector and national welfare, like many empire-born projects, sought to solve problems of agricultural overproduction and poor health outcomes in the metropole. By combining economic and individual health, the proponents of the new nutritional guidelines were creating a measure of wealth and poverty. Except that the measure was never scientifically applied in Africa. The nutritional information collected by experts for a 1936 report came from Australia, Michigan, the UK and other European countries. It was applied in Africa on the basis that, if malnutrition could exist in those high-income parts of the world, 'it must be even more prevalent' in Africa. As during Buxton's day, 'underutilized productive capacity' was deemed to be the culprit.[35]

But as Jane Guyer writes in the introduction to her book on the economic anthropology of Equatorial Africa, *Marginal Gains*, in the 1930s it was Britain that was known for nutritional deficiencies, not Africa. The Nobel Peace Prize winner Wangari Maathai writes of her own childhood in colonial Kenya that she was well fed and that hunger was almost unknown.[36]

In the period after the Second World War, European countries were suffering from a lack of food, rationing was widespread and refugees from the war were malnourished. In this situation the Food and Agriculture Organization of the United Nations (UN) asserted that it was a *world* crisis, and so they put African nutrition on their agenda. The Food and Agricultural Organization's work on hunger and nutritional access in Europe was effectively ended by the 1950s. What was this organization left to do? They could apply their knowledge of and expertise in famine prevention from post-war Europe to famines in developing countries. The historian Vincent Bonnecase has investigated how the idea of African starvation became a trope in the twentieth century. He notes that a board member of the Food and Agricultural Organization described Africa as 'a continent of the starving, all of it'.[37]

The image of a starving East African population had first made its way to readers in Britain at the end of the nineteenth century through the publication of sketches of captured slaving dhows in the Indian Ocean and Red Sea. *The Illustrated London News* and *The Graphic* published regular news items on the East African slave trade and helped to shape the idea of the region as being in the grip of irascible slavers preying on the population. Images of emaciated men on board British anti-slavery naval patrol vessels were splashed across the pages of the papers.[38]

Slave-raiding had created and fed on certain conditions of poverty that had arisen in the wider Great Lakes region of East Africa at the beginning of the nineteenth century – a severe drought had transformed the area between 1780 and 1830.[39] Combined with shifting demand for plantation workers in the Indian Ocean littoral and the abolition of the West African slave trade, East African slave-trading became a new *cause célèbre* from the 1870s. With the dwindling need for a West African slave patrol as the century progressed, humanitarian campaigners began a crusade on behalf of the East African populations documented by the Scottish missionary David Livingstone. In 1872, Sir Bartle Frere was sent to Mombasa and Zanzibar by the British government to determine the extent of the East African slave trade and what could be done about it. But even then, a caravan passing through the region around Lake Victoria noted the abundance of food and 'the generally contented and well-to-do air of the inhabitants'.[40] In fact, the view of the people around south-eastern Uganda at the end of the century was that it was missionaries and colonial administrators who were 'the cause of the long drought'.[41]

Despite the rhetoric about the need for economic investment to bring Africa into modernity, and despite the belief in the poor standard of living in Africa among well-meaning missionaries and even technocratic colonial administrators, the reality that they failed to see – or wished not to see – was a much more variegated landscape. And in places where living standards were low it was often as a result of very recent civil wars or the Europeans' own policy of using forced-labour taxes – believing that hard work had to be taught to otherwise 'lazy' people – that created or exacerbated the problems.

The scholars Alexander Moradi, Gareth Austin and Jörg Baten brought together a data set comprising the heights of army recruits in the Gold Coast colony (Ghana) throughout the period of British rule. Using army enlistment books (over 10,000 men were enlisted from Ghana during the First World War and 65,000 in the Second, since the army was yet another destination for the labour-tax conscripts) and the Ghana Living Standard Surveys from 1987 to 1988, the researchers were able to determine evidence of nutritional changes. These surveys showed, across a large sample population, that there was a birth-cohort average height gain of one inch (2.54cm) between 1875 and 1884, as well as a drop during the 1930s, the years of the Great Depression.

People's heights in northern Ghana were a surprise to the researchers because it was assumed that that region was poorer since it was farther from coastal trade networks. But the Northern Region grows groundnuts, and a dietician in 1940 reported that children in the north ate 'whole grain millet flour in water in the morning, and raw groundnuts at mid-day', in contrast to southern children who ate roast plantain only.[42] In fact they cite an early-nineteenth-century source which reported that in Asante, 'the food of the higher orders is principally soup of dried fish, fowls, beef or mutton . . . and ground nuts stewed in blood. The poorer class make their soups of dried deer, monkeys' flesh, and frequently of the pelts of skins.' Which is to say that in the 1930s' and 1940s' nutritional understanding of wealth and poverty, Asante was flourishing.

This is an important piece of evidence. Asante had been in a period of civil war and British military conquest at the start of the survey in 1875, which could account for the appearance of improved living standards over the first period of colonial occupation, when stability was reintroduced at the barrel of a gun. But the authors also point to Ghana's integration into British trading networks as providing new markets for Ghana's producers in the period leading up to the 1930s. Integrating the Gold Coast into one colony, and that colony into the broader empire, facilitated new trade networks for farmers, fishermen and herdsmen across the different regions of the colony – often using infrastructure like roads and railways built by their own forced labour. This not only had the effect of increasing access to nutritious calories, but also increasing disposable incomes. The scholars write that 'it is notable that the episodes of rising average heights occurred among the cohorts born when aggregate cocoa income was expanding before the First World War and in the twenty years after 1945', but not during the Depression.[43]

In other words, the problem that well-meaning economists and nutritionists were trying to solve in Africa was not really an African problem. And so the solution, which was intended to be 'mutually beneficial' – Africans would receive access to nutrients they were previously denied; British farmers would receive new consumers of their produce – was in fact a one-sided deal, destined to damage the only benefit that empire had provided for Africa: access to imperial markets.[44]

Because what is particularly notable about Moradi, Baten and Austin's research is that they dismiss most European interventions as having little impact on the health outcomes

that they observe in the data. It was the increase in income –
something made possible by the forced labour contributed
by Gold Coast recruits on development projects and the
entrepreneurial decisions of Ghana's farmers and merchants –
that led to the improved health of the population.

Gold Coast farmers, for instance, saw the opportunities
offered by cocoa. Beginning in the 1890s, migrants from southern
Ghana used earnings from selling in-demand palm oil and palm
kernels to invest in land to the north where cocoa could be grown.
They interplanted cocoa trees among their other staple crops
and were able to reap the benefits of harvesting both a cash crop
and food crops simultaneously for the first few decades until
the cocoa trees overtook the other crops. They used their land
extensively as well as intensively, as described by the economic
anthropologist Polly Hill, saving up to buy more land either
individually or in 'groups or clubs, known as companies'.[45]

In fact, in Ghana, by the 1920s if not earlier, land had become
a source of value and something that could be capitalized, as
Hill puts it, 'to the extent that many farmers regarded land
as the only reliable "savings bank"'.[46] Those same farmers
used the new road networks and railways built by their own
forced labour, but also 'were unimpressed by the colonial
administration', and even before 1914 'had hired contractors
to build three bridges over the river Densu', which Hill notes
was financed by a cash investment recouped through charging
a toll for its use; 'and a little later they invested at least £50,000
in the building of motorable access roads' between north and
south.[47] Later, Gold Coast farmers invested their profits from
cocoa-farming in importing lorries. This capital investment
was practical – it allowed them to transport their own produce

to distant markets, including coastal trading ports – but it was also speculative. Owning a lorry was an expensive bet on the future growth of the market and a hedge that diversified the capital investment of the new lorry owner.

◆ ◆ ◆

Increasingly, union leaders, business owners and student activists in African colonies began taking the lead in demanding protection, regulation and an investment in welfare and development in the colonies. They argued that the justifications for European rule in Africa were based on the argument that Europeans would help Africans progress through the stages of economic development, but there seemed to be little in the way of evidence that local economic development and the success of European businesses actually went together at all. High commodity prices were noticed by the people living and working in Africa. And the rapid investment in infrastructure and implementation of more widespread elementary education 'for the benefit of Africans' raised questions about how imperial authorities were deciding these policies, and the authoritarian ways in which these 'improvements' were being implemented without public consultation or consideration of impacts on communities and the environment.

It was Batten's contention that 'in Europe there has long been established a strong tradition of voluntary, unpaid work in the service of the community'. He suggested that Africa lacked this, and 'a new conception of the duty of individuals to undertake voluntary work to assist the less fortunate members of their communities must be accepted'.[48]

In fact, in Uganda, at the time when Batten was explaining that there was little to no African leadership at the community level, there was a cooperative movement making exactly that kind of attempt. Despite the concern among the empire's well-meaning educators and technical experts, there were plenty of local farmers who were concerned about the same changes that worried Batten. These farmers sought their own ways of organizing to mitigate their effects. A few different farmers' cooperatives emerged in Uganda, beginning in 1913 and spreading over the 1920s and 1930s, to try to retain some bargaining power for the farmers.

Uganda was transformed into a commodity export economy by the colonial government through a system of agricultural incentives, taxation and land redistribution policies. Cotton and coffee were the two major cash crops. Batten wrote that 'cotton cultivation in Uganda has increased between 1916 and 1936 from 133,000 acres to 1,500,000 acres'. He described a depleted male labour force, drawn into 'paid employment' and therefore abandoning what he believed was the traditional model of 'peasant agriculture'. The need to feed more people led to the land being used continuously, without the period of fallow that had been part of 'shifting cultivation'. Batten lamented that 'from the serious situation which has now arisen there can be no going back. Where the sale of cash crops has enabled Africans to become used to a higher standard of living it is inconceivable that they would be content to return to former conditions.' While African farmers took the initiative in planting new crops, he doubted that they would be able to deal with the problems arising from it on their own: 'Thus one of Africa's most urgent needs is the education of the African peasant in the ways by which he can improve his agriculture.'[49]

What Batten advises in his *Problems of African Development* is a plan of education not so dissimilar from Buxton's model farm: educate people about modern farming, put them to work on modern model farms to learn the techniques and send them back to their farms with these new ideas.

As Polly Hill put it, 'farmers are often considered to be people who would choose to take up other economic occupations were they better educated or more intelligent'.[50] The condescending assumption was that Africans were poor farmers because they were uneducated and unintelligent.

Behavioural economists have begun to explore this relationship between education and poverty in the past few decades. For example, Jane Costello looked into the impact of casino earnings on poverty in North Carolina Cherokee populations. Her research showed that the increase in cash led to better education outcomes, not the other way round. In his book *Give a Man a Fish*, James Ferguson's research on direct cash transfers in Africa shows that, while external aid organizations and funders favour market-focused solutions to poverty such as microfinance, government austerity and privatization, the governments themselves were seeing success with 'monthly cash payments' to, in South Africa's case, 'more than sixteen million individuals'.[51] It is not a lack of education that makes people poor; it is a lack of money.

Nor are people poor because of a lack of moral character. Yet this was something that many Western interventionists believed, particularly the missionaries who sought to introduce 'civilization'. And moral character was apparently essential for self-government. Batten quoted Woodrow Wilson in the introduction to the second part of *Problems of African Development*: 'self-government is not a mere form of institution, to be had when desired, if only the proper pains are taken. It is a form of character.' As Batten summarized, 'real freedom is not something which can be given and accepted. Poverty, disease, prejudice and self-seeking are its enemies no less than conquest by a foreign power.'[52]

So if poverty is actually caused by a lack of money rather than a lack of education or a lack of morals, did the colonial government of Uganda facilitate access to money? Well, sort of. But instead of giving cash they provided credit. The Credit and Savings Bank was created by the colonial government in 1951. Only registered cooperatives were allowed to apply for credit. In the first year of the bank's lending, individuals applied for loans amounting to 4,533,900 shillings, but only 829,300 shillings were lent.[53]

The prices paid to African farmers remained low even in the commodity price boom of the Second World War. Part of the problem, according to both the Ugandan farmers and the British administration, was the role of Indians as moneylenders and capitalists within the system of cash-crop marketing. Their role as middlemen – buyers and ginners of cotton – was the target of Ugandan frustration. By 1945, farmers as well as labourers, factory workers, public works employees and tobacco workers were fed up. Strikes led to riots and spread across Buganda. Soon the Post Office workers, hospital staff, servants and printing offices joined in. Their demands included 'increased rates of pay' and 'better prices for crops'.[54]

The colonial government responded swiftly and violently, believing that at their core these strikes and protests were the machinations of powerful Baganda political actors who were trying to overthrow the colonial government, rather than widely popular protests against the organization of the economy. And then the government passed a new law on cooperatives, requiring them to be registered and overseen by the Registrar for Cooperatives. The registrar had complete authority to determine whether a cooperative was or was not legal, and those that did register were given favourable treatment, including the ability to apply for credit at the new Credit and Savings Bank.[55]

But Ignatius Musaazi, leader of the Uganda African Farmers Union, refused to participate with the Registrar for Cooperatives. Musaazi, previously a trade union leader in Kampala, believed in the economic power that farmers could wield. His cooperative purchased all of the cotton of its members in 1949 – 22 million pounds – and refused to sell it to the cotton ginners and buyers. They wanted to gin it themselves, adding value, and then sell it at the market price rather than at the reduced price forced on African producers. A percentage of the higher sale price would then go back into community projects. Musaazi and the cooperative aimed 'at improving agriculture which would lead to better homes, better health, better recreation, the widening of intellectual horizons, the enrichment of rural life through music, drama and other forms of arts and the revival of the old community spirit'.[56]

What is strange is that when Batten was writing and publishing *Problems of African Development* in Uganda, he was surrounded by this. He knew exactly how powerful the cooperative movement was, and exactly how important it was as both an economic and a social force for mobilizing new community connections. The Ugandan cooperative approach was precisely the kind of leadership that Batten wrongly argued Africa was lacking. And it was not an isolated incident.

The Ghanaian Winifred Tete-Ansá, for instance, argued in his 1930 book *Africa at Work* that 'education and business training have produced Africans who have realized that not only can the African carry on his own business with the world, but that the Africans can meet the world in the Trade Markets and reap for themselves and their colored descendants of the world the benefits of this trade, and the profits'.[57] Tete-Ansá's response to the clear exploitation of Ghanaian cocoa farmers in the 1920s had been to establish his own cooperative 'to act as "Commission House" in marketing their products and the importing of general merchandise from abroad for the benefit of its members and patrons', and to set up a bank, based in Nigeria, 'with capital subscribed by the African producers' in the second half of the 1920s.[58]

Fundamentally, the European rural development experts did not believe that national – rather than imperial – governments could work in the interest of the people because the development experts didn't trust them. The experts assumed that the national governments were unthinking, 'inefficient' and selfish, and that only a benevolent outsider could mediate in the best interests of everyone. They believed this even with evidence of the exploitation carried out by European private firms in front of their eyes, because those private firms were assumed to be trying to make money as efficiently as possible.

Only the humanitarian technical expert could be trusted to ensure the best welfare outcomes (in the long run) for African farmers because otherwise they would be taken advantage of by unscrupulous businessmen and politicians – both European and African.

Batten argued, for instance, that 'the peasant has no knowledge of world markets by which to judge the reasonableness of the prices offered'.[59] This is something that he knew was not true. Also untrue was his argument that cooperatives had 'so far made little progress in any part of British tropical Africa' because 'the peasant members are unskilled in handling money and credit and are ignorant of the conditions of world trade'. Once again, he pointed to a condition of general ignorance and innocence, something that a small African elite would be only too happy to take advantage of by 'sowing mistrust among members about the honesty of their representatives'. 'It is for these reasons that governments have been careful not to encourage a sudden increase in the number of cooperative societies,' Batten told his readers. The colonial governments 'fear that too quick a growth may make it impossible for their officers to give sufficient help in the early stages when the societies most need it; that this would lead to too many failures through avoidable mistakes'.[60]

But as demands for welfare provisions and development investment increased, European states in Africa had to ask themselves what they could afford, both at home and abroad, whose welfare mattered, and who was responsible for it. Margery Perham, writing in *Foreign Affairs* in 1951, explained: 'The West has the desire, the science, the energy and the capital to develop Africa. Africa has a desperate need of all these things. The question is whether Africans will be able to accept them. Their poverty and weakness allowed (it might almost be said to have necessitated) a subjection so complete that when Africans became aware at last of their history and position in the world, the discovery created a deep bitterness.'[61]

Batten saw development and self-rule as intricately connected, but purely in one direction: development, *then* self-rule. The two could not happen in tandem, and it certainly couldn't be the case that self-rule led to development. So what did that precondition for development look like?

As Batten argued, 'Sufficient economic development . . . [is] now generally accepted as essential for the well-being of the modern state.' Again, this seems like common sense: the state needs to provide things for its people, otherwise why does it exist? But, of course, this was very much reflective of the time, as even Batten admits with his use of 'now generally accepted' and 'modern state'. These were not timeless economic principles but the contemporary concerns of mid-twentieth-century governments.

◆ ◆ ◆

As the Second World War drew to a close, the colonial contributions to victory began to recede into memory. Posters celebrating Sierra Leone's efforts – 'Your Iron Ore makes front-line TANKS and GUNS. Thank you, Sierra Leone!' – which had been an important part of wartime propaganda were not replaced by posters celebrating Sierra Leone's independence. Instead, governments in Europe were facing a post-war financial crisis of epic proportions. India was clamouring for independence, and other Asian countries erupted into justified revolt over its recolonization by European powers as the Japanese were forced out.

Africa, it seemed, would be the last frontier of colonialism. Which was a lucky thing for the colonizers. In 1948, after years of activism and planning, the British state introduced a National Health Service. This was part of an expanding 'welfare state' – built on the idea of the state's role as the provider of development for its people. Similar welfare policies in France, Belgium, the Netherlands and West Germany were important aspects of post-war reconstruction. The NHS was a victory for the people of Britain, and particularly those living in poverty, who had benefited only tangentially from the economic spoils of imperial conquest: roads, railways, some public investment in sewage disposal and, after 1918, free elementary schools.

The most important consequence of empire for the working classes of Europe had been access to cheap consumer goods. This had important consequences for employers too, since the low cost of imported food meant that wages could stay low. During the Great Depression of the 1930s and throughout the Second World War, having an empire ensured access to raw materials at fixed prices.[62] But after the war, Western Europe's governments needed to rebuild and there was political pressure to ensure that the rebuilt Europe would recognize the sacrifices that people had made for their country during the war. Access to US Marshall aid helped with the rebuilding, and so did access to empire.

Commodities produced in Africa, in particular, were in demand. Rubber, which had been grown in South East Asia as well as Africa, was needed for the booming car industry. With anti-colonial wars spreading in then-colonial Indochina and

Malaya, prices of African rubber increased. Metals like bauxite from the Gold Coast and copper from Northern Rhodesia allowed Britain to earn dollars which it could use to buy US goods. In 1950, 86 per cent of the world's cobalt was mined in Africa. Around 50 per cent of the world's gold, chrome and manganese was African. The crops grown in Africa were extensive and the lack of investment in Africa before the war meant that there were plenty of easy gains to be made for investors after it ended. A UN report from 1955 noted that 'to the extent that these products can replace comparable items from the dollar area, their importance to the metropolitan Powers, the majority of which suffer in varying degrees from foreign exchange difficulties, is enhanced'.[63]

With such low levels of pre-war investment in the continent, there was lots to do that would increase productivity and provide quick and easy returns on investment. The 1940 Colonial Welfare and Development Act and the French version, *Le Fonds d'investissements pour le développement économique et social* (FIDES) in 1946, have been seen by scholars as the start of a new wave of interest in Africa and a new phase of colonialism that they have come to call 'developmental colonialism'.

But within the argument for development were the seeds of empire's destruction. Why, Africa's returning soldiers, labour unions and students asked, should development be driven by the priorities of London and Paris? A crucial part of this frustration was that the financing of development was still supposed to come from the colonies. This was easy when the commodities being produced in African countries were in high demand for the reconstruction of post-war Europe: iron ore from Sierra Leone, aluminium from Guinea, rare-earth metals from Congo and uranium from Niger. And African business leaders and politicians naturally wondered why it should be Britain, France, Belgium and Portugal that were using Africa's resources to fund Europe's rebuilding after the war; why weren't the various African colonies using the money earned from these resources for their own building efforts?

By 1952 it was clear that the winds were blowing in Africa's favour. The Gold Coast elections in 1951 in favour of self-government called for a rapid reassessment of the progress of economic development across British possessions in Africa. Colonial governments attempted to loudly justify their continued presence. The arrival of a new governor for Uganda in 1952 led to a rapid change in policy towards the farmers' cooperatives. Both cotton and coffee cooperatives were recognized, the Registrar of Cooperatives was scrapped and a new Cooperative Development Council was established, with Ugandan representatives making decisions. Following this success Musaazi pivoted to politics, spearheading the new Ugandan Congress Party and making cooperatives the basis for his argument that economic development was a national, not an imperial project, and one that would be best achieved for Ugandans by Ugandans.

Batten, in the end, agreed that the *hopes* for self-rule were justified. But he just couldn't believe that a national system would be able to provide economic development. He concluded the two-volume *Problems of African Development* with a caution: 'Good intentions are not enough.'

CHAPTER 6

FINANCING FREEDOM

In 1944, a group of men (there were no women present) met at the Mount Washington Hotel in Bretton Woods, New Hampshire. The sprawling white building played host to 730 delegates from forty-four countries. These were not presidents, though; they were economists.

The UK sent John Maynard Keynes – one of the chief architects of the system that the conference established. The United States sent four delegates: Henry Morgenthau Jr, Fred Vinson, Dean Acheson and Harry Dexter White. China sent a prominent banker, Kung Hsiang-hsi, as well as a higher-education pioneer and a historian, all nationalists friendly to the US. The Soviet Union was represented by its Assistant People's Commissar for Foreign Trade, Mikhail Stepanovich Stepanov.

The forty-four countries represented were the sovereign allied nations. Standing in for India was the British Finance Member of the Government of India, Jeremy Raisman, alongside several Indian delegates. Standing in for all of the African continent, save Liberia, Egypt, Ethiopia and South

Africa, were representatives from Belgium, France and Britain.

The Bretton Woods system that emerged from the conference governed monetary relations by agreement among member countries to fix their currencies to the dollar. The US agreed to fix the dollar to gold. This, alongside the establishment of new international lending institutions – the International Monetary Fund and the International Bank for Reconstruction and Development – would help to keep money flowing in the system and prevent a global post-war economic contraction, or worse, another Great Depression.

Twenty-nine countries were present at the ratification of the treaty, becoming the first group members. Despite Soviet participation in the initial conference, and their signature on the final act of the conference, the USSR did not end up ratifying the Bretton Woods Agreement. The wartime bridge between the USA and the USSR– in part maintained through the credit of the Lend-Lease Program – was beginning to crumble. The USSR withheld its ratification in December 1945, citing concerns about the establishment of the new financial institutions as 'branches of Wall Street'.

African leaders working with 'development politics' felt the need to provide modernity for their people; after all, this was the promise of nationalism. Shared prosperity was the glue that held new countries together. By facing down colonial rule with an argument for a united, future-facing nation state rather than a backward-looking pre-colonial past, leaders like Kwame Nkrumah in Ghana, or Nnamdi Azikiwe in Nigeria, or Léopold Senghor in Senegal were able to unite peoples who had been deliberately played off against each other under colonial 'divide and rule' strategies.

In the 1950s and 1960s, the growing US military–industrial complex may have been peddling perpetual war, but it was also making cars cheaper every year, improving the standard of living through technologies that finally solved (some of) the household labour problem, and finding new ways of addressing physical constraints – like the amount of grain that could be grown on an acre of land – that had previously held back growth.[1] Enormous government investment in Africa, largely financed by borrowing from the US or the Soviet Union, had led to sudden leaps in productivity. Investment in railways, for instance, linked up parts of Nigeria's groundnut economy to the coast for export. Investment in hydroelectric dams brought electricity to industries, expanding their productive capacity. Investment in universities expanded the 'human capital' of states, drawing on a much wider pool of talent and reaping the gains of meritocracy.[2]

But there was legacy infrastructure that needed to be upgraded *and* new infrastructure to be installed. And one thing was for sure: development wasn't cheap. As the Cold War pitted capitalist and communist plans for rapid social and economic development against each other, costs skyrocketed. A 'developed economy', which had once meant simply an economy with basic infrastructure, now came to include high-quality education, health care and state pensions, as well as access to the latest industrial technologies. And in the mid-twentieth century, for a short period of time, it came to mean these things through a reduction in national inequality. These were the contemporary hallmarks of modernization theory.

In order to be taken seriously as a newly independent nation, these were the new goalposts.[3]

♦ ♦ ♦

The British delegate at Bretton Woods, John Maynard Keynes, believed that government spending facilitated growth in the rest of the economy. Keynes proposed an argument that the economy was driven by aggregate demand. A healthy, stable, government-employed middle class would spend money, creating demand for manufacturing and service-sector jobs in the private sector. In other words, governments should stimulate the economy by spending money.

The newly emerging field of development economics included people like the West Indian Nobel laureate W. Arthur Lewis, and they made the case for economic growth:

Man has to struggle for subsistence. With great drudgery he succeeds in wresting from the soil barely enough to keep himself alive. Every year he passes through a starvation period for several months, because the year's crop barely lasts out until the next harvest. Regularly he is visited by famine, plague or pestilence. Half his children die before reaching the age of ten, and at forty his wife is wrinkled and old. Economic growth enables him to escape from this servitude.[4]

Growth was the way to enable development. It would allow countries to take on debt to fund projects. And development would enable further growth as these countries became reliable borrowers. Growth, in other words, would spiral into further growth, as increased wealth led to the abandonment of behaviours associated with poverty. And this would free Africa.

In postcolonial Africa, newly independent states had some easy – and popular – wins up their sleeves. In the 1960s, with commodity prices booming, it looked like the African leadership would have their pick of interest rates. And with the Cold War clouding everything, the Western powers and their financiers were keen to win the ideological support of the newly independent countries. Economic development would bring prosperity to the people living in new nation states, enhancing the popularity (and power) of the new leaders, which would in turn ensure that their Western backers didn't have to worry about a communist popular uprising. Win-win-win.

◆ ◆ ◆

The Egyptian economist Samir Amin arrived in Bamako, the capital of the new Republic of Mali, in 1960. Like many of the expat experts who came to help Africa's governments manage the transition to independence, Amin found himself living in unexpected splendour. For the first month in Bamako he stayed in the Grand Hotel, an old colonial building with a piano bar propped up by French aristocrats. After that, a villa.

Amin's time in Mali was dedicated to helping the left wing of the governing party to implement educational, health and governance reforms that would make the country run effectively, including promoting light industry, reforming public finances and reducing bureaucracy. His specific role was calculating investment and return, in his own words, 'to ensure that these programmes were coherent at the level of both public and external funding'.[5]

But how to set about doing that? He explained: 'Instruments had to be devised for the measuring of coherences and efficiency,' and that meant 'I therefore had to work out an ad hoc national accounting framework that built in the deficiencies of information and the nature of the fundamental objectives.' Because there wasn't enough money or manpower to conduct statistical surveys, the national accounts were based on the knowhow of two former colonial officials: the secretary of the Chamber of Commerce and a former administrator of one of Mali's colonial districts. This approach, Amin felt, set up Mali rather well to understand the costs and benefits of different forms of government economic policies. He was proud of the way he pieced together information from local informants, officials and his own observations, and that it was based on technical details rather than on the ideological shibboleths that Soviet or World Bank experts intoned. Amin rejected both sides of the Cold War as too hung up on proving their own view correct. He found both the Soviet-aligned Sékou Touré of Guinea and the British-influenced Liberal Ghanaians frustrating. The latter he accused of being 'susceptible to all the World Bank nonsense about "comparative advantages", even though such a strategy has absolutely nothing to offer modern Africa'.[6]

However, Amin was working with flawed data and he knew it. In a 1961 paper he pointed out the problem with the trends in national accounting that had spread with the rise of postcolonial development experts. He argued that 'basic concepts of national accounting were forged for market economies' but were being applied to economies that were not fully marketized.[7] Amin argued that subsistence agriculture, rather than production of agricultural commodities for sale, was a major category of African economic activity. But since it was not the *only* category, African economies were complex. True accounts would need to adjust for the fact that some productivity was impossible to account for in GDP measures. Despite this complexity, UN reports on African economies around the time of independence were regularly publishing statistics on the economic output of various countries as though all production was for the market. Amin knew that it was not possible to measure growth in a comparable and accurate way when the national accounts on which the loans were based were not reliable.

This mattered because the ability of the newly independent states to finance their development rested on their creditworthiness. Creditworthiness was a measure that was calculated based on the total GDP of economies as well as capacity for gathering revenue to pay back interest to lenders. If GDP wasn't being calculated accurately, and if tariffs and taxes were being applied in ways that potentially damaged trade competitiveness, then these new states would be punished on the bond market.

◆ ◆ ◆

Financing growth had been the problem facing Liberia, one of only two independent states in Africa through the period of high colonialism. Imperial systems had allowed for financing at favourable rates for those colonies linked to a wealthy metropole. Being able to raise money for Nigerian or South African companies on London's Stock Exchange gave a distinct benefit to business operations in those colonies, but it also gave them a lender-of-last-resort who was tied to the interest of capital. Being able to cover labour, or food, or capital shortages from *within* the empire was a valuable tool of the European empires to smooth over the cracks in an increasingly fragile system. The French could respond to labour shortages in Congo by importing labour from another part of French Equatorial Africa. Cash crop labour shortages in Ghana or Nigeria were covered by labour migration from within the empire, incentivized by taxation.[8] The Congo–Océan Railway was funded by an initial French loan, which was effectively a loan to a French company backed by the taxpayers of Congo. When Southern Rhodesia required a loan in 1924 it was able to borrow £2 million 'on about the same terms as a large English borough would have to pay'.[9]

When Liberia wanted to undertake development projects it had no such recourse. Liberia had to rely on market terms. The historian Leigh Gardner's research on bond spreads in the period before the First World War, comparing British West African colonies and Liberia, shows that they were significantly higher for Liberia, while spreads for the British West African bonds were all similar, despite the differences in the economies of Gambia, Sierra Leone, Gold Coast and Nigeria.[10] Any financing that Liberia was able to receive required oversight by the international community, something that Britain and France's colonies did not experience. Liberia was in a tricky position. It had to demonstrate effective occupation by 'pacifying' and taxing its hinterland. It had to show that it was taking steps towards economically developing the interior of the colony, in part by funding capital-intensive infrastructure projects. But taxation was insufficient to pay for these projects outright, and so financing was required.

European empires were able to loan money to European companies and loan labour to help build these projects without worrying about international oversight. They argued repeatedly, and with conviction, that these projects were improving the lives of the peoples of Africa by bringing them consumer goods, incentivizing their work ethic and helping them to overcome the primordial jungle. But they were extremely wary of the gravitational pull towards enslavement in settings with little other than human capital, and without significant injections of foreign direct investment – which never really took off. This paved the way for a general sense in the 1940s and 1950s, discussed in the previous chapter, that economic trusteeship meant not only developing the economy but also protecting certain groups from the predations of the elite. And for many progressives, Liberia provided the perfect example of what might happen to minority groups if Africa were left to develop itself.

Kwame Nkrumah accused the West of extending Liberia's fate to the rest of the continent, just before his own Ghanaian government was overthrown by a coup in 1966. Nkrumah argued, in *Neo-colonialism: The Last Stage of Imperialism*, published in 1965, that 'neo-colonialist control is exercised through economic or monetary means . . . for the exploitation rather than the development of the less developed parts of the world'.[11] Nkrumah also decried neocolonialism as worse than straightforward imperial rule: 'for those who practise it, it means power without responsibility and for those who suffer from it, it means exploitation without redress'.[12]

◆ ◆ ◆

In 1968 and 1969, Samir Amin attended the Social Science Council Conference at the University of East Africa in Dar es Salaam, the capital of the new country of Tanzania. It had only been a few years since Zanzibar and Tanganyika had formed the United Republic of Tanzania in 1964. Amin, at thirty-seven, was already an important economic thinker. But his reason for being in Dar es Salaam was not to explain his take on world systems theory or his theory of economic underdevelopment: he was there to discuss how to teach economics in Africa.

The results of that conference were published in a book a few years later, after three of Amin's books had been published in quick succession – *Accumulation on a World Scale* (1970), *Neo-Colonialism in West Africa* (1971) and *Unequal Development* (1973), a set of titles that hinted at some of the problems facing postcolonial African economies. The Foreword to *The Teaching of Economics in Africa* (1973) argued that economics needed to be taught differently in African universities in order to address real problems: 'the need to eliminate poverty and to achieve true national independence'.[13]

The University of Dar es Salaam, where Amin gathered with other teachers interested in how economics training was taking place in Africa, was a classic example of the problems facing newly independent countries struggling to be free. The university had been established in 1961, first as a constituent part of the University of London, then as a part of the University of East Africa. It awarded degrees on behalf of the members of the East African Federation – Uganda, Kenya and Tanzania – a union formed as part of an attempt to counter the problem of economic decolonization.

The University of East Africa was part of a project of federalism in the newly independent countries. Pan-Africanists and economists like Samir Amin and Walter Rodney could see that economic cooperation, open trade and shared services would give newly independent states a broader tax base, a bigger market for their goods and more power to negotiate outside the continent. And for a brief moment around independence, this was tried in East Africa (Uganda, Tanganyika, Kenya), Central Africa (Nyasaland, Northern and Southern Rhodesia) and West Africa (Mali, Guinea and Ghana). Federation was supposed to act as a bulwark against what the economist Paul Streeten termed the 'small countries' problem: economic vulnerability, isolation and the high costs of administration. Samir Amin, visiting Kwame Nkrumah during the short-lived Mali–Ghana–Guinea union, suggested that the union would 'require a linked-up railway system, joint development of major rivers' and the division of some import-substitution industries to 'achieve economies of scale in relation to the world market'.[14]

Federation made sense because modern economies needed to approach the world market, not necessarily to sell their products but to sell themselves as an investment. Modern states don't fund things with taxes. What they *actually* do is raise money on international markets. Then they pay debt interest with taxes. What these new African nation states needed was a regular stream of tax income that could be used to pay interest on debts. They needed access to financing.

Loan rates were favourable in the 1960s, right after African countries gained independence. And there were lots of clear capital investments that newly independent countries could make which would have the potential to dramatically increase output and productivity. Electrification. Education. Transportation improvements, especially roads. And creditors loved a good, clean, one-time project like the Aswan Dam in the Nile to electrify Egypt, the Kariba Dam in Zambia, the Volta (Akosombo) Dam in Ghana and the Inga Dams in what was then Zaire (the Democratic Republic of Congo).

Loans would facilitate growth through capital investment. Dams would lead to electrification, and electrification would lead to increased production efficiency. A virtuous circle of development would follow.

◆　◆　◆

When Julius Nyerere led Tanganyika to independence in 1961, he helped to produce a five-year development plan. While five-year plans may bring to mind Stalinist Russia or Maoist China, in this period they were a standard 'modernization' tool. Like many emerging decolonized countries, Tanganyika's five-year plan was premised on foreign investment and the ability of the country to finance development through loans.

The UN *Economic Survey of Africa Since 1950*, published in 1959, showed Tanganyika to be fairly diversified within agricultural commodity production. It listed decent amounts of cattle production, cotton, sweet potatoes and yams, cassava, sugar, tea, coffee beans, sesame seeds, groundnuts, cotton seed, copra, rice, millet and sorghum. The country also produced gold, lead, tin and diamonds, and made its own beer and cigarettes. Its population was 96.5 per cent rural, and although there was a lot of production for export because the colonial economy was interested in extraction, the dominant sector was subsistence agriculture. In other words, the population were largely self-sufficient farmers with, in 1957 dollars, something like $48 per capita. Compared with Ghana's $194 per capita in the same year, it's clear why Nyerere felt the pressure to invest in development.

But soon the country found itself in debt and with little income to show for it. By the mid-1960s, Nyerere joined other African leaders in seeing debt as just another form of colonialism. They turned away from the assumptions peddled by the technical experts of the Bretton Woods institutions that the best route to development was through continued participation in what Samir Amin was starting to call the 'world system' that kept Africa in an inferior economic position to industrialized countries.

In 1967, Nyerere abandoned the five-year-plan and published his 'Arusha Declaration'. Nyerere's new approach would be *Ujamaa* – brotherhood. It would also be known as African socialism.[15] The first aim of the Arusha Declaration was to consolidate independence. But Nyerere's controversial plan, which advocated collectivized farming, was based on principles that put him on the 'wrong' side in the Cold War. And with that choice came consequences.

For socialist-leaning countries, import substitution was a popular approach to establishing an independent economy. This meant imposing large tariffs on imports of goods. This was common sense in some quarters, even for capitalist countries. Both Marxist and capitalist promoters of modernization embraced the argument that investment in infrastructure and industry could rapidly raise the standard of living. Growth and development in the mid-twentieth century meant industrialization. Independent African states had tried to industrialize. In fact, they had been encouraged to industrialize. The UN was concerned as early as 1955 that 'It is quite clear that export income plays so dominant a role that any major fluctuations in exports would, if not compensated, jeopardize the stability of the economies.'[16]

In fact, the US had plenty of history with import tariffs. Right from the establishment of the post-revolutionary US government in the eighteenth century, the country embraced tariffs as an important protection for the new country, enabling it to raise funds to pay back war debts and to cultivate infant industries. The US was no fan of mercantilism and in fact had broken away from the British Empire for, among other things, its taxation policies. But it recognized the role that tariffs had played in British development.

The British textile industry had provided a particularly strong example of this. As we saw with the Spitalfields weavers, the East India Company had been importing Indian cloths since the seventeenth century as part of its own monopoly. These were widely popular within England, but also had a huge re-export market in the Americas and Africa. But because the mercantilists were still concerned about 'draining' national wealth to India, they put into place tariffs on Indian cloth imports (not re-exports) in order to protect infant manufacturing in Britain. This initially spurred a new high-wage-paying industry to respond to the strong levels of demand and the protected prices that manufacturers would get for their goods. But, as the tech industry has recently experienced, high-wage industrial work didn't last long: soon manufacturers found new ways to economize on labour to make bigger profits.

US wannabe manufacturers looked to Britain and saw protection. They saw tariffs. And they recognized that this was the approach they should take to build up their own national industry too, even as Britain moved away from its mercantilist past to embrace free trade.

The attempts at import substitution tariffs in postcolonial Africa followed the same logic, yet here they were seen by former colonizing powers as frustrating growth.

Once again, the diagnosis of problems and the solutions on offer revealed misunderstandings and misreadings based on the economic ideas circulating at the time and their connection to the Cold War view of the world. Some new African states like Ghana wanted to introduce high import tariffs to incentivize industrialization. Others, like Nigeria, continued to focus on exports of primary commodities. Tanzania attempted collectivized farming. But all of these economic policies were read by outsiders as endorsing a particular side in the Cold War. And if the new African states wanted loans from the West to be able to start the development projects – electrification, hospital- and school-building, road and airport construction – which they had promised their citizens they could deliver where the colonial powers couldn't (or wouldn't), then they had to toe the line or face the political consequences.

To the economists at the World Bank and IMF, who worried about policies like import substitution or industry nationalization, the strengths in African economies lay in their 'traditional' (colonial) production of agricultural commodities for the world market; and import substitution seemed illogical. Why should Senegal try to produce its own cars when it was so good at groundnut production? Why should Kenya produce its own clothes when it was so good at coffee production? These countries should focus on what they had a comparative advantage in and leave the factories to the countries that were good at them.

Trade was helpful because it had 'broken' what a UN report on the *Structure and Growth of Selected African Economies* referred to as 'the vicious circle of stagnancy in which the traditional economies were caught'. 'Foreign business enterprise and government administrations' had 'provided the means and incentives to bring certain of the products of Africa within reach of world markets'. If Senegal had to make all of its own cars, they would be too expensive for anyone to buy because their scale of production could never reach a high enough level. If Kenya and Tanzania were both producing clothes for their own home consumer markets, how would they ever achieve regional integration? And if African consumers were denied the cheap global goods that everyone else had access to, how would their standard of living improve? Comparative advantage had saved the day for the African consumer.[17] Regional integration plans collapsed by the end of the 1960s as different leaders responded to development plans, loan conditions and the needs of their constituents. In 1970, the University of East Africa became the University of Dar es Salaam.

◆ ◆ ◆

Samir Amin was losing heart. He noted that 'apart from the difficulties due to the absence of statistics, the task of the national accountant seems to us to be complicated by three orders of phenomena' which were: 'subsistence activities represent an important part of economic activity in Africa . . . there are hardly ever integrated national economies in Africa . . . [and] economic quantities particular to such and such a year often do not have much significance'.[18]

The authors who featured in *The Teaching of Economics in Africa*, including Samir Amin, were concerned that if there were a continued preference for British, French and US-trained economists in university lecturing in African universities, assumptions would 'creep in', assumptions which 'may be locally appropriate in the social and economic conditions where and for which the models are devised, but they are by no means applicable in Africa'.

Samir Amin worried in particular about the trend in economics towards becoming 'an algebra of deductions from a set of assumptions defining the so-called economic rationality of Man isolated from Nature'. Amin and the other authors of *The Teaching of Economics in Africa* were concerned by what the historian Joseph Hodge has described as the 'Triumph of Experts'.

By 1973, Samir Amin and the other Africa-based economists who had spoken at the conference in Dar es Salaam were arguing that 'a university has an essential role to play in liberating "public opinion" from the fantasies that stand in the way of development, notably an overly optimistic view of the possibility of developing painlessly as an appendage of the existing world system'.[19] How had people come to the idea that economic development was a painless proposition? That the economy could be one that featured only winners, only upsides, only positive externalities?

Now, there are not many places where democracy and development – big, destructive, infrastructure development – have gone hand in hand. Sometimes *part* of the population has a democracy (as in the US, UK, most of Europe). Or sometimes full democracy comes soon after development. But these kinds of projects often result in displacement, if not worse.

When implicit government support reassures ratings agencies about the creditworthiness of entities ranging from public universities to municipalities to whole states that function as part of a broader federation or empire, the risk and reward of debt become an entirely different calculation to the fiscal responsibility imagined by the experts at the World Bank. But these moments of fiscal tension have also historically seen the transformation of relationships between political representation and fiscal responsibility – often to the detriment of local and democratic governance.

In his book *In a Bad State*, David Schleicher argues that in the case of the United States, the problem really comes down to the fact that state and local governments are undemocratic because specific interest groups have undue sway at the state and local level of politics, where voter turnout is low and competition is inefficient. He cites a worrying trend that local government borrowing costs increase when local newspapers close. Schleicher argues that local budget crises create a trilemma for the US federal government: they want to ensure that states and cities can use debt to finance infrastructure improvements; they want to avoid cuts to essential services, cuts that have the effect of exacerbating recessions; and they want to avoid the moral hazard of giving democratic leaders of states and cities the impression that they will always be bailed out. They can't have all three.[20]

Take, for instance, the construction of Interstate 95 along the US East Coast. In each major city the highway passes through, the areas that were torn down to make way for construction were the homes of the poor and disfranchised. In Philadelphia, where the city planner Ed Bacon placed the route of the six-lane elevated highway straight through historic neighbourhoods, the city's Black community were displaced. I-95 now carries 150,000 vehicles per day and in 2006 was estimated to contribute something like $5.1 trillion to US GDP. Was it worth it? Well, it depends what measurements you use. If the measurement of well-being is purely based on GDP, then you get one answer. If the measure of well-being is based on another factor, like community cohesion, for instance, you would have quite a different answer.

Or take New York's development in the period of the urban planner Robert Moses. Moses set out to improve the city – its infrastructure, its civil service, its housing and recreation areas – and had a lasting legacy on its development. As Moses's biographer Robert Caro argues, for New York's Black and Hispanic residents that legacy was overwhelmingly one of displacement as their communities were bulldozed to make way for new highways, upscale housing for white residents and new cultural areas like the Lincoln Center.[21]

Pushing these residents out of the heart of New York echoed what was taking place in South Africa, where Black

South Africans were moved out of the cities they worked in and forced to commute from underserved Black townships. A similar consequence played out with the dam construction for electrification in Ghana and Zambia. Development entailed utilitarian calculations about costs and benefits. The benefits to GDP ensured access to financing. The costs to individuals and communities could be swallowed for the greater good.

Success in independence was being measured by the ability to get development done, to improve the standard of living. But the easiest, most efficient way to achieve these goals was through high-modernist central planning, an approach that conflicted with arguments for autonomy, for democracy. And a variety of thinkers in the postcolonial period began to see a problem with how the state operated. For instance, the influential scholar James Scott laid out his prescription of how and why high-modernist states in the Global South were unable to complete their development plans and why they were, in fact, catastrophic failures. As he writes in *Seeing Like a State*, 'much of this book can be read as a case against the *imperialism* of high-modernist, planned social order'. Specifically, he argues against 'an imperial or hegemonic planning mentality that excludes the necessary role of local knowledge and know-how'.[22]

Increasingly, the job of president in newly independent countries was to make these kinds of hard decisions about how to sell their country as a good investment. They were representatives of their country on a world market rather than representatives of their people's needs.

◆ ◆ ◆

During the 1960s, hard decisions were being made, but mostly everyone was experiencing some improvement to their standard of living. This was possible because commodity prices were high. The things that Africa could sell on the world market were in demand. In fact, they were so in demand that newly independent states were having to fight to keep control over them.

In 1960, the UN intervened in Congo to prevent Katanga Province from seceding from the whole-of-Western-Europe-sized country. The UN operation in Congo was initially a response to the disordered decolonization of the territory by the Belgian government. It quickly became a mission to preserve the territorial integrity of the new state.[23] It also established a precedent for the UN to reject secessionist claims. Of course, the irony of this position was not lost on secessionist movements. European powers had carved up Northern Ireland and the Republic of Ireland, Israel and Palestine, India and Pakistan, North and South Korea, North and South Vietnam. The idea that there were only specific ways that borders could be determined was so obviously arbitrary that it was laughable.

Nigeria offered a test of this principle. At independence in 1960, Nigeria retained the federal structure that had been inscribed into its constitution in 1946. Three regions, representing different ethnic majorities, were linked together in a loose federal structure. The Yoruba, in the Western Region, were represented by the Action Group (AG); the Hausa–Fulani North – the region that was the model for Lugard's indirect rule – was represented by the Northern People's Congress (NPC); and the Igbo-dominated East by the National Council of Nigeria and the Cameroons (NCNC).

Because the new states had very tenuous legitimacy, and because the economy was not growing evenly, the developmental promise of a shared national future started to fracture. Part of this was an attempt to respond to demands for self-determination by various minority groups within the three regions, who felt dominated by the regional majority.[24] The country had been rocked by strikes, coups and counter-coups between 1965 and 1966. The Igbo were suspected of targeting the dominant Hausa–Fulani elite, and their celebrations after the execution of several NPC military and civilian leaders, while the Igbo president was out of the country, compounded growing conspiracy theories. Pogroms against Igbos in the north reflected growing distrust of the Igbo ethnic group.

At the end of this series of coups the new president, Yakubu Gowon, was installed as a compromise candidate, an attempt to reconcile the Northern Region and Eastern Region. Gowon was from the north but was Christian and not Hausa or Fulani. But for the Eastern Region Igbos it was still clear that they needed to be independent in order to be in control of their economic fate. And so, after an official vote of secession, the Military Governor of the Eastern Region, Colonel Odumegwu Ojukwu, declared the independence of a new state, the Republic of Biafra, on 30 May 1967.

Political decolonization was one thing. Economic decolonization proved to be a trickier prospect. Nigerian President Gowon's decision to partition the country further (despite promises to the Governor of the Eastern Region that he wouldn't) and then to blockade the Eastern Region (with the exception of oil exports) showed a shrewd understanding of where the country's economic future lay.

As the scholar Stephanie Decker has argued, political reform was 'the subject of political decision-making between nationalist politicians and the Colonial Office executive, while economic development was left to technical staff and economic experts'.[25] Responding to the changing political winds, international businesses based in Africa in the 1960s began a process of 'Africanization' of their local leadership, a strategy that in some ways mirrored the policy of indirect rule practised by the British political leaders. Businesses understood that their continued legitimacy – and ability to avoid nationalization by new states – relied on representation. Where colonial states had lost power through their approach to 'Africanization', multinational businesses sought to use the process as a chance to retain control.

Back in 1958, Shell-BP had begun oil production at the Oloibiri field in the Niger Delta. Royalties were divided up by the colonial government, with 50 per cent going to the region of origin (in this case the Eastern Region), 20 per cent to the federal government, and 30 per cent divided between the other two regions. But these were royalties, not profits. In other words, the system that had evolved to manage resource extraction by private firms under colonial rule was a return to the kinds of annual gifts given by the slave traders to the African states that enabled the trade. Historian Frederick Cooper has dubbed these 'gatekeeper states', pointing out that colonial governments and their successors were both run to collect a toll at the proverbial gate rather than risk popular revolt by imposing unpopular taxes on their citizens.[26]

The Federal Government of Nigeria's war against Biafra was a war to continue controlling the gate toll. Secession was not an option for the countries whose companies had invested in Nigeria's oil-exporting economy. And while breakaway movements like the Republic of Biafra were extreme cases, the same principle began to apply across the continent. From the perspective of the external institutions that had financed early postcolonial development, governments that responded to the demands of the people rather than the needs of GDP growth were unstable and unpredictable.

Instead of democracy, *representation* was what was deemed to be most important. If states were unable to fulfil the development promise for their citizens, they risked being voted out. The early moment of decolonization had provided newly independent states with a newfound power to negotiate development financing, as both sides in the Cold War competed over whose path to modernization was better. But as independent African states sought new ways to convert their export-oriented economies to longer-term growth, this risked access to both African raw materials and African consumers. It risked a turn to socialism. It risked the ability or willingness of African governments to take on and pay back debts.

◆　◆　◆

The Bretton Woods Agreement that had dominated the post-Second World War modernization era of state-led development imploded in the wake of the economic recessions of the late 1960s and 1970s. The countries that had not been at the Bretton Woods Conference because they were represented by the colonial powers had now, theoretically, a seat at the table of global governance. By 1976, all of the former African imperial colonies had joined the UN.* But they were there with a declining sense of agency over the futures of their states.

When the promise of continuous growth failed at the end of the 1960s, people began to worry about who might be winning at their expense and whether their share of the limited future was secure. 'The appearance of millionaires in any society is no proof of its affluence; they can be produced by very poor countries like Tanganyika just as well as by rich countries like the United States of America,' wrote Julius Nyerere, 'for it is not efficiency of production, nor the amount of wealth in a country, which make millionaires; it is the uneven distribution of what is produced.'[27]

The question of distribution was central to the Cold War. As the immediacy of the Second World War recovery receded, a new emphasis on individualism and the power and the health of the private sector became a major focus of development policy in Africa.

* Zimbabwe and Namibia were still ruled by white minority governments in Africa, and neither joined the UN until majority rule was established. South Africa, which had white minority rule until 1994, was one of the first UN member states in 1945.

CHAPTER 7

HELPING YOU TO GET RICH QUICK

In 2005, teenagers and college students in countries from Australia to Canada, the US to Finland wore white silicone bracelets inscribed with 'Make Poverty History 2005'. I still probably have one sitting in a drawer somewhere. The Make Poverty History campaign targeted the G8 meeting at Gleneagles, Scotland. The campaign brought together 540 member organizations in Britain alone. Oxfam was a leading voice in the movement. In the United States, television ads featured Tom Hanks.

The campaign was part of a broader push from the aid and development sectors to throw light on the problems that countries across Africa had experienced since the end of its post-independence growth. The 1980s and 1990s had been particularly terrible decades for the continent. First, the constraints of the Cold War on democracy had allowed the 'representative' governments in Africa to prioritize debt-servicing and the strictures of the IMF structural adjustment policies that accompanied it over everything else. Then, when the Cold War ended, support for these regimes disappeared overnight, alongside whatever foreign direct investment had remained. The massive fire sale of Eastern Bloc state assets was a much better bet for private capital investment. The instability caused by the end of the Cold War erupted into civil war in twenty-six countries across Africa in the 1980s and 1990s. By 2005, most of those civil wars had ended. But scepticism of government and of state institutions ran deep. And not only among the citizens of those states.

In 1995, Oxfam released an annual report calling out the Bretton Woods institutions for their preference for 'laissez-faire' policies that promoted trickle-down economics. It chafed at the idea that market solutions would solve poverty in a system where state debts made investment in the poor impossible. But by 2005, while still campaigning for debt cancellation, Oxfam was one of many humanitarian organizations that had shifted towards microeconomic, market-based solutions to poverty. The thinking was that if individual behaviours could be changed, if incentives could be activated in the right ways, then a little bit of money could go a long way towards reducing poverty. States didn't need to spend a huge amount of money – money they didn't have – to make a big difference.

◆ ◆ ◆

In the early 1990s, in Masvingo Province, Zimbabwe, Oxfam was working with Dorothy Chiredze, a farmer in the village of Katule. Chiredze's story is told in Oxfam's 1995 *Poverty Report* to show what the day-to-day lives of the global poor are like. She grows maize on her one-hectare farm, typically producing three sacks' worth in a season. She has to carry water from two hours away to irrigate her land and she has no access to fertilizer.

Chiredze explains that the difference between her farm and that of her wealthier neighbours is that they have a cow, which can act as a draught animal. Oxfam explains that Chiredze finds herself in a poverty trap because of insecurity. The slightest bad luck pushes the family over the edge – her husband loses his factory job; the school raises fees; there is a drought.[1]

Insecurity was an issue that many post-war European countries dealt with through the establishment of welfare states. But welfare states require wealth and state capacity to build and enormous amounts of buy-in from the public, who are able to sacrifice a portion of their income to create a social safety net for others. Historian Frederick Cooper points out that it was the demand for a welfare state at home that led European countries to decolonize.[2] Unwilling and unable to afford to match welfare-funding both at home and in the empire, they cut their colonies loose. But, more subtly, the bargain in welfare spending at home was that it was for European nationals only. A more equal and stable standard of living at home would be possible, but only by closing the borders on those from the colonies.

But this welfare nationalism wasn't a sustainable or humane solution. Oxfam's 1995 *Poverty Report* made a strong case for rich countries to be interested in problems of poverty: 'the forces unleashed by conflict and global poverty will not respect national borders, however well-defended they may be'. Oxfam argued that 'enlightened self-interest and moral concern' needed to be extended 'to developing countries' – global poverty was everyone's problem.

◆ ◆ ◆

'The Long, Slow Death of Global Development', an article published in 2022, reports that 'large numbers of jobless youth in economies that have seen little real development over the last few decades will only aggravate the recurring political and social crises on the African continent'.[3]

When the development economist Arthur Lewis was defining the role of labour supply in development economics in the 1950s, Africa did not fit his model 'of unlimited supply of labour in subsistence activities'. In Africa in the 1950s, labour was still scarce.

But across the 1960s and 1970s, African countries became, almost universally, labour-abundant. Government investment in hospitals, maternal health and education helped to decrease mortality. The post-war and post-independence boom times had made people wealthier; they could buy better-quality food. African government investment in extending supplies of running water and electricity, building new roads to connect rural villages and the establishment of bus services had all contributed to both a population boom and an aspirational labour class who wanted to work for wages in the city. But as government revenues dried up, the middle classes were laid off. The continent's 'unemployment problem' shifted from a colonial concern with 'labour scarcity' to the persistent downward spiral of underemployment.

Now, increasing efforts were focused on the lack of demand for labour. In his memoir *Born a Crime*, the South African comedian Trevor Noah recounts the life of unemployed young men living in Alexandra, the Johannesburg township near where he grew up:

you're always working, working, working, and you feel like something's happening, but really nothing's happening at all. I was out there every day from seven a.m. to seven p.m., and every day it was: How do we turn ten rand into twenty? How do we turn twenty into fifty? How do I turn fifty into a hundred? At the end of the day we'd spend it on food and maybe some beers, and then we'd go home and come back . . . It was a whole day's work to flip that money . . . There were many days we'd end up back at zero, but I always felt like I'd been very productive.[4]

One survey classified between 80 and 95 per cent of Sub-Saharan African employment as taking place in the informal sector. In South Africa that number was lower – around 38 per cent. But this was still a new problem. A shift had taken place, from a history in which slavery was one of the ways that labour was ensured, despite its scarcity, to a new reality where apparently 38 per cent (and up to 95 per cent in some places) of a county's adult population were not employed 'formally', and by the middle of the 2010s 'self- and family-(largely urban) employment rose sharply as a share of the labour force'.[5]

Development sceptics, ever ready with a policy proposal, blamed aid dependency. Resource-rich countries were said to be suffering from Dutch oil disease – the over-reliance of a country on one sector, leading to a decline in other sectors, and especially in manufacturing. Development experts also blamed a weak private sector and the legacy of corruption in preventing people from starting and maintaining businesses.

Comparative advantage – a crucial part of arguments for structural adjustment policies – promised to integrate the world by ensuring that different countries would be able to participate by selling their most advantageous output on a global market. So, in theory, Sierra Leone would sell iron ore, coltan and diamonds. With the money it made from those products the country would be able to buy the food and manufactured goods it needed. What this meant in practice, though, was that there was no need for local industrial skills, or even agricultural skills, when both manufactured products and food could be imported so cheaply into Sierra Leone.

According to structural adjustment logic, it simply wouldn't make sense to produce cars or grow rice in Africa when these things can be had more cheaply abroad. And this is great if you're a country that has a comparative advantage in a product – or even better, multiple products – that is in demand and you have some power in the global economy to, for instance, dictate the price of that product.

If, for example, Sierra Leone had a monopoly on coltan, or was part of a coltan cartel, and it could make sure it was getting enough money for its resource, then it really could fund a domestic economy off it, employing enough people to create demand for service-sector jobs. Instead, African workers made use of their comparative advantage in service-sector jobs within their own local economies. The global marketplace can't fix your car when it breaks down, or cut your hair; it can't officiate at a funeral or bake a cake for your wedding. In other words, the rise of service-sector jobs in Africa should be seen as a sign of its integration into the global market. This has worked out for Saudi Arabia, for instance.

But in general, it's hard to keep everyone employed when an economy is geared towards only one sector (the one with the comparative advantage). For Saudis, John Maynard Keynes's 1930 prediction of a fifteen-hour work week, facilitated by redistribution, proved true. Underemployment there is endemic, but with the ability to redistribute oil income the service economy is able to thrive.

But comparative advantage does not always work as cleanly as this. There are inherent problems in relying on an export that is subject to unpredictable fluctuations in price on the international market. Exporting coltan may not always create the foreign income necessary to buy all the imports that free trade makes available. It may be theoretically cheaper to buy imported rice, but if people aren't making any money because there aren't any jobs and there's not enough export money to redistribute, then even imported rice is probably still too expensive.

◆ ◆ ◆

Oxfam's report appeared at a time when spending on welfare programmes in rich countries was in decline too. US President Bill Clinton had campaigned in 1992 on the promise to 'end welfare as we have come to know it'. The Personal Responsibility and Work Opportunity Act was passed in 1996. For welfare reformists, the problem of a too-generous safety net was that it was disincentivizing people from working. What people needed, they argued, was the fear of poverty and insecurity to motivate them into being productive labourers.

For the United States, the argument for welfare reform was about who were and were not the 'deserving poor'. Women and children typically fell into the category of 'deserving', although with Ronald Reagan's invocation of a purely fabricated 'Welfare Queen' there was an explicitly racialized edge to that calculation.

But the United States wasn't just cutting welfare spending. It was also thinking about more efficient and effective welfare spending.

The sociologist Elizabeth Popp Berman has called the emergence of a form of neutral economic language in policymaking from the 1960s 'Thinking Like an Economist'.[6] The point of thinking like an economist was to see all policy problems as, fundamentally, microeconomic ones. If people could be expected to behave as rational economic actors (*ceteris paribus*), then the government's job was to create the right incentives for growth. Economic thinking was premised on the assumption of austerity and scarcity of resources. Governments, like private companies, should be interested in the bottom line. They should be after value for money.

This style of economic thinking was epitomized by World Bank President, Robert McNamara. McNamara had been brought into the Kennedy administration as Secretary of Defense during the Vietnam War, but he had started out at the Ford Motor Company. When the car manufacturer began to decline after the Second World War, McNamara had been part of a team who had organized themselves around the new ideas of business efficiency, using computers to streamline production and analyse data trends in the wider market.

As McNamara moved his skills into government in the 1960s, and then to the World Bank in 1968, he took with him a desire to facilitate growth and eliminate poverty. But he also brought along a view of the state that was sceptical of politics and sought to improve everyone's outcomes without having to deal with the question of redistribution. Like other development economists, he had hoped that growth would allow capitalist countries to dodge the uncomfortable question of wealth distribution put to them by their rival communists. Instead, McNamara and other efficiency-minded economists tried to focus on 'trade-offs at the margin   what the benefits of an additional unit would be relative to the cost, and what else those same resources might be used for'.[7]

The priority would no longer be economic growth, but how to most effectively allocate funds to improve the lives of the poor. The development economist Thandika Mkandawire noted that 'the choice between targeting and universalism is counted in the language of efficient allocation of resources subject to budget constraints'.[8]

♦ ♦ ♦

In 2005, the economist Jeffrey Sachs published *The End of Poverty*. In it he proposed something called 'clinical economics', a crucial component of which was that 'monitoring and evaluation are essential to successful treatment'.[9]

Campaigns like Make Poverty History put poverty firmly on the agenda of meetings of rich-country leaders like the G8. One of the campaign's key aims was for more and better aid. In 2005, the Paris Declaration on Aid Effectiveness set out principles for ensuring that 'better' was a measure of effectiveness. Between 2008 and 2012 the Organisation for Economic Co-Operation and Development (OECD) published a series of books on Better Aid, 'examining strategies for making aid more effective'. Its principles rested in part on incentive structures and ensuring value for money.

Empirical research into how poverty affected economic behaviours proliferated. Would people be more likely to use malaria nets if they were given them for free or if they had to pay a small amount for them? How did people living in poverty think about investment and risk? What, in other words, would be the most efficient and effective ways to invest small amounts of money in Africa for the largest results?[10]

In 2007, in his hit book *The Bottom Billion*, the economist Paul Collier explained why he thought that so many people were trapped in poverty.[11] Beyond the problem of African governance, he blamed the development industry's 'headless heart'. Rather than moralizing about poverty, they needed to come up with small and effective policy solutions. Heeding his call for efficiency, and tired of top-down, state-based development solutions, organizations like Oxfam, but also state agencies, sought more effective return on investment at the development margins. Impressed with books critical of the aid complex, they began to seek out better ways of measuring effectiveness.[12]

The idea was that humanitarian organizations would deliver aid as efficiently as a business. Everyone was encouraged to be on the lookout for potential quick fixes for poverty. The satirical blog Stuff Expat Aid Workers

Like noticed a pattern in the use of the language of tech entrepreneurship: 'patient zero was definitely a grad student with a solid academic background from a well-respected university, who noticed a problem in the developing world while volunteering or backpacking. This specimen then also noticed a technology that made that problem less bad and INNOVATEd! a solution. There's no question that patient zero was an E[xpat]A[id]W[orker]-to-be. (He is now a social entrepreneur.)'[13]

With tech start-up and management consulting as models, NGO reporting to donors became more stringent. The corporate language of consulting began to filter into aid. Stuff Expat Aid Workers Like lampooned the proliferation of toolkits, org charts and technological innovation. But the humanitarian organizations needed to borrow these methods to show effectiveness.

One consequence of this transformation was that donor whims also became more pronounced. Tools from the corporate sector helped to identify the impact of donor money on outcomes, rather than overheads. A wave of books appearing in the 2000s pointed to the staffing costs and other inefficiencies of most NGOs and charities. The ideas and tools of value-based management, where management is responsible for maximizing shareholder value, were brought into the aid sector.

Charity evaluators began to emerge, with their own measures of effectiveness and efficiency. GiveWell was founded in 2007 by hedge funders; Giving What We Can in 2009 by William MacAskill and Toby Ord, Oxford philosophers. They measured charities by things like the extent to which they 'demonstrably maximise the good they do with each dollar raised', but also ranked the charities for being research-based and third-party evaluated.[14] NGOs and charities began competing over their effectiveness and efficiency. One consequence of this was the shift of overheads – fundraising and administrative jobs – off the books to 'overburdened program staff, untrained volunteers, and external consultants'.[15]

My very first experience working in retail, in high school, was for a shop that sold items made in Fair Trade women's cooperatives. The shop relied on volunteer labour (including mine). But that was good, because it meant that more of the price consumers paid for the baskets, scarves and other things we sold went directly to the women's cooperatives making them. Fair Trade sought to make more efficient markets between the world's poorest producers and the world's richest consumers. Giving hand manufacturers and farmers access to the people who wanted to buy their goods was an attempt to solve the inefficient allocation of labour.

But wouldn't it be great if you could make money *while* being effective? Do well by doing good? MacAskill and Ord's Giving What We Can not only rated charities based on their effectiveness. It also served as a meta-charity for the emerging Effective Altruism movement. Effective Altruism brought together aspects of utilitarianism – the argument that we should be aiming for the greatest possible good for the greatest number of people – with some of the kinds of ideas that had been around since the Sierra Leone Company and Thomas Fowell Buxton: business could be a force for good. Giving What We Can's members pledged to give at least 10 per cent of their income to *effective* charities. Effective Altruists even worked out the cost of saving a life in the developing world: around $4,000.[16]

A big part of their philosophy was to encourage people not to go directly into the charity sector but, in order to have the most impact, to make as much money as they possibly could, the more effectively to redistribute their wealth: earning to give. As MacAskill posed the question in a lecture, 'What if I became an *altruistic banker*, pursuing a lucrative career in order to donate my earnings?'[17] They were going to do good by doing well. By 2022, Giving What We Can had received pledges of more than $2.5 billion from 7,000 people. The Oxford University news story celebrating this milestone in 2022 lists the cryptocurrency entrepreneur Sam Bankman-Fried as a significant donor and booster of the Effective Altruism movement, having promised 'the vast majority of his net worth' to the organization's efficient charities.[18]

♦ ♦ ♦

One of the major targets of research into effectiveness was the problem of insecurity and insuring against risk. Picking up on Dorothy Chiredze's comment about the wealthier farms in her village, Oxfam created a way for people in the Global North to 'invest' in a cow or a goat. I could buy a goat for my parents for Christmas, giving families in the Global South access to an asset that would generate returns in the form of milk, but also as an object of collateral that could be used to finance microloans or sold for a profit to fund a child's place at school. Providing a cow or a goat was a way of providing security. Having access to an asset was a way to insure against risk.

But having access to an asset also *allowed* for risk: entrepreneurial risk and the promise of exponential developmental growth that both individuals and nations hoped for. Across the board, these were largely hard-working people who didn't see a return on the investment of their labour – just more of the same day after day, and very little promise of anything better for their children. Credit could change that.

External aid agencies weren't the only ones trying to innovate solutions to the problem of the lack of capital. In Kenya, Uganda, Botswana, Ghana and Mozambique, mobile phone airtime credits were being used to pay small amounts for services as early as 2002; people would top them up when they had cash. Then, when they needed to make a small payment for a haircut, they would text some of that airtime credit to the mobile phone of the barber. The barber could then use that airtime to make calls, but equally could text it to another user to make a payment for something as well. Airtime was both valuable in its own right and fungible. It could also be broken down into very small units. Just as with cowries, a local solution to the small-change problem was developed.

In 2005, operatives from Safaricom, the largest telecoms operator in Kenya, partnered with Vodafone in the UK and approached the Department for International Development (DFID) to secure funding for a pilot launch of the product that would become M-Pesa mobile money. Using the tech start-up model, they sought to leapfrog the problem of a lack of banking services. The idea behind the M-Pesa bid was that Safaricom and Vodafone could fill the gap in banking services in East Africa by tapping into something that people were already doing.

Vodafone and DFID were interested in mobile banking options because of the craze for microfinance that was sweeping the development economics world in the first decade of the 2000s. Instead of relying on aid and going through formal, government-controlled channels, microfinance promised to kick-start entrepreneurship and get straight to those most in need of help.

The economist Muhammad Yunus had founded the first microfinance lender, Grameen Bank, in Bangladesh in 1976.[19] He saw that there was demand for credit among a part of the population that had trouble accessing financing because of high barriers to formal financial institutions. Yunus proposed that these could be overcome by taking advantage of existing lending networks, where women contributed to a small shared pot of money and then took it in turns to make larger withdrawals. By the early 2000s the idea had spread to development projects beyond Bangladesh. Parts of Africa where there were existing lending clubs and mutual aid societies seemed like a good opportunity.

The problem that Grameen Bank sought to solve was a big one: how to get poor people into the credit economy. The poor could never gather enough capital to start businesses, buy assets or invest in education. The growth required for economic development to continue had hit a wall. And that wall was *not* demand – there was plenty of that – but access to money. So why not solve that problem by creating money? Not printing it, of course, since we know that central bankers hated quantitative easing after the inflation of the 1970s. No, instead we could create *future* money. Give people credit and they will create the money to pay you back in the future. Give aspiring entrepreneurs access to small amounts of credit and they will be able to start a small business, satisfying a demand in their community and also creating money to pay back their investors. Invest in people.

◆ ◆ ◆

Microfinance lenders hoped that M-Pesa accounts would become an easy way to slowly repay small credit loans. Most people didn't end up using M-Pesa in the way Safaricom and Vodafone had intended. Instead, the pilot group used M-Pesa to send money to relatives and pay for goods and services. This was what the phone-credit system had been used for before M-Pesa was set up. Once M-Pesa was established, children who moved to the cities or migrated beyond the country continued to use it to send remittances back to their parents, families, extended families and age-mates in villages. They were earning to give.

As was the case with the Effective Altruists, there were already ideas in circulation about how to maximize investments, most of which were about a family making as much money as it could through efficient allocation of capital and redistribution. To release investment capital, a family might sell land to invest in one child going to university in the United States or in Europe. The child would pay the investment back in full and then provide a regular stream of remittances to family members.[20]

Those with less family capital might simply try to migrate anyway through less legal routes, picking up work along the way, only able to return home when they had capital to bring with them, when they had made their families proud, and when they could invest in another relative or age-mate's dreams.

Prior to COVID-19, remittances made up nearly the same amount of external financing as overseas development aid ($48 billion in 2019 versus $50 billion), compared to around $20 billion in foreign direct investment or in portfolio debt and equity flows.[21] And M-Pesa was one of the innovations that made remittances easier than ever in the twenty-first century. If securing foreign investment from official sources was difficult, then remittances from family living abroad were a way round the institutional barriers needed to convince foreign investors. Families and friends could tap into their wealth in people.

Wealth in people was about building up value in human beings. But this value came from a variety of sources: from the imagined value of those people to other people; from the value of the relationships that owning or controlling people facilitated; from the productive capacity of the people; from the reproductive capacity of the people; and from the status accumulation that wealth in people conferred. People are poor if they are without relationships.

♦ ♦ ♦

Peer-to-peer schemes, like the spate of get-rich-quick seminars and books that were proliferating in the US from the 1990s, also played on the idea that people were poor because they were not well connected or because they were not 'in the know' or willing to take clever risks. For those on the receiving end of help from the Global North there was a hazy border between solutions devised as 'one quick trick to end poverty' and 'one quick trick to get rich'.

In 1989, the Russian entrepreneur Sergei Mavrodi set up Mavrodi Mondial Moneybox. MMM promised investors 30 per cent returns. It had the tag line: 'Today you HELP someone. Tomorrow You will be Helped!!' MMM was successful because it traded on hopes: why shouldn't hard work yield prosperity? Why shouldn't people be able to work for themselves? Why shouldn't the standard of living improve every year? Why shouldn't neighbours help each other?

The Soviet Union was on the brink of collapse. Mavrodi, a bespectacled maths and engineering graduate with a prior history of economic manipulation, took advantage of the impact of the West's 'Shock Doctrine' on Russia's economy to convince people to invest their savings in his 'joint stock company'. With state assets being grabbed by oligarchs and people racing to capitalize on the uncertainty amid the collapse of the communist regime, Mavrodi's was only one of dozens of such schemes across the former Eastern Bloc countries. Taking advantage of people's fear and insecurity, Mavrodi billed his fund as giving 'a system and tool to people to fight against financial slavery' and to 'stop American Dollar Monopoly'.

What Mavrodi was offering was a voucher investment fund. MMM was a place for people to invest the privatization vouchers they received as state enterprises were sold off. But of course, when these vouchers were invested with Mavrodi they were not invested in anything real.

Like others who capitalized on the Soviet Union's privatization, Mavrodi had served in the government. He was elected to the Duma in 1994, which granted him immunity from prosecution. When MMM was declared bankrupt in 1997, Mavrodi disappeared. He was eventually sentenced in 2007.

After serving time in prison for defrauding millions of Russian investors, Mavrodi relaunched his fund in 2011, spreading to India, China, South Africa, Zimbabwe and Nigeria. Using Facebook and WhatsApp, the scheme brought in investors by relying on existing social networks and calling itself a 'social financial network'.

Schemes like MMM tap into wealth in people. Like microfinance, they also play on the language of 'mutual aid'. Building on those *esusu* clubs and other Indigenous credit institutions – where women banked their money together and took turns getting access to the pot to make a large purchase for their families – microlending was supposed to build on pre-existing trust networks and a sense of self-help. MMM also sold itself as 'a community of ordinary people, selflessly helping each other, a kind of Global Fund of mutual aid'. To get the returns on their investment, early investors were encouraged to sell the scheme to others. The more people who invested, the better the returns for the original investors. Unlike many other multilevel marketing schemes that proliferated at the same time using the same kinds of social networks, MMM Global was upfront about the pyramidal structure of this scheme. It was, unashamedly, a Ponzi scheme.

MMM was able to draw in investors because of the novelty of the technologies it used, combined with its appeals to pre-existing trust mechanisms. In Zimbabwe, EcoCash, the mobile payment platform, was advertised as being accepted for

MMM investments. This link between MMM and EcoCash legitimized the Ponzi scheme in the marks' minds. One of the Zimbabwean victims was quoted in a Nigerian newspaper warning its readers against investing in MMM. The victim commented that 'we believed that by using EcoCash to do the transactions, things were in order'.[22]

In multilevel marketing, microfinance and other innovations that facilitated individual entrepreneurship through technological innovations, networks of friendship and the idea of trust are sold as the key to success. They all appeal to the idea that through pure hustle and hard work, through mobilizing social networks and by having access to start-up capital – especially start-up capital that comes from those who trust your business sense – people will be able to propel themselves into a higher standard of living.[23] The uncertainty of the state and the seemingly endless decline of the standard of living provided the perfect economic culture for a scheme like MMM to blossom.

Mavrodi's death in 2018 didn't slow MMM's progress as it spread around Africa. The promise of 30, 50 or even 100 per cent returns attracted hundreds, then thousands, then millions of investors. And, like all Ponzi schemes, the later investors were inspired by the apparent success of those who got in first.

♦ ♦ ♦

MMM's second scheme, which launched in 2011 when Sergei Mavrodi was released from prison, was also based on the developing idea of cryptocurrency. MMM encouraged people to buy 'Mavro currency'. Mavros generated 525 per cent returns for investors who got in at the start of the pandemic and out at crypto's peak in April 2021. This cryptocurrency is still trading, though it is not available on the Binance or Coinbase trading platforms.

But plenty of other cryptocurrencies have emerged to compete with Mavro and build on the idea of a virtual currency de-linked from national financial institutions. Bankman-Fried's plan to donate billions to Effective Altruism causes rested on his exchange's ability to facilitate global crypto markets beyond the regulation of the state. Cryptocurrency took an African technology   mobile money that was a commodity-based unit of account and store of value, rather than a government-backed one – and globalized it.

Bitcoin, founded two years after M-Pesa, took this model a step further. If money wasn't 'real' in the sense that its worth derived from its perceived value relative to other currencies, or from the perceived worthiness of the state producing it, then – Bitcoin and other cryptocurrencies proposed – the state really wasn't necessary at all. But the susceptibility of crypto to bubbles and scams, perpetrated on populations struggling from the growth of the informal economy and declining standards of living across the West as well as Africa, showed that this supposedly new technology really was a commodity currency and would be subject, once again, to the old tests of trust and value.

Internet technologies were important in the rise of the new politics of the twenty-first century in Africa. But they were also carving out new paths in commerce. Tech became the latest tool for solving Africa's economic problems. Mobile phones had helped African people 'leapfrog' the problem of landlines.

Could individual solar panels help rural farmers leapfrog the electricity grid? Could blockchain do . . . something?

It's no surprise that the countries which were most susceptible to MMM are some of the most unequal in the world. But it's not poverty alone that incentivizes people to seek out get-rich-quick schemes. NGOs and movements like Effective Altruism are also susceptible to fraud. The same excitement about a quick fix for poverty had incentivized investment in tech-based approaches. And with the pressures on accountability, 'many NGOs feel pressure not to report fraud for fear the news of the defrauding would reduce public trust and deter future donations'.[24]

The reason for the appeal of get-rich-quick schemes is the obvious disconnect between hard work and the kinds of lifestyles people see around them. It is the sense that a declining public infrastructure, a retreating public sector, leaves the standard of living in an individual's hands. When the lights fail in Nigeria or South Africa, people who can afford private generators and the fuel to run them don't notice. When there is too little public transport and roads are clogged for hours, people who can afford air-conditioned cars instead of crowding into sweltering *danfo* taxis barely notice. When the naira or the rand crashes, people who have parked their money in 'safer' investments like crypto or British real estate, or who have invested in sending family abroad so they have access to forex from family remittances, don't feel the pinch.

Insuring against insecurity is an effective and efficient means of eradicating poverty for some. For others, it's a way to get rich quick. And for many, the line between those is non-existent. Doing good by doing well and doing well by doing good were two sides of the same (crypto) coin. The reward seemed worth the risk.

◆ ◆ ◆

In 2023, the MMM GLOBAL 2022/2023 OFFICIALS Facebook page had 7,800 members. My view of the page notified me that '24 members said they went to University of Oxford'. They were in my social network. We may even have met back in 2005, when I was wearing my Make Poverty History bracelet to lectures. MMM still relies on social networks, on trust, on wealth in people.

When you open the page today it is covered in South African multilevel marketing – referred to as 'network marketing' on the site – for Air Rose air fresheners. Members of the MMM Global group are exhorted to 'Join AIR ROSE and have financial freedom'. Air Rose has 'a dual income stream' model for its affiliates. They buy stock for 500, 1000, 1,500 or 2,000 ZAR and 'get from 100 per cent Profit into your pocket' from sales. The other aspect of the income stream is explicitly laid out as a pyramid: 'You get paid when you recruit other people to join the business under you.' This was, at least, more upfront than Effective Altruist Sam Bankman-Fried's crypto fund. When Bankman-Fried was convicted of fraud in November 2023, his crypto exchange, FTX, 'began trying to claw back donations'.[25]

Nigerian filmmaker Ike Nnaebue, who attempted to migrate illegally to Europe at twenty years old, recently made a film called *No U-Turn* exploring the risky routes that migrants try to use to get out of West Africa to Europe in search of work. Along the way his film encounters people at all stages of their attempt, including a woman stuck in Mali who had migrated from Nigeria. As she tells her story, she proudly insists that she cannot go back since she has not yet made the money she needs to help her family. Returning now would make her a burden. But she won't resort to prostitution. She is a businesswoman. She runs a business. She is selling air fresheners.

CHAPTER 8

WOMEN ARE NOTHING MORE THAN SLAVES

In 2023, USAID reaffirmed 'that gender equality and women's empowerment are fundamental for the realization of human rights and key to sustainable development outcomes'. Christian Aid, the British Anglican charity, identified that 'unequal distribution of power – most pervasive between women and men – is at the heart of poverty'. A quick look through the websites of your favourite international charities will show you that empowering 'women and girls' in the economy is an important and omnipresent goal. Surely, also, one that is fairly uncontroversial.

As the twentieth century drew to a close, humanitarian concerns about women coincided with a growing women's peace movement in places like Liberia to generate a new focus on the place of women in development. Women were on the development agenda because their perceived lack of emancipation in African societies was deemed an economic problem. Women couldn't set up businesses, women were having too many children, women were holding back the economic boom. Inequality was growing and women were being left behind.

The rebuilding of numerous African states devastated by conflicts after the collapse of Cold War regimes in the 1990s and early 2000s gave intervening states and organizations the opportunity to promote women's entry into the workforce through education, training, job placement and empowerment initiatives. Many of these were based on the idea that, traditionally, women were stuck in the household. Because Africa as a whole was seen to be 'developmentally' fifty years behind the West, the logic followed that its women must be stuck in the 1950s too. This was hardly a new idea. Victorian missionaries had also identified a gender problem at the heart of African poverty. Still attempting to save African women from drudgery, the new generation of foreign experts with good intentions commanded that, this time, a modern economic woman must be part of the workforce rather than a homemaker.

◆　◆　◆

When missionary and anti-slavery activists began to intervene in African economies in the nineteenth century, the European system of primogeniture was on its way out everywhere but Britain. The French Revolution had abolished the system in which the eldest male heir inherited everything and most European countries had followed suit. But in nineteenth-century Britain it was still common for the eldest son to inherit all the property in a family. British families were expected to provide dowries to the men who married their daughters, and that wealth would be transferred directly to the much-hoped-for male heir. Primogeniture led to the preference for sons, as daughters were a drain on family resources while sons could accumulate wealth to the family through marriage. This is the social problem at the heart of stories like *Downton Abbey* or *Pride and Prejudice*.

But having many daughters in a wide variety of African cultures was not an economic problem in the same way it was for Mr Bennet, who had to find dowries for five daughters. In fact, in 'labour-scarce' societies, having multiple wives was a solution to the problem of labour-intensive self-sufficiency. This was important because, as the economic historian Robert Allen has argued, the amount of work needed to produce food for a family in a 'subsistence'-style setting would have required a woman to work six hours a day, assuming a man was helping for two hours.[1] If two hours doesn't sound like much, bear in mind that the OECD's current estimate of the 'second shift' that people do in domestic chores after their waged job is about four hours a day for women and about two and a half for men.[2] In addition to being able to rotate chores – taking turns to cook, for instance – having more wives meant (potentially) more (legitimate) children as well, adding much-needed labour to the community.

In wealth-in-people societies women were highly valued because of their reproductive capacity, as well as their productive capacity. In the Cold War era, early economic anthropologists thought of the household and the marketplace as distinct but interlocking economic institutions. The anthropologists Laura and Paul Bohannan, working in Nigeria, for instance, argued that while to 'modern Western or Soviet types of societies, the question of family organization is peripheral . . . among the Tiv, the primary institutionalized means by which people obtain their subsistence is the domestic unit'.[3] Crucial to the domestic unit in these contexts was the institution of polygyny, which allowed the (extended) household to farm, cook, reproduce and go to market.

In the nineteenth-century US enslavement economy, women of prime childbearing age were valued at nearly the same price as men of prime working age.[4] And although enslaved men were valued at a premium in the New Orleans market, 'female prices actually exceeded male prices for young slaves'.[5] In Northern Nigeria, which had a similar plantation-based economy in the mid-nineteenth century, 'a young male slave, from thirteen to twenty years of age, will bring from 10,000 to 20,000 cowries [$5–10]; a female slave, if very handsome, from 40,000 to 50,000 [$20–25]; the common price is about 30,000 [$15] for a virgin about fourteen or fifteen'.[6] Within Equatorial African societies, a wife who bore no children 'became designated as *metut* – low status women' who could be 'exchanged at a husband's discretion, for example, to settle a debt'.[7]

Marriage and household-building were an important cultural aspect of wealth-in-people value systems. The extended household model of enslavement doesn't fit the grim realities faced by enslaved people who were far from treated as part of a kin-based domestic unit. But from the perspective of flexibility of labour, slavery provided the equivalent of an enlarged household. Economist Christopher Hanes argued that 'because the transfer of labour in any form involved transactions costs, the labour of any employee was (and is) more costly than a potential employer's own labour, or the labour of his family'. He explains that 'an employer could not compete with family production unless the optimal scale of production demanded more labour than one family could provide'.[8]

In plantation economies the scale of production did require more labour than one family could provide, but it was also labour that was unevenly distributed across the year – something that sharp-eyed liberal abolitionists noted when they discussed the inefficiency of enslaved labour. They thought that having enslaved people 'on the books' in the off season was a luxury that made slavery a purely aristocratic status symbol. But the reality, as the economist Suresh Naidu highlights, is that slavery – like family labour – is the most responsive economic system for the allocation of labour to demand.[9]

◆ ◆ ◆

Among people like the Tiv in Nigeria or the Maradi in Niger, it was the husband who had to pay a family in order to marry and not (as in the UK) the other way round. In the Maradi Valley both enslaved women and free women were 'tied' to a man, but 'in principle the transfer of a *sadaki* (bridewealth) payment stated publicly and unambiguously the freeborn status of the woman'.[10] The *sadaki* consisted of a cow, goat or camel and 'was generally considered to be the property of the bride . . . it served as both a symbol and a source of . . . prosperity, fertility, and wealth – by producing wealth in the form of offspring for the bride . . . when you had it for a while it would give birth, and then the offspring was yours as well. You wouldn't slaughter it.'[11]

Because of women's clear value, girls were in fact a boon, because women carried the family bridewealth with them into marriage. Bridewealth was not exactly a payment for a bride. It was meant to be a recognition of the fact that the family who was losing a daughter would be losing a productive member of the household. Elopement without the payment of bridewealth threatened any future claim the husband might have on litigation, adultery complaints, or his children.[12]

In matrilineal societies, such as among groups in Ghana and Senegal, Zambia and Angola, men did not inherit in the same way as they did in countries with primogeniture. Fathers, in fact, only had sole responsibility for children born to enslaved women. Decisions about the future of children of free women in these societies were referred to their mother's brothers. When a man died it was his sister's sons who would inherit, rather than his own children. And when a daughter married, the bridewealth would be paid to her maternal uncles as well as a share to her father. If a man wanted to marry he needed to earn the 'bridewealth' he would use to pay to his future wife's family, or he could seek support from his mother's family.

And even in patrilineal African societies there are plenty of examples of women's value. A folk tale from south-eastern Nigeria, recorded by a British district commissioner in 1910, told the story of a tortoise with a beautiful daughter whom the prince wanted to marry. The moral of the story was 'always have pretty daughters, as no matter how poor they may be, there is always the chance that the king's son may fall in love with them'.[13]

So if this was the reality – that women were highly valued for their economic contribution – then how did the idea that African women needed economic rescue get started?

◆ ◆ ◆

By the second half of the nineteenth century, a mission to rescue Africa's women from drudgery was in full swing. The era of Victorian ideals, with the wife in charge of a separate domestic economy of efficient and sanitary household management, had replaced the Georgian period's more liberated attitude towards women's rights. Helping Africa's women to have the 'correct' role in the economy became a major rallying cry for European intervention and colonial expansion.

In many rural communities, the women of the household – wives, enslaved women, daughters, grandmothers – shared responsibilities for certain household duties that would be recognizable to European women missionaries and teachers, but their living arrangements were deemed unseemly and premodern. The institution of polygyny especially was seen as contrary to Christian ideals. Middle-class Victorians may have relied on a range of women as domestic servants, but only one woman in the household was allowed to have conjugal rights.

The concern among colonial officials and abolitionist women was twofold: on the one hand, women's role in society could be virtually indistinguishable from enslavement, particularly in polygynous societies. 'Bridewealth' reeked of purchase price. Plural marriage was a clear display of wealth. And the work that women did in expanding and labouring for the household went unremunerated while contributing to its growth. But on the other hand, anti-slavery activists were certainly not promoting the abolition of the family! As the scholars Benedetta Rossi and Joel Quirk argue, 'The end result can be best described as a patriarchal bargain, with European colonial authorities – who were overwhelmingly male – reaching a tacit bargain with African political elites – also overwhelmingly male – to minimize disruption of the status quo by establishing pathways that enabled them to uphold their authority within the household'.[14]

It was, in fact, the *imposition* of European gender norms of work and household economy that led to the elision between slavery and marriage. Europeans assumed that wives had similarly limited rights under African legal traditions as under European ones. They therefore struggled to see the forms of economic autonomy that women had in African society, and thought that slavery and marriage were pretty similar. Because they refused to compensate slave owners in Africa, they would never have paid them to emancipate their enslaved women and girls. And so, instead, African slave owners used the assumptions of European men about the status of African wives to merge their enslaved women and girls into their households under the rules accepted by European society.

◆　◆　◆

From their first interventions into the slave trade economy, European philanthropists had been attracted to the idea of supporting women and girls. When British missionaries began to arrive in Sierra Leone they saw an opportunity to help the people who had been resettled there as 'recaptives' from the slave trade. The British anti-slave-trade squadron brought hundreds of people a year to Freetown after they had been intercepted on illegal slaving ships. But they weren't really sure what to do with them once they arrived. Freetown wasn't their home; it was a refugee station. So when missionaries stepped up with a plan for educating the former captives in Christianity and in skilled work, the British state was happy to hand responsibility over to them.

Individual girls could be sponsored by women's church groups in Britain to attend missionary schools. As the apparent benefits of attaining a European education became clear to local parents, who wanted their daughters to continue to be valuable to their families as society changed, the mission schools also became a popular option for those who could pay for their children to attend.

The historian Silke Strickrodt looked at a variety of sewing samplers from a girls' school set up by missionaries in colonial Sierra Leone to identify the clash in ideas and values between the British sponsors and the Sierra Leone parents. Time and again, the parents who could afford private education were interested in the same things as their British counterparts were: the attributes that would make their daughters more valuable on the marriage market, including French lessons, dancing, painting and politics. Julia Sass was the leader of the upper-class Female Institution, a boarding school that operated for West Africa's emerging elite in the 1850s and 1860s. Parents paying for their daughters' education told the school that 'it had become absolutely necessary for girls to read, write, cast up accounts, work and "know well to mind the house"'.[15] To become, in other words, like upper-class European women.

The missionaries, on the other hand, were interested in teaching what they thought of as 'humble domestic skills' to help the girls become 'quiet sensible housewives': skills like sewing, cooking and hygiene.[16] According to Strickrodt, girls spent around two hours a day, five days a week, learning to sew. And what did the girls sew? – 'upwards of 100 shirts for the Liberated African Boys'.[17]

The skills of needlework were valued by local parents, but not for the same reasons that the missionaries valued them: girls left the school to become dressmakers in Freetown, living independently or with other girls who had the same skills. The missionaries, according to Strickrodt, resented this. In fact, one of the reasons they promoted sewing was to encourage women to stay at home. But in Freetown, as in many growing market towns in Africa, 'women were used to earning their own money rather than being financially dependent on their husbands'. In the 1831 census of Freetown there were 217 'market women' listed – 7 per cent of the total population.[18]

When Catholic missionaries arrived in the 1860s and set up their own school for girls, parents used the denominational competition to induce the Female Institution to reluctantly offer the kinds of subjects they wanted: 'water colours, Music, French language, artificial flowers, Ancient and modern history'.[19] It looked as if the competition between Europeans would work to the advantage of African parents.

But when a new head teacher arrived in the late 1870s, the school changed direction again. The new head and his wife reoriented the curriculum along the lines of an industrial school model, with the broader implication that African women should be trained for service rather than as middle-class homemakers and wives. They were to do their own laundry and make their own food rather than learn languages and arts and other 'accomplishments' that ladies should be expected to know.

This was part of that earlier-discussed swing towards industrial and 'practical' education that was taking place in Britain at the same time, a backlash against lower-middle-class and working-class people getting above themselves in their demands for destinies that matched their education. What countries needed, economists and sociologists argued, were people with industrial and agricultural skills.

The particular manifestation of this argument in colonized Africa was that African workers needed the kinds of skills that were valuable to the colonial economy. That value came from two directions: they could be valuable as consumers, and they could be valuable as labourers. These changes filtered into the economy in unexpected ways. One example of the shift in work patterns was the emergence of Akwete cloth in south-eastern Nigeria. Scholars have identified the emergence of this cloth in the late nineteenth century as a response to the overwhelming importation of cheap British cloth. Akwete cloth was high-end, intended for special occasions. It was expensive – a luxury – rather than a staple. It was produced exclusively by women, on a wider loom than had been traditionally used by the men who had been weavers before colonial rule. And Akwete was made with imported thread as a labour-saving innovation. In previous cloth-making traditions in the region women had been the thread spinners, and thread had never needed to be imported. But since men were working wage-labour jobs or engaged in commercial agriculture and women were doing the weaving as a full-time occupation, spinning the thread was effectively outsourced to Britain.[20]

As we saw in earlier chapters, during the colonial period men were increasingly under pressure to take on wage-labour jobs in agriculture or go to big cities or work in mines to earn money to pay the new colonial taxes. Women's domestic work allowed men to go out to wage-earning jobs. This shift to a more patriarchal model of organizing labour around wage-earning rather than household production meant that men, who earned higher wages than women outside the household, were valued, while women, who either did not earn wages outside the house or did so at a lower wage rate, were less valuable. In both cases, colonial rule sought to suppress the wages of African workers to ensure that European companies were profitable. Men were expected to be wage earners, but they weren't paid enough to make up for the loss of their labour at home or to improve the standard of living of their families. And so, despite government disincentives and missionary arguments, poverty meant that most women were also needed for wage labour.

The calculation in which large families had provided wealth in people began to falter. Daughters were newly a drain on family resources because they did not contribute wages. Where families could not survive without women's wages they sent their daughters to cities where they undertook informal employment in cash work – providing meals to migrant workers or prostitution or beer-brewing. But these were paid poorly, and in the case of prostitution were not respected. Some became live-in domestic servants for European expats, colonial officials and settlers, where their maintenance was outsourced to their employer and wages could be sent back home. Education became less of a priority, and in places where girls did attend schools, the education they needed to contribute to the economy primarily consisted of skills associated with being domestic servants: ironing, laundry, mending clothes, cooking, cleaning.[21]

The impact of wage labour was complex. In the region of Nigeria around Abeokuta, for example, women had always 'processed the palm oil from the palm fruit and also dominated its retail sale'.[22] With the expansion of the palm oil trade in the colonial period women had profited and 'also dominated the retail trade in cloth and foodstuffs in the town's markets'.[23] Then with the gradual end of enslavement came (as we have seen) a general labour shortage and the imposition of labour taxes. At this point marriage (and offspring) became an important alternative source of labour. Bride prices shot up and families were incentivized to marry their daughters off rather than send them to school. But at the same time, divorce rates increased because monogamy was incentivized by the state. One way of continuing to have an expanded household and wealth in people without polygyny is to undertake successive marriages rather than simultaneous ones. British colonial officials complained that 'the family system is breaking down' because husbands did not have what one official assumed was their 'absolute power over their wives as heretofore'.[24]

These mixed feelings about the economic empowerment of women and its social consequences led colonial policymakers into different means of trying to incentivize European models of domesticity for women. In Nigeria, sanitation fines, for instance, were imposed only on women, whom the colonial government deemed responsible for maintaining the tidy appearance of neighbourhoods. Later colonial taxation included wives in the assessment of the value of a household, the first wife being included in the £1 annual tax rate with 'a further tax of 10/- per annum for each additional wife' in order to try to disincentivize polygyny.[25] But at the same time, Egba women were taxed independently, on the basis of Yoruba precedent and because so many Egba women were proprietors in their own right.

In other words, the propensity to view women's agency primarily through the lens of economic contribution (which can be taxed) or household contribution (which had reproductive value) was a problem that persisted from the abolition of slavery onwards. Inequality of power was a structural feature of enslavement. The complexities of concubinage and the use of enslavement to 'reproduce' both the family labour force and the wealth of the patriarch made women's economic power a continually problematic site of intervention in African economic life. But it was European ideas of marriage that conflated slaves and wives, rather than a standard interpretation stemming from African ideas.

It was this position that led to the Egba Women's Tax Riot of 1947. Joining together to protest against the unfair treatment of women under the tax codes, members of the Abeokuta Women's Union, led by local headteacher Funmilayo Ransome-Kuti, had come together to, among other goals, 'cooperate with all organizations seeking and fighting genuinely and selflessly for the economic and political freedom and independence of the people'.[26] Objecting to intrusive tax collection policies – including stripping girl traders to determine if they were old enough to pay the taxes that women paid – they also demanded representation as taxpayers. In Nigeria, the Lagos Market Women's Association and the Abeokuta Women's Union were at the forefront of seeking women's economic empowerment. The Egba Women's Tax Riot pushed back against the presumption that wage-earning was the correct economic realm for men and that women as traders were an aberration. In particular, the women were frustrated that they were taxed without representation in government. These protests played an important role in shaping the argument more generally for representative government and national self-determination.

◆ ◆ ◆

When national governments came to power in the 1960s, one of the signs of economic and social modernity and a rising standard of living that they embraced was the ability of a single male wage earner to provide for the family. The 'breadwinner' would enable the modern woman to step back from the backbreaking and demoralizing labour imposed on her by the inequalities of colonial rule.

And so the Victorian goal of relieving women of 'drudgery' re-emerged as a project of late-colonial development and the nascent field of development economics. Arthur Lewis, in making the case for economic growth, argued that

In most under-developed countries woman is a drudge, doing in the household tasks which in more advanced societies are done by mechanical power – grinding grain for hours, walking miles to fetch pails of water, and so on. Economic growth transfers these and many other tasks – spinning and weaving, teaching children, minding the sick – to external establishments, where they are done with greater specialization and greater capital, and with all the advantages of large-scale production. In the process woman gains freedom from drudgery, is emancipated from the seclusion of the household, and gains at last the chance to be a full human being.[27]

Many of the improved conditions that Lewis pointed to actually relied on the state. Investment in infrastructure, for instance: building water and sewage systems and connecting them to houses.

Polly Hill explained that there was a 'women problem' in development economics in the 1970s because of assumptions made in data collection about where economic activity was taking place, how to account for it in understanding household wealth, and in calculating GDP. For instance, 'particularly in their trading activities, women are sometimes richer than their husbands, to whom they often grant loans'. And 'in many West African societies it is common for wives to receive partial maintenance only, as they are expected to procure some of the food required by themselves and their children, especially at certain seasons'. The assumption in the 1960s and 1970s that men were the primary breadwinners and that their wages accounted for the household wealth was flawed. As Hill explained, rural women's involvement in farming and marketing made it 'entirely conceivable that women . . .

are responsible for a larger proportion of the gross domestic product than are men'.[28]

In newly independent states in the 1960s lower-middle-class women might have aspired to stay at home and to fill their houses with the labour-saving appliances being advertised by US and European manufacturers. With big state investment in electrification projects, refrigerators, electric cookers, washing machines and hoovers looked poised to shift the labour burden of domestic economy for the middle class. But for the vast majority, work outside the home, for the market, was part of the mix of activities that they contributed to the household economy. A lower-middle-class family might still send children out before and after school to hawk food cooked by a stay-at-home mother to help supplement the family income.

And when the economic decline of the 1980s hit African economies and the provision of electricity began to be intermittent, the proportion of women who could afford to shift fully away from domestic labour decreased. It looked as if they would carry the burden of household labour indefinitely. The labour-saving technologies that had allowed women in wealthy economies to go into the workforce without shifting the gendered ideas of housekeeping as 'women's work' were not as widely available in African contexts, where electrification was increasingly sporadic and imports of white goods were inconsistent. And so the way of 'relieving' middle-class women of 'drudgery' was simply by employing other women to do it for them.

◆ ◆ ◆

What is interesting about the shifting attention of development economists to the role of women is the way that it aligns with a move towards needing to explain *all* values as economically motivated. In development circles, the case being made is that the cultural practice in 'less developed countries' holds girls back; more investment in specifically girls' education and women's empowerment would yield economic gains 'in the order of $5–6 trillion'; and an 'ambitious and shared commitment' is needed for 'closing gender gaps and promoting girls' and women's empowerment'.[29]

Gender equality isn't a neutral idea. It is a culturally and historically specific one. It happens to be one I agree with. But accepting that it is historically and culturally specific means that imposing it on someone else comes with shades of imperialism. This isn't, in fact, a universal value, even if we think it *ought* to be. So rather than risk the appearance of yet another dance around the 'the way you do gender is wrong' imperial game, well-intentioned people have decided to find an incontrovertible, measurable, materialist rationale for gender equality: it's good for your economy. Rather than focusing on human rights or equality, the economic framing of women's and girls' empowerment emphasizes the gains in GDP to be made through 'getting women into the market'.

For instance, in the spring of 2019 the UK launched a global fund to 'help end "period poverty" by 2050'. This was not merely a government-driven initiative; in fact they were responding to a groundswell of interest across rich countries. The World Economic Forum explained that 'period poverty is a reality to many women and girls in low- and middle-income nations', including in Africa, where 'discussions around puberty is [*sic*] still considered a taboo' for 'cultural or religious' reasons. The World Economic Forum celebrated a project in Abuja, Nigeria 'teaching girls to manufacture reusable sanitary pads' and noted that 'the skill in learning how to make these products could be commodified and a source of income'.[30] It couldn't just be good in its own right, something to make women's lives better. It had to be economically beneficial and, specifically, commodifiable. Something that would boost GDP and/or reduce poverty.

Fundamentally, none of these approaches address the elephant in the room: the problem of trying to quantify the work of the household in a society where only labour outside the home is considered 'work'. A lot of the well-meaning remedies to the 'drudgery' of household domestic tasks assume that people gain a sense of selfhood and dignity in their work through specialization, rather than control over the environment of production. Do I want to spend all day cleaning my house? I do not. Does my house need to be cleaned? Probably. Is 'the economy' better off if I hire someone to clean my house, or if I do it myself? What about if my husband and I shared it? How would 'the economy' know? How would you even measure the economic impact of a clean division of labour?

Polly Hill's *Development Economics on Trial* was an important text that challenged many of the assumptions made by modernization theorists in their development plans in the post-war and postcolonial era. Modernization theorists were preoccupied by the debate between Marxist and capitalist ideas about the progress of development. This preoccupation led them to centre ideas of industrial labour, breadwinner households and the role of the export economy in facilitating growth. But Hill and other economic anthropologists began to note the importance of domestic economy, the under-reporting of internal markets, and assumptions about how household labour was divided that held no water in (particularly West) African rural contexts.

Measures of economic development, she argued, took for granted that workers – labourers, peasants, traders – were men, while 'the very word *work* is seriously biased against women, if only because it normally excludes domestic labour performed within the home'.[31]

But this isn't a problem only for development economics, as Polly Hill points out: 'this is, incidentally, a statistical problem for the first as well as for the third world where, for example, increasing participation of women in part-time paid employment sometimes leads, as in present-day [1970] Britain, to the simultaneous and confusing rise in rates of both unemployment and employment'.[32]

Economists haven't figured out how to account for the economic value of housework, unless the labour for it was bought in from the market. And the assumption is that by 'freeing' women of housework they can add to the welfare of the country by monetizing their economic contributions. But the '$5–6 trillion' that could be added to the economy by enhancing girls' education seems to be countered by another '$6 trillion' that would be added just by counting the hours spent changing nappies, doing laundry, preparing dinner and the other housework that isn't usually outsourced.[33]

In calculating social and cultural goods in economic terms there is an appeal to universality and neutrality that Adam

Smith would have recognized. It is the neutrality of Popp Berman's 'economic thinking'. In eras of polarized morality when it seems impossible to get people to agree, the economy seems to offer a clean, mathematical measure of what is good. But the idea that the economy is divorced from social norms and cultural values is a false hope.

♦ ♦ ♦

The recent trend of 'redshirting' boys in US schools – holding them back to the next school year – and policy debates around universally starting boys a year later in school than girls proceed in part from the suggestion that boys are biologically different in their rate of development.[34] Research identifying that boys born at the start of the school year do better in sports has spilled over into other applications. Anecdotally, from discussions in the playgrounds and at the school gates in Britain, parents think it is just a matter of scientific fact that girls develop more quickly. But rather than recognizing this phenomenon as a social and cultural development that stems from a shift in expectations, measures and outcomes, the assumption is that poor economic outcomes for a particular demographic of boys leaving school are biological: boys need more time; girls are too quick for them; we need to level the playing field.

The consensus in countries where girls have overtaken boys in school outcomes (though not in later career advancement or in average earnings) is that empowering girls was good, but now we need to empower boys. Masculinity crises have been identified on both the left and right as one of the potential causes of the rise of far-right politics across countries like the United States and UK.[35] There is certainly a lot of research to suggest that expectations about the gendered nature of certain jobs have made the transition from an industrial labour force to a service economy difficult for many young men. They struggle to see a role for themselves in the economy that will allow them to be providers, improve their family's standard of living and fulfil all the gendered expectations that parents, friends, wives and the wider culture place on them. This has also been a feature of the shift towards telling young women that they are expected to do everything that a young man can do in work *and* also be mothers, household managers and fulfil all the gendered expectations that come with being a woman.

There are educational and cultural issues underlying these economic changes, largely stemming from expectations of what is 'men's work' and what is 'women's work'. But very few people in rich economies seem to buy the idea that simply freeing up women for employment in the formal economy and educating people about the economic benefits that their wages contribute to GDP have 'solved' the problems of the gender wage gap, the unequal division of household labour, or the crises of a declining industrial sector.

All of which is to say that turning to Africa and saying that 'their economic problem is that they need to release the potential of their girls and women' is not as straightforward a proposal as many Western do-gooders might hope. As has been the pattern with well-meaning economic interventions for two centuries, a problem that rich countries think they have solved, and think explains their wealth, is then identified in Africa. And people, only too eager to help, set out with ready-made solutions.

◆ ◆ ◆

Women in Africa are definitely working, and they are working outside the home. A UN Development Programme and World Bank report on African development indicators in the 1980s showed that around 40 per cent of the Sub-Saharan African labour force was female. This ranged from 50 per cent in Tanzania to 40 per cent in Kenya to 17 per cent in Mali.[36] In 2021, the total labour force participation rate in Ghana was 71 per cent. Men's participation was 70 per cent and women's was 65 per cent.

While women's unemployment is a problem, men's unemployment is also a problem. And while, in theory, the idea of bringing more productive human capital into the formal, waged economy could expand consumer power and increase GDP growth, this is most useful in places where labour is expensive rather than where it is made cheap by high unemployment. Not measuring the informal sector and not measuring domestic work create the impression of a non-productive labour force – the 'lazy' myth resurfacing – rather than recognizing the lack of formal-sector jobs for men *and* for women as a problem of global capital allocation.

In one recent study of long-term trends, historians showed that in Sub-Saharan Africa, 'If gender gaps are primarily dynamic, the implication is that they can be best resolved through investment in overall educational expansion.'[37] In places and times where families have had to cut back on their daughters' school attendance, it isn't because they haven't been taught the value of women. It is because of a lack of funding. Where more *people* go to school, more girls go to school. Where there are more formal-sector jobs, more women work in the formal sector. Where there is less inequality, there is less male–female inequality. This is a two-genders problem.

But it is also the inverse of the 'economic thinking' framing: it is not that targeting girls' education will expand the economy, it is not that a quick policy or cultural fix will boost the economy and solve poverty and inequality, but that *spending* money on education, state services and jobs across the board will improve girls' outcomes, and outcomes for everyone.

HOW TO THINK DIFFERENTLY ABOUT AFRICAN ECONOMICS

Thomas Sankara was born in 1949, the son of a policeman in the French colony then known as Upper Volta (Burkina Faso). He was a good student at school and, when the government of the newly independent Upper Volta introduced military academies as part of a range of investments in the state and education, Sankara chose to attend. His teacher for history and geography, Adama Touré, was a member of PAI, the African Independence Party. He taught Sankara about socialism and gave him books to read about imperialism. When Sankara was sent thousands of miles away to Madagascar in 1969 for officer training, he got to witness some of the principles of development economics in action. He learned about agriculture and economics as well as more traditional military leadership. After the training ended he stayed to work with the green berets there, a public-service corps dedicated to development projects. He took these ideas back with him to Upper Volta's capital, Ouagadougou, where he was assigned to the army engineering corps to oversee construction and other development projects.

Over the course of the 1970s – a decade that put an end to the hopes of independence as a political *and* an economic project – Sankara worked his way up the ranks of the army, impressing his superiors and making a name for himself as a socialist interested in local development projects.

In 1980, Colonel Saye Zerbo staged a coup against President Sangoulé Lamizana, who had been in office since 1966. Zerbo gave Sankara his first government post, as Minister of Information. Zerbo's government was supposed to be fighting corruption. Sankara took that seriously, allowing the press the freedom to investigate corrupt officials. This went down like a proverbial lead balloon. Sankara left the government and retained his anti-corruption image.

Throughout his career, the danger of gifts – the under-standing that gifts are usually reciprocal, which the Temne were aware of, as we saw in Chapter 1 – was the target of Sankara's anti-imperialism. He saw that gifts of aid commit-ted African governments to pursuing international priorities. The conditions of aid were undermining African independence.

Sankara also pointed out something that is regularly overlooked in the story of international debt relief: the role of Africa in the rebuilding of Europe at the end of the Second World War.

The Marshall Plan – the economic recovery plan – put in place by the United States in 1948 transferred $13.3 billion to France, Britain, West Germany, Portugal, Italy, Greece, Turkey, Ireland, Iceland, Sweden, Norway, Denmark, the Netherlands, Switzerland (why? No, but seriously, why?), Austria, Belgium and Luxembourg (really?!). The idea was that the Marshall Plan would help Europe to boost production, provide new consumer markets and trade partners for the United States, and contain the Soviet threat. Development would make people happy, which would keep them away from communism.

Sankara looked at the Marshall Plan and saw an example of lending that was perfectly compatible with social welfare spending, with autonomy about where and how the money was spent and with the priorities of the people. But this was not Africa's experience of international aid after the war. Sankara spoke at the Organization of African Unity in 1987, arguing that 'We hear about the Marshall Plan that rebuilt Europe's economy. But we never hear about the African plan which allowed Europe to face Hitlerian hordes when their economies and their stability were at stake. Who saved Europe? Africa.'[1] The 'gift' of African aid sent to Europe – in the form of the continent's raw materials and soldiers – helped Europe to pay off its debts to the United States.

But as Sankara saw it, instead of recognizing their debts to Africa, the Europeans were acting as though they were the ones giving a gift. Money – in the form of aid – is intended to keep the giver in a position of power: it is good for 'stability', which is good for credit, which is good for long-term infrastructure development. But, as the 1970s and 1980s showed, this way of framing aid as a personal gift was a disaster for the people of West Africa who, like Sankara, thought that the personal indebtedness that accompanied the money meant that politicians owed favours to the people who gave it. Instead of working for the people of their country, they work for their gift givers.

And Sankara did not buy into that. So when, after a series of coups and counter-coups, he was announced as the new President of Upper Volta in August 1983, France and the United States were worried. Sankara had met with Libyan President Muammar Gaddafi. He publicly repudiated the neocolonialism of debt. And he suggested that Upper Volta – whose name he changed to Burkina Faso, or 'land of the upright people' – should concentrate on making its own food, its own consumer goods.

Sankara's tendency to play many different aid and trade partners off against each other was an attempt to re-establish some of the power and autonomy held by African leaders during the eighteenth century. France and, to a lesser extent, the United States were concerned about the appeal of Burkina Faso to socialist countries like Libya, Cuba and China.

People always want to talk about China, so this is as good a time as any to digress. Isn't what China is doing in Africa a form of colonialism? Aren't they entrapping African countries in debt? They only want access to resources, they have no good intentions, surely EU/British/American investment is *better* for the continent because it comes with goodwill and the 'right' values. But for leaders like Sankara, having multiple options – even some that Western countries deemed un-savoury – meant having agency and power. Sometimes this can be good for African economies.

Of course, what is good for African economies is not always the same thing as what is good for the people of those countries. Countries are made up of people with a huge range of interests – importers, exporters, service industries, parents, farmers, tech entrepreneurs, politicians, religious figures. In foreign relations, international financing and aid it can be tempting to equate one of those groups with the interests of the nation. A dam will be good for the country, even if it's bad for the people who live in the area that will be flooded. Tariffs on imports are great for burgeoning industry, but possibly bad for consumers' pockets.

This is why people worry about China. There is concern that if African leaders take Chinese investment then those leaders will feel they owe China a favour, and that favour can be called in at any point. The West is concerned that China's favours are good for one group or one corrupt leader, but not for everyone. This is the old problem that people from abolitionists to T. R. Batten identified: the need to protect ordinary African victims from predatory African elites. It's not like the West has such a great record of picking the good guys.

And the West needn't always be worried. The Zimbabwean political economist Godfrey Kanyenze shows that African people are not powerless in the face of their governments' relationships with Chinese favours. In 2008, a Zimbabwean trade union and their 'network of unions and social movements' from South Africa, Mozambique, Namibia and Angola blocked a Chinese container ship carrying 77 tons of weapons to the Zimbabwean regime during violently contested elections. Regional solidarity, rather than Western intervention, prevented the Chinese from arming the government.[2]

But back in Burkina Faso, Western ambassadors also worried about Sankara's friendship with Ghana's military leader Jerry Rawlings. Burkina Faso was also a major source of cheap labour supply for Ivory Coast's booming cocoa agriculture industry, a cocoa industry that competed with Ghana's on the world market. In a way, Ivory Coast needed Burkina Faso to stay poor. As France's most reliable ally in the region, Ivory Coast's President, Félix Houphouët Boigny, began telegraphing his concern about Sankara. It was important to France that Houphouët Boigny, their friend and ally, be kept on side.

Sankara embarrassed other leaders. If it turned out that the people didn't need to suffer from austerity measures because ministers and presidents could take the hit instead, there would be pressure across the continent to cut back on presidential planes and ministerial perks. And without presidential planes and ministerial perks there were three potential concerns. First was the risk that Western countries wouldn't take them seriously as peer nations. Second was that this indicated a shift towards socialism. And third, that the tendency towards corruption might grow.

Many people now agree with Sankara. While the Cold War was ongoing, corruption was a pretty low priority. But at the end of the Cold War people began to see what Sankara was talking about. His plans for empowering women, for managing child mortality, for community-led development were all dismissed in his lifetime but he is now praised as being 'ahead of his time'.

Sankara's People's Development Programme was launched in October 1984. Lasting fifteen months, the programme built 351 schools and 314 maternal health centres, as well as wells and boreholes. Burkinabè (the people of Burkina Faso) planted more than 10 million trees during his presidency.[3] Targeting gifts and corruption, though, was his undoing.

In the end, Sankara was undone by the interests of the old elite in his country and those of external players – Ivory Coast, France and the US – in maintaining a strong anti-socialist front. Sankara's debt speech, where he invoked the Marshall Plan and argued that African countries should default on their debts, was one of his last. A few months later he was murdered by order of his second-in-command, Blaise Compoaré, with the support of those who preferred to take the gifts.

◆ ◆ ◆

The people who were working to intervene in enslavement, poverty and underdevelopment in Africa ran into repeated obstacles because of their misunderstanding of where wealth came from, how slavery was connected to development, and how to balance wealth creation and economic growth with development for all. They misunderstood where their own economic power came from. They misunderstood the forms of and choices about economic power that they encountered in Africa. And they did it over and over again.

This book has not set out to answer the question 'Why is Africa poor?' Instead it asks how ideas about labour, money and value change: how are we measuring wealth and poverty? What are the goalposts for success? Is development a process or a goal? What assumptions about how the economy works, or should work, are we making in answering those questions?

These are the questions that I have asked my students to think about over the past fifteen years of teaching. These are the questions that have been at the heart of scholarship on African economic history and colonialism, and I hope that by bringing them to a wider public we can open up new conversations about global and national inequality, about racial prejudice and about the way we imagine the economy.

We can kid ourselves that the wealth enjoyed in certain parts of the world is somehow separate from the problems facing the poorer parts, but everything is linked. Wealth in one nation has so often been facilitated by extraction and a lack of redistribution at a global scale. The problem of trying to separate economic development from the slave trade is that the slave trade was foundational to economic development. The problem of trying to separate the accumulation of wealth from extraction and exploitation is that they are two sides of the same coin.

The patterns of misunderstanding set in motion by the anti-slavery interventionists in the early nineteenth century have been repeated for over two centuries. A problem is observed. Assumptions are made about the causes of this problem, based on ideas about Africa's relationship to Europe in the history of 'civilization' and development. Solutions to the problem are proposed and, as global power shifts away from Africa towards Europe and European settler nations, imposed.

So many of the ideas about how economics functions at both a micro and a macro level are completely entangled with the observations, experiments and interventions that have taken place in African states, colonies and countries as the discipline of economics developed in tandem with the spread of colonial rule. By the time colonial rule was dismantled in the mid-twentieth century, ideas about the history of barter and money, about the relationship between slavery and debt, about tariffs and free trade, about labour incentives and the role of women in the home or in the workforce had become fundamentally assumed truths about how humans interact economically.

This book has set out to question those assumed truths. It suggests that we need to stop approaching African economies as if they are automatically in need of Western intervention. It argues that misunderstanding the causes of observed economic behaviours can have profoundly negative outcomes, and so truly understanding those observations – in their cultural and historical context – is vital if we want to stop repeating the same mistakes.

Economic imperialism isn't only exploitation. It can also be the superiority of good intentions. If development has had a historic problem with trusting people to make decisions for themselves, then maybe it's time to give real democracy its chance. Maybe it's time to trust in people to have power over their own choices.

Part of the tyranny of economic thinking about Africa stems from the sense that every piece of data, every story that comes out of the continent has to be tinged with a sense of tragedy. New evidence is immediately read within the context of whether or not it affirms the sense that Africa's people are exploited and lacking agency, or are exploiters and dastardly agents. This is what the Nigerian author Chimamanda Ngozi Adichie described as the 'danger of a single story' and Nigerian Nobel Laureate Chinua Achebe lamented as the 'image of Africa' problem: 'The West seems to suffer deep anxieties about the precariousness of its civilization and to have a need for constant reassurance by comparison with Africa.'[4]

The basis of so much economic intervention, from the end of the slave trade down to our present, has been an assumption that 'we know better'. What I hope this book has shown is that, time and again, people who have tried to 'fix' Africa's economies don't know better than the people living and working there, raising families and making ends meet. We only ever have a partial knowledge about how changes in global commerce, in monetary systems, in labour supply and demand and in government regulation really interact. Pretending we know that a new recession will play out like the recession of 1931 rather than 1873 or 1973; assuming that money only has one meaning to people; misunderstanding the reasons people take the jobs they do – all of this happens within economies in the Global North on a daily basis. And yet, when confronting African economies, individuals, institutions and foreign governments conveniently put economic culture out of their minds in order to prescribe the discipline's scientific remedies, *ceteris paribus*.

This short history of Western economic thought about Africa is not meant to suggest that African economic thought is culturally informed and therefore exotic and unknowable. Instead we need to understand that *all* economic thought is culturally informed. The assumptions people make about what is normal and rational economic behaviour in one era or one geographical context can suddenly appear so obviously of their time or place. In other words, believing that the West's economies are 'modern' and 'developed' and those of Africa's fifty-four countries are 'traditional' or 'underdeveloped' is a matter of perspective.

Does the Global North have more money to spend on public infrastructure, health services, education and social services? Yes. Does it know why that is the case? Partially. But since a large part of the answer is 'through the integration of the global economic system', it seems difficult to look at, for instance, America's or the UK's or France's economy in isolation and turn to Africa with advice about monetary policy, education, or debt management. Poor people are not poor because they are stupid; they are poor because they don't have money. Poverty is a technical term for a lack of money. It also implies a lack of relationships in some African contexts. And among the wealthy and the well-meaning, it implies a lack of knowledge.

And so, armed with ignorance and good intentions, generation after generation has arrived in Africa prepared to share its assumptions about why some countries are rich and developed and why Africa's are not.

ACKNOWLEDGEMENTS

Thank you to my students for helping me to articulate this narrative over the years (and for babysitting!). It would never have been possible without the incredible intellectual community of the Cambridge African Economic History Seminar. Gareth Austin has been a wonderful and supportive colleague, and we have been lucky to have such talented MPhil and PhD cohorts, a steady stream of postdocs and visiting fellows, cutting-edge seminar presenters and stalwart attendees like Tony Hopkins and Laura Channing. Jonnie, Bryony, Harriet and Felicity have always been troupers about these Tuesday-evening seminars ('sebidars'). Thank you to everyone at the Cambridge Centre of African Studies, and especially for the help of its incredible librarians, Jenni Skinner and Ben Carson. Michael Wells and the staff at Harvey's kept me caffeinated. Thank you to all the many colleagues and friends in Nigeria, Sierra Leone, Liberia, Senegal, Gambia, Kenya, Egypt, Morocco, Zimbabwe and South Africa who shared your hospitality and your expertise, put up with my endless questions, and supported my research. I am grateful to my agent, James Pullen, and to Shoaib Rokadiya for believing in the project from the start, to Margot Tudor for inspiring the title that wasn't to be, to my editors Rozalind Dineen, Eva Hodgkin and Arabella Pike and the team at William Collins.

NOTES

A note about sources: the African Economic History Network Working Paper Series hosts open-access (non-paywalled) research papers. While many of these go on to be accepted by major journals in the field, I have cited their African Economic History Working Paper Series number where available for ease of access. https://www.aehnetwork. org/working-papers/

◆ ◆ ◆

CHAPTER 1: A KING WITH HOLEY STOCKINGS, OR MEASURING WEALTH

1 Anna Maria Falconbridge, *Two Voyages to Sierra Leone* (London, 1793).
2 Adam Smith, *The Wealth of Nations* (London, 1776).
3 Sibel Kusimba, 'Embodied value: Wealth-in-people', *Economic Anthropology* 7, 2 (2020), pp. 166–75; Igor Kopytoff and Suzanne Miers, 'African slavery as an institution of marginality', in Suzanne Miers and Igor Kopytoff (eds),

Slavery in Africa: Historical and Anthropological Perspectives (Madison, WI, 1979), pp. 3–81.

4 Jane Guyer and Samuel Eno Belinga, 'Wealth in people as wealth in knowledge: Accumulation and composition in Equatorial Africa', *Journal of African History* 36, 1 (1995), pp. 91–120.

5 Eric Williams, *Capitalism and Slavery* (London, 2022).

6 See José Lingna Nafafé, *Lourenço da Silva Mendonça and the Black Atlantic Abolitionist Movement in the Seventeenth Century* (Cambridge, 2022).

7 British National Archives T 70/1262.

8 Ty M. Reese, 'Controlling the company: The structures of Fante-British relations on the Gold Coast, 1750–1821', *The Journal of Imperial and Commonwealth History* 41, 1 (2013), pp. 104–19.

9 Ty M. Reese, 'Wives, brokers, and labourers: Women at Cape Coast, 1750–1807', in Douglas Catterall and Jodi Campbell (eds), *Women in Port: Gendering Communities, Economies, and Social Networks in Atlantic Port Cities, 1500–1800* (Leiden, 2012), p. 295. See also Kwasi Konadu, *Many Black Women of the Fortress* (London, 2022).

10 Archibald Dalzel, Governor at Cape Coast Castle, *The History of Dahomy, An Inland Kingdom of Africa* (London, 1793), pp. xii–xiii.

11 Joseph Inikori, 'The credit needs of the African trade and the development of the credit economy in England', *Explorations in Economic History* 27, 2 (1990), pp. 197–231.

12 Gary B. Magee and Andrew S. Thompson, *Empire and Globalisation: Networks of People, Goods and Capital in the British World, c.1850–1914* (Cambridge, 2010).

◆ ◆ ◆

CHAPTER 2: LEARNING TO BE FARMERS

1 Thomas Fowell Buxton, *The African Slave Trade and Its Remedy* (London, 1841), p. 193.

2 As quoted in Charles Buxton (ed.), *Memoirs of Sir Thomas Fowell Buxton, Baronet* (London, 1849, third edition), p. 323.

3 Papers of Thomas Fowell Buxton, vol. 1, 19 September 1806 to Hannah Gurney.

4 Ibid., 19 January 1812 from Berwick, to Hannah Buxton.

5 Robert Allen, 'Why the industrial revolution was British: Commerce, induced invention, and the scientific revolution', *Economic History Review* 64, 2 (2011), pp. 357–84; Jane Humphries, 'Childhood and child labour in the British industrial revolution', *Economic History Review* 66, 1 (2013), pp. 395–418.

6 Bernard Mandeville, *Fable of the Bees* (London, 1713), p. 122.

7 Duncan Foley, *Adam's Fallacy* (Cambridge, MA, 2006), p. 64.

8 Report of the Commissioners of Inquiry, Sierra Leone Part I, pp. 27; 29.

9 Ibid., Part I, p. 30.

10 Hansard, Debate 9 May 1823, vol. 9, cc143–50 'Spitalfields Silk Manufacture Acts – Petition for the Repeal Thereof'.

11 Maxine Berg and Pat Hudson, *Slavery, Capitalism and the Industrial Revolution* (Cambridge, 2023), location 889 in Kindle edition.

12 Papers of Thomas Fowell Buxton, vol. 1, 10 September 1839 to Hannah Gurney.

13 Buxton, *Slave Trade and Its Remedy*, p. 240.

14 Papers of Thomas Fowell Buxton, vol. 1, 10 September 1839 to Hannah Gurney.

15 No. 23, Copy of a Despatch (no. 8) from Her Majesty's Commissioners of the Expedition to the Niger to Lord John Russell, 30 August 1841.

16 Mohamad Bashir Salau, *Plantation Slavery in the Sokoto Caliphate* (Rochester, NY, 2018), p. 55. Kabiru Sulaiman Chafe, 'Challenges to the hegemony of the Sokoto Caliphate: A preliminary examination', *Paideuma*, 40 (1994), pp. 99–109; Paul Lovejoy, 'Plantations in the economy of the Sokoto Caliphate', *Journal of African History* 19, 3 (1978), pp. 341–68.

17 Buxton, *Slave Trade and Its Remedy*, p. 194.

18 Heinrich Barth, *Travels and Discoveries in North and Central Africa, Vol. IV* (London, 1858), p. 163.

19 C. C. Ifemesia, 'The "civilizing" mission of 1841: Aspects of an episode in Anglo-Nigerian relations', *Journal of the Historical Society of Nigeria* 2, 3 (1962), p. 305.

20 Salau, *Plantation Slavery*, p. 72.

21 Ibid., pp. 67–8.

22 Hansard, 16 December 1902, 'Sultan of Sokoto and the Niger Company', vol. 116, Mr Austen Chamberlain.

23 Lugard cited in Paul E. Lovejoy and Jan S. Hogendorn, *Slow Death for Slavery: The Course of Abolition in Northern Nigeria, 1897–1936* (Cambridge, 1993), p. 27.

24 Frederick Lugard, *The Dual Mandate in British Tropical Africa* (London, 1922), p. 523.

♦ ♦ ♦

CHAPTER 3: GETTING PEOPLE BACK TO WORK

1 'H.W.L.' cited in Keletso Atkins, '"Kafir Time": Preindustrial temporal concepts and labour discipline in nineteenth-century colonial Natal', *Journal of African History* 29 (1988), p. 230.

2 Klas Rönnback, 'The idle and the industrious – European ideas about the African work ethic in precolonial West Africa', *History in Africa* 41 (2014), pp. 117–45.

3 George Nicholson, *The Cape and Its Colonists: with Hints to Settlers in 1848* (London, 1848), p. 161.

4 Erik Green, 'The economics of slavery in the eighteenth-century Cape Colony: Revising the Nieboer-Domar Hypothesis', *International Review of Social History* 59, 1 (2014), pp. 39–70.

5 Marlous van Waijenberg and Ewout Frankema, 'Structural impediments to African growth? New evidence from real wages in British Africa, 1880–1965', *Journal of Economic History* 72, 4 (2012), p. 896.

6 Keletso Atkins, *The Moon Is Dead! Give Us Our Money!* (London, 1993).

7 E. P. Thompson, 'Time, work-discipline, and industrial capitalism', *Past and Present*, 38 (1967), pp. 56–97.

8 Pim de Zwart, 'South African living standards in global perspective, 1835–1910', *Economic History of Developing Regions* 26, 1 (2011), pp. 49–74.

9 Reuben Loffman, 'Rubber Production in Africa', *Oxford Research Encyclopedia of African History*, 2023; Dean Pavlakis, *British Humanitarianism and the Congo Reform*

Movement, 1896–1913 (Abingdon, 2015); Kevin Grant, *A Civilised Savagery: Britain and the New Slaveries in Africa, 1884–1926* (London, 2005); Adam Hoschschild, *King Leopold's Ghost: A Story of Greed, Terror, and Heroism in Colonial Africa* (Boston, 1998).

10 Nicholson, *The Cape and Its Colonists*, pp. 32–3.

11 Christian Frederick Schlenker, *A Collection of Temne Traditions, Fables and Proverbs* (London, 1861).

12 Pierre Bourdieu, *Algeria 1960* (Cambridge, 1972), p. 19.

13 Nicholson, *The Cape and Its Colonists*, p. 158.

14 A. G. Hopkins, 'Property rights and empire building: Britain's annexation of Lagos, 1861', *Journal of Economic History* 40, 4 (1980), pp. 777–98.

15 Frederick Cooper, *Decolonization and African Society: The Labor Question in French and British Africa* (Cambridge, 1996), p. 45.

16 Earl of Selborne cited in Laura Channing, 'Taxing chiefs: The design and introduction of taxation in the Sierra Leone Protectorate, 1896–1914', *Journal of Imperial and Commonwealth History* 48, 3 (2020), p. 400.

17 Ibid., p. 403.

18 Olatunji Ojo, 'The Southern Nigeria Native House Rule Ordinance (1901)', *African Economic History* 40 (2012), p. 127.

19 Belinda Archibong and Nonso Obikili, 'Prison labour: The price of prisons and the lasting effects of incarceration', African Economic History Working Paper Series no. 52/2020, pp. 19–21.

20 Cited in ibid., pp. 13–14.

21 Ibid., pp. 19–21.

22 Mary Rose Whitehouse, 'Modern prison labour: A reemergence of convict leasing under the guise of rehabilitation and private enterprises', *Loyola Journal of Public Interest Law* 18 (2017), pp. 89–113.

23 Lugard as cited in Michael Twaddle, 'The ending of slavery in Buganda', in Suzanne Miers and Richard Roberts (eds), *The End of Slavery in Africa* (Madison, WI, 1988), pp. 127–28.

24 Portal as cited in Twaddle, 'Buganda', p. 130.

25 Thomas Fuller, 'African labour and training in the Uganda colonial economy', *International Journal of African Historical Studies* 10, 1 (1977), p. 79.

26 Parliamentary Papers, Colonial Reports – Miscellaneous no. 57, Uganda, Report by the Governor on a Tour Through the Eastern Province, 1908.

27 Marlous Van Waijenberg, 'Financing the African colonial state: The revenue imperative and forced labour', African Economic History Working Paper Series no. 20/2015, p. 41. See also Dacil Juif and Ewout Frankema, 'From coercion to compensation: Institutional responses to labour scarcity in the Central African copperbelt', African Economic History Working Paper Series no. 24/2016.

28 J. P. Daughton, *The Violence of Empire: The Forgotten History of the Congo-Océan Railroad* (Cheltenham, 2021).

29 Ibid., p. 54.

30 Lieut. Barnard, Royal Navy, *A Three Years' Cruize in the Mozambique Channel, of the Suppression of the Slave Trade* (London, 1848), pp. 78–9.

31 Albert Sarraut cited in Daughton, *Violence of Empire*, p. 51.

◆ ◆ ◆

CHAPTER 4: MONEY PROBLEMS

1 Richard Burton, *To the Gold Coast for Gold* (London, 1883), p. viii.

2 'To the Gold Coast for Gold', *Pall Mall Gazette*, 2 January 1883, p. 5.

3 For the best overview of Burton's life see Dane Kennedy, *The Highly Civilized Man: Richard Burton and the Victorian World* (Cambridge, MA, 2005).

4 Burton, *Wanderings in West Africa Vol. 2* (London, 1863), pp. 104–31.

5 Domenico Cristofaro in Karin Pallaver (ed.), *Monetary Transitions: Currencies, Colonialism and African Societies* (London, 2022), p. 33.

6 Philip Curtin, *Economic Change in Precolonial Africa: Senegambia in the Era of the Slave Trade* (Madison, WI, 1975), p. 312.

7 John Matthews, *A Voyage to the River Sierra-Leone on the Coast of Africa* (London, 1788), p. 141.

8 Marion Johnson, 'The cowrie currencies of West Africa, Part I', *Journal of African History* 11, 1 (1970), pp. 17; Johnson, 'The cowrie currencies of West Africa, Part II', *Journal of African History* 11, 3 (1970), pp. 331–53; see also Jan Hogendorn and Marion Johnson, *The Shell Money of the Slave Trade* (Cambridge, 2003); see also, Toyomu Masaki, 'Spheres of Money, Payments and Credit Systems in the Colony of Senegal in the Long Nineteenth Century', in Pallaver (ed.), *Monetary Transitions*, 55-79.

9 Jan Hogendorn, 'Slaves as money in the Sokoto Caliphate', in Endre Stiansen and Jane Guyer, *Credit, Currencies and Culture: African Financial Institutions in Historical Perspective* (Uppsala, 1999), p. 63.

10 See e.g. Joshua R. Greenberg, *Banknotes and Shinplasters: The Rage for Paper Money in the Early Republic* (Philadelphia, 2020).

11 Thomas J. Sargent and François R. Velde, *The Big Problem of Small Change* (Princeton, NJ, 2003), pp. 261–90.

12 Hogendorn, 'Slaves as money in the Sokoto caliphate', pp. 62–77; Akanmu Adebayo, '*Kòse-é-máni*: Idealism and contradiction in the Yorùbá view of money', in Stiansen and Guyer (eds), *Credit, Currencies and Culture*, pp. 146–74.

13 A. G. Hopkins, 'The currency revolution in south-west Nigeria in the late nineteenth century', *Journal of the Historical Society of Nigeria* 3, 3 (1966), pp. 471–83.

14 Jane Guyer, *Marginal Gains: Monetary Transactions in Atlantic Africa* (Chicago, 2004), p. 65.

15 Dalzel, *History of Dahomy*, p. xii.

16 William Stanley Jevons, *The Theory of Political Economy* (London, 1879), p. 13.

17 Eli Cook, *The Pricing of Progress* (Cambridge, MA, 2017), p. 245.

18 Robin Law, 'Posthumous questions for Karl Polanyi: Price inflation in pre-colonial Dahomey', *Journal of African History* 33, 3 (1992), pp. 399; 396.

19 A. G. Hopkins, *An Economic History of West Africa* (London, 1973; second edition, 2020).

20 Jane Guyer, *Marginal Gains*, p. 12.

21 Kate Ekama, Johan Fourie, Hans Heese and Lisa Martin, 'When Cape slavery ended: Evidence from a new slave emancipation dataset', African Economic History Working Paper no. 53/2020; Igor Martins, *Collateral Effect: Slavery and Wealth in the Cape Colony* (Lund, 2020); Legacies of

British Slavery, https://www.ucl.ac.uk/lbs/; Bronwen Everill and Khadidiatou Diedhiou, 'Profiting from slavery and emancipation: Compensation, capital, and collateral in nineteenth-century Senegal', *Business History Review* 97, 2 (2023).

◆ ◆ ◆

CHAPTER 5: UNEQUAL DEVELOPMENT

1 George Lovell, 'T. R. (Reg) Batten and Madge Batten, non-directivity and community development', https://infed.org/mobi/t-r-reg-batten-and-madge-batten-non-directivity-and-community-development/

2 Ibid.

3 Aaron Windel, *Cooperative Rule: Community Development in Britain's Late Empire* (Berkeley, CA, 2022).

4 Lugard, *Dual Mandate*, pp. 79–93, as cited in P. S. Zachernuk, 'African history and imperial culture in colonial Nigerian schools', *Africa* 68, 4 (1998), p. 487.

5 Raymond Leslie Buell, *The Native Problem in Africa*, vol. 2 (New York, 1928), p. 221.

6 Emma Hunter, 'A history of maendeleo: The concept of "development" in Tanganyika's late colonial public sphere', in Joseph Hodge, Gerald Hodl and Martina Kopf (eds), *Developing Africa* (Manchester, 2014), pp. 87–107.

7 Damilola Adebayo, 'Electricity, agency and class in Lagos Colony, c.1860–1914', *Past & Present* 262, 1 (2024), pp. 168–206.

8 Margery Perham, 'A re-statement of indirect rule', *Africa* 7, 3 (1934), p. 325.

9 T. R. Batten, *Problems of African Development*, vols 1 and 2 (London, 1947), p. 13.

10 Article 22, Versailles Peace Treaty.

11 Margery Perham, 'The British problem in Africa', *Foreign Affairs* 29, 4 (1951), p. 640.

12 Windel, *Cooperative Rule*, p. 20.

13 Cited in Tim Rogan, *The Moral Economists: R. H. Tawney, Karl Polanyi, E. P. Thompson, and the Critique of Capitalism* (Princeton, NJ, 2017), p. 20.

14 As described in the Preface to T. R. Batten, 'Community development in the colonies', *African Affairs* (1951), p. 321.

15 Batten, *Problems*, vol. 1, p. 73.

16 Ibid., pp. 9–10.

17 Ibid., p. 14.

18 Ibid. p. 4.

19 Batten, 'Community development in the colonies', p. 324.

20 Thomas Malthus, *An Essay on the Principle of Population* (1826, sixth edition), Appendix.

21 Buell, *The Native Problem in Africa*, vol. 2, p. 219.

22 Ibid., p. 727.

23 Ibid., pp. 748–9.

24 Ibid., p. 780.

25 Rhiannon Stephens, *Poverty and Wealth in East Africa: A Conceptual History* (Raleigh, NC, 2022), p. 78.

26 Ibid., pp. 80; 79.

27 Ibid., p. 153.

28 Ibid., p. 160.

29 Twaddle, 'Buganda', p. 139.

30 Batten, *Problems*, vol. 2, pp. 82–3.

31 Twaddle, 'Buganda', p. 144.

32 Andrew Porter, 'Margery Perham and British rule in Africa', *Journal of Imperial and Commonwealth History*, 86.

33 Douglas Rimmer, '"Basic needs" and the origins of the development ethos', *Journal of Developing Areas* 15, 2 (1981), p. 217.

34 Ibid., p. 219.

35 Ibid., p. 222.

36 Guyer, *Marginal Gains*; Wangari Maathai, *Unbowed: A Memoir* (New York, 2006).

37 Josué de Castro cited in Vincent Bonnecase, 'When numbers represented poverty: The changing meaning of the food ration in French colonial Africa', *Journal of African History* 59, 3 (2018), p. 474.

38 E.g. *The Graphic*, 8 March 1873. See Lindsay Doulton, 'The Royal Navy's anti-slavery campaign in the western Indian Ocean *c.*1860–1890: Race, empire and identity', PhD thesis, University of Hull, 2010, p. 86.

39 Stephens, *Poverty and Wealth*, p. 146.

40 Ibid., p. 150.

41 Anthony Vanterm, 1900, cited in ibid., p. 151.

42 Dr F. M. Purcell, 1940, as cited in Alexander Moradi, Gareth Austin and Jörg Baten, 'Heights and development in a cash-crop colony: Living standards in Ghana, 1870–1980', African Economic History Working Paper no. 7/2013, p. 20.

43 Ibid., p. 25.

44 Alfonso Herranz-Loncan and Johan Fourie, '"For the public benefit"? Railways in the British Cape Colony', *European Review of Economic History* 22, 1 (2018), pp. 73–100.

45 Polly Hill, *Studies in Rural Capitalism in West Africa* (Cambridge, 1970), p. 26.

46 Ibid., p. 27.

47 Ibid., p. 28.

48 Stephens, *Poverty and Wealth*, pp. 12–13.

49 Batten, *Problems*, vol. 1, p. 53.

50 Hill, *Studies in Rural Capitalism in West Africa*, p. 21.

51 James Ferguson, *Give a Man a Fish: Reflections on the New Politics of Distribution* (Durham, NC, 2015), p. 6.

52 Batten, *Problems*, vol. 2, p. 3.

53 British Foreign and Commonwealth Office, Uganda Credit and Savings Bank, Report of the Board of Management for the period ended 31 December 1950, p. 2.

54 *Uganda Herald*, 24 January 1945, as cited in Gardner Thompson, 'Colonialism in crisis: The Uganda disturbances of 1945', *African Affairs* 91, 365 (1992), p. 607.

55 Windel, *Cooperative Rule*, pp. 112–41; Charles Kabuga, 'I. K. Musazi memorial lecture: Tracing cooperative steps in the struggle for Uganda's economic development', Uhuru Institute, https://www.uhuruinstitute.org/wp-content/uploads/2018/06/IK-Musaazi-lecture-Article.pdf; British Foreign and Commonwealth Office, Uganda Credit and Savings Bank, Report of the Board of Management for the period ended 31 December 1950.

56 As cited in Windel, *Cooperative Rule*, p. 116.

57 W. Tete-Ansa, *Africa at Work* (New York, 1930), p. 79.

58 Ibid., p. 81.

59 Batten, *Problems*, p. 150.

60 Ibid., pp. 155–6.

61 Perham, 'The British problem in Africa', p. 650.

62 Moses Ochonu, *Colonial Meltdown: Northern Nigeria in the Great Depression* (Athens, OH, 2009), p. 74.

63 United Nations, *Review of Economic Activity in Africa, 1950 to 1954* (New York, 1955), p. 10.

◆ ◆ ◆

CHAPTER 6: FINANCING FREEDOM

1 Chirag Dhara and Vandana Singh, 'The delusion of infinite economic growth', *Scientific American*, 20 June 2021. See also Morten Jerven, *Africa: Why Economists Get It Wrong* (London, 2015).

2 Tinashe Nyamunda, 'Complexities of decolonization: The political economy of independence and development', *Afriche e orienti* 16, 3 (2014), pp. 209–21.

3 Corey Decker and Elisabeth McMahon, *The Idea of Development in Africa: A History* (Cambridge, 2020), pp. 143–63.

4 W. Arthur Lewis, *The Theory of Economic Growth* (London, 1955), p. 421.

5 Samir Amin, *A Life Looking Forward: Memoirs of an Independent Marxist* (London, 2006), p. 114. Ingrid Harvold Kvangraven, Maria Dyveke Styve and Ushehwedu Kufakurinani, 'Samir Amin and beyond: The enduring relevance of Amin's approach to political economy', *Review of African Political Economy* 48, 167 (2021), pp. 1–7.

6 Amin, *A Life Looking Forward*, p. 135.

7 Samir Amin, *Problèmes de Planification : Les Bases d'établissement d'une comptabilité nationale dans une planification socialiste (économies africaines)* (Paris, 1961), p. 8.

8 Michiel de Haas and Emiliano Travieso, 'Cash-crop migration systems in East and West Africa', in Ewout Frankema and

Michiel de Haas (eds), *Migration in Africa: Shifting Patterns of Mobility from the 19th to the 21st Century* (Abingdon, 2022), pp. 231–55.

9 John Maynard Keynes cited in Leigh Gardner, 'Colonialism or supersanctions: Sovereignty and debt in West Africa, 1871–1914', *European Review of Economic History* 21, 2 (2017), p. 236.

10 Ibid., figure 4.

11 Kwame Nkrumah, *Neo-Colonialism: The Last Stage of Imperialism* (London, 1965), p. 3.

12 Ibid., p. 5.

13 Ian Livingstone (ed.), *Teaching of Economics in Africa* (Brighton, 1973), p. 11; see also Decker and McMahon, *The Idea of Development in Africa*, pp. 143–63.

14 Amin, *A Life Looking Forward*, p. 135.

15 Emmanuel Akyeampong, 'African socialism; or the search for an indigenous model of economic development', African Economic History Network Working Paper Series no. 36/2017; Julius Nyerere, 'Ujamaa – the basis of African socialism', in Julius K. Nyerere (ed.), *Ujamaa: Essays on Socialism* (Dar es Salaam, 1968), pp. 1–12.

16 United Nations, *Scope and Structure of Money Economies in Tropical Africa* (New York, 1955), p. 5.

17 United Nations, *Structure and Growth of Selected African Economies* (New York, 1958), p. 1.

18 Amin, *Problèmes de Planification*, p. 6.

19 Livingstone, *Teaching of Economics in Africa*.

20 David Schleicher, *In a Bad State: Responding to State and Local Budget Crises* (Oxford, 2023), p. 7.

21 Robert Caro, *The Power Broker* (New York, 1974), pp. 7; 1013–14.

22 James C. Scott, *Seeing Like a State: How Certain Schemes to Improve the Human Condition Have Failed* (New Haven, CT, 1998), p. 6.

23 See for instance, Margot Tudor, *Blue Helmet Bureaucrats: United Nations Peacekeeping and the Reinvention of Colonialism, 1945–1971* (Cambridge, 2023).

24 See for instance, Samuel Fury Childs Daly, *A History of the Republic of Biafra: Law, Crime, and the Nigerian Civil War* (Cambridge, 2020).

25 Stephanie Decker, 'Africanization in British multinationals in Ghana and Nigeria', *Business History Review* 92, 4 (Winter 2018), p. 705.

26 Frederick Cooper, 'From colonial state to gatekeeper state in Africa', the Mario Einaudi Center for International Studies Working Paper Series no. 04-05 (October 2005).

27 Julius Nyerere, 'African Socialism: Ujamaa in Practice', *The Black Scholar* 2, 6 (1971), p. 2.

◆ ◆ ◆

CHAPTER 7: HELPING YOU TO GET RICH QUICK

1 Kevin Watkins, *Oxfam Poverty Report* (Oxford, 1995), pp. 12–13.

2 Frederick Cooper, *Citizenship Between Empire and Nation* (Princeton, NJ, 2014).

3 David Oks and Henry Williams, 'The long, slow death of global development', *American Affairs* 6, 4 (2022).

4 Trevor Noah, *Born a Crime* (London, 2017), p. 217.

5 Stephen Golub and Faraz Hayat, 'Employment, unemployment and underemployment', in *The Oxford*

Handbook of Africa and Economics, vol. 1 (Oxford, 2015), p. 139.

6 Elizabeth Popp Berman, *Thinking Like an Economist: How Efficiency Replaced Equality in U.S. Public Policy* (Princeton, NJ, 2022). See also Joseph Hodge, *Triumph of the Expert: Agrarian Doctrines of Development and the Legacies of British Colonialism* (Athens, OH, 2007).

7 Popp Berman, *Thinking Like an Economist*, p. 35.

8 Thandika Mkandawire, 'Targeting and universalism in poverty reduction', Social Policy and Development Programme Paper no. 23 (UN Research Institute for Social Development, December 2005), p. 1.

9 Jeffrey Sachs, *The End of Poverty: How We Can Make It Happen in Our Lifetime* (New York, 2005).

10 Esther Duflo, 'Poor but rational?', in Abhijit Vinayak Banerjee, Roland Benabou and Dilip Mookherjee (eds), *Understanding Poverty* (Oxford, 2006); Abhijit Vinayak Banerjee and Esther Duflo, *Poor Economics: A Radical Rethinking of the Way to Fight Global Poverty* (New York, 2011); Abhijit Vinayak Banerjee and Esther Duflo, 'The economic lives of the poor', *Journal of Economic Perspectives* 21, 1 (2007), pp. 141–68.

11 Paul Collier, *The Bottom Billion: Why the Poorest Countries Are Failing and What Can Be Done About It* (Oxford, 2007), p. 12.

12 E.g. Dambisa Moyo, *Dead Aid* (New York, 2009); William Easterly, *The White Man's Burden* (Oxford, 2006).

13 E.g. https://stuffexpataidworkerslike.com/2012/11/19/182-innovation-tourettes/

14 https://www.givingwhatwecan.org/best-charities-to-donate-to-2024

15 As cited in William Therford Jr, 'Evaporating aid: Dangers besetting NGOs in sub-Saharan Africa and what NGOs can do about it', *JGJPP International Human Rights Scholarship Review* 2, 21 (2016), pp. 26–7.

16 Gideon Lewis-Kraus, 'The reluctant prophet of Effective Altruism', *The New Yorker*, 15 August 2022.

17 Michael Lewis, *Going Infinite: The Rise and Fall of a New Tycoon* (London, 2023), p. 49.

18 https://www.ox.ac.uk/news/2022-03-01-oxford-based-charity-receives-more-25-billion-pledges-community-effective-givers

19 Muhammad Yunus, *Banker to the Poor* (PublicAffairs, 1999).

20 Aderanti Adepoju, *African Families in the Twenty-First Century: Prospects and Challenges* (Lincoln, NE, 2005).

21 Dilip Ratha, 'Keep Remittances Flowing to Africa', *Brookings*, 15 March 2021.

22 Felex Share and Reason Razao, 'Zimbabwe: Thousands lose money to Ponzi scheme', *The Herald*, 3 September 2016.

23 A. Akinyoade, A.J. Dietz, and Chibuike Uche, *Entrepreneurship in Africa* (Brill, 2017).

24 William R. Thetford Jr. 'Evaporating aid: Dangers besetting NGOs in Sub-Saharan Africa and what NGOs can do about it', https://jgjpp.regent.edu/wp-content/uploads/2021/12/EVAPORATING-AID-DANGERS-BESETTING.pdf, p. 31.

25 https://www.bbc.com/worklife/article/20231009-ftxs-sam-bankman-fried-believed-in-effective-altruism-what-is-it; Gideon Lewis-Kraus, 'Sam Bankman-Fried, Effective Altruism, and the question of complicity', *The New Yorker* 1 December 2022.

◆ ◆ ◆

CHAPTER 8: WOMEN ARE NOTHING MORE THAN SLAVES

1 Robert Allen, 'From foraging to the first states: An economic history', Ellen Macarthur Lectures, University of Cambridge, March 2022.

2 Dewan K. Farhana, 'How "second shift" impacts women physicians' finance', 13 April 2021, https://mypmg.com/blog/how-second-shift-impacts-women-physicians-finances

3 Paul and Laura Bohannan, *Tiv Economy* (Chicago, 1968), p. 14.

4 Sarah Eiland, 'The unspoken demands of slavery: The exploitation of female slaves in the Memphis slave trade', *The Gettysburg College Journal of the Civil War Era* 10 (2020), p. 27.

5 Allan Kotlikoff, 'The structure of slave prices in New Orleans', *Economic Inquiry* 17 (1979), p. 510.

6 Clapperton cited in Paul Lovejoy and David Richardson, 'British abolition and its impact on slave prices along the Atlantic coast of Africa, 1783–1850', *Journal of Economic History* 55, 1 (1995), p. 273.

7 Jane Guyer, 'Wealth in people and self-realization in Equatorial Africa', *Man*, new series, 28, 2 (1993), p. 256.

8 Christopher Hanes, 'Turnover cost and the distribution of slave labour in Anglo-America', *Journal of Economic History* 56, 2 (1996), p. 313.

9 Suresh Naidu, 'American slavery and labour market power', *Economic History of Developing Regions* 35, 1 (2020), pp. 3–22; Calumet Links, Johan Fourie and Erik Green, 'Was slavery a flexible form of labour? Division of labour and location specific skills on the eastern Cape frontier', African Economic History Working Paper Series no. 42/2018.

10 Barbara Cooper, 'Women's worth and wedding gift exchange in Maradi, Niger, 1907–89', *Journal of African History* 36, 1 (1995), p. 124.

11 Ibid.

12 Flexon Mizinga, 'Marriage and bridewealth in a matrilineal society: The case of the Tonga of Southern Zambia: 1900–1996', *African Economic History* 28 (2000), p. 59.

13 Elphinstone Dayrell, *Folk Stories from Southern Nigeria, West Africa* (London, 1910), p. 5.

14 Benedetta Rossi and Joel Quirk, 'Slavery and marriage in African societies', *Slavery and Abolition* 43, 2 (2022), p. 251.

15 Church Missionary Society (CMS) CA 1/0 187/1, Julia Sass to Henry Venn, 21 February 1849, as cited in Silke Strickrodt, 'If she no learn, she no get husband: Christianity, domesticity, and education at the Church Missionary Society's female institution in nineteenth-century Sierra Leone', *Comparativ*, 5–6 (2007), p. 30.

16 CMS CA 1/0 187/44, Julia Sass to Mr Venn, 19 December 1865, as cited in Strickrodt, 'If she no learn', p. 25.

17 CMS CA 1/O 219.53, J. Weeks, Report of the Bathurst Schools, 25 December 1833, as cited in Silke Strickrodt, 'African girls' samplers from mission schools in Sierra Leone (1820s to 1840s)', *History in Africa* 37 (2010), pp. 189–245.

18 British National Archives, CO 267/111 Census of Freetown, 1831.

19 Strickrodt, 'If she no learn', p. 32.

20 Gareth Austin, 'Labour-intensity and manufacturing in West Africa, *c.*1450–*c.*2000', in Gareth Austin and Kaoru Sugihara, *Labour-Intensive Industrialization in Global History* (Abingdon, 2013), p. 210; Colleen Kriger, *Cloth in*

West African History (Lanham, MD, 2006); Judith Byfield, *The Bluest Hands: A Social and Economic History of Women Dyers in Abeokuta (Nigeria), 1890–1940* (Oxford, 2002).

21 David Damtar, 'A history of gold mining in the Asante region of Ghana (1950–1972)', DPhil thesis, University of Oxford, 2021; Luise White, *The Comforts of Home: Prostitution in Colonial Nairobi* (Chicago, 1990).

22 Judith Byfield, *The Great Upheaval: Women and Nation in Postwar Nigeria* (Athens, OH, 2019), p. 40.

23 Judith Byfield, 'Taxation, women, and the colonial state: Egba women's tax revolt', *Meridians* 3, 2 (2003), p. 252.

24 Ibid., p. 253.

25 Ibid., p. 256.

26 Ibid., p. 267.

27 Lewis, *The Theory of Economic Growth*, p. 422.

28 Polly Hill, *Development Economics on Trial: The Anthropological Case for a Prosecution* (Cambridge, 1986), pp. 144–5.

29 World Bank, https://www.worldbank.org/en/topic/gender/overview

30 World Economic Forum, https://www.weforum.org/agenda/2022/09/period-poverty-menstruation-nigeria-education-global-shapers/

31 Hill, *Development Economics on Trial*, p. 141.

32 Ibid., p. 142.

33 Annie Lowrey review, *Who Cooked Adam Smith's Dinner?* by Katrine Marçal, *New York Times*, 10 June 2016.

34 Ezra Klein, 'The men – and boys – are not alright', *New York Times*, 10 March 2023, https://www.nytimes.com/2023/03/10/opinion/ezra-klein-podcast-richard-reeves.html

35 Idrees Kahloon, 'What's the matter with men?', *The New Yorker*, 23 January 2023.

36 UNDP and World Bank, *African Development Indicators* (New York, 1992), p. 282.

37 Joerg Baten, Michiel de Haas, Elisabeth Kempter, and Felix Meier zu Selhausen, 'Educational gender inequality in sub-Saharan Africa: A long-term perspective', *Population and Development Review* 47, 3 (2021), p. 816.

◆ ◆ ◆

EPILOGUE: HOW TO THINK DIFFERENTLY ABOUT AFRICAN ECONOMICS

1 Thomas Sankara, 'A united front against the debt', speech given at the African Unity Organisation Conference, Addis Ababa, 29 July 1987, https://www.documenta14.de/en/south/37_a_united_front_against_the_debt

2 Godfrey Kanyenze, *Zimbabwe Leaving So Many Behind: The Link Between Politics and the Economy* (Harare, 2021), p. 167.

3 See e.g. Ernest Herst, *Thomas Sankara: An African Revolutionary* (Athens, OH, 2014).

4 Chimamanda Ngozi Adichie, 'The danger of a single story', TED Talk, https://www.ted.com/talks/chimamanda_ngozi_adichie_the_danger_of_a_single_story/transcript; Chinua Achebe, *An Image of Africa* (London: Penguin, 2010), p. 19.

INDEX

Abeokuta Women's Union 229, 230, 231

Abyssinia 142

Achebe, Chinua 249–50

Acheson, Dean 168

Action Group (AG) 188

Adichie, Chimamanda Ngozi 249

Africanization 190

African socialism 180–81

agriculture
cash crop 14, 89–90, 156, 158, 160, 175
cocoa 155, 156–7, 162, 246
Coinage Act (1873) and 130
commodity trades and 38, 90–91, 106, 158, 174, 179–80, 183
cooperatives 158, 160, 161, 162, 163, 167, 180, 182
day-to-day lives of global poor and 194–5
education in 3, 13–14, 38, 81, 82, 159, 161, 227
inequality and 81
model farms 13, 38, 60, 61, 62, 63, 65–6, 67, 159
Mouride Sufi movement and 89
natural abundance of, work ethic and 55

Niger Expedition and 70

nutritional guidelines and 150, 151, 152

peasant farmers 64

prices paid to African farmers 160

slavery and 8, 13, 31, 38, 43, 44–5, 57–8, 65, 90–91

Sokoto economy and 64–5, 67, 69

subsistence 54, 64, 150, 174, 180

time and 77

wage-labour jobs in 228

women and 10, 232

aid
dependency 197
Make Poverty History see Make Poverty History
market-focused solutions to poverty and 159
Marshall Plan 165, 242–3, 247
mutual aid 207, 211
OECD books on Better Aid 202
Paris Declaration on Aid Effectiveness (2005) 201–2
personal gift, framing as a 243
Sankara and 242–4
Stuff Expat Aid Workers blog 202–3
value-based management and 203–6
workers 2, 3, 10, 12, 15

Akwete cloth 227–8
Albert, Prince 61
Allen, Robert 48, 219
Alliance Marine Assurance Company 56–7
aluminium 167
American Board of Commissioners for Foreign Missions 79
American Civil War (1861–5) 90–91, 95
American Colonization Society 66
Americas 8, 20, 27, 28, 29, 31, 48, 71–2, 181
Amin, Samir 172–4, 177–8, 180; The Teaching of Economics in Africa 177, 184
Angola 30, 78, 79, 222, 245
Ankobra River 108
Archibong, Belinda 94
Arusha Declaration 180
Asante, Kingdom 33, 106–7, 108, 109, 121, 154–5
Aswan Dam, Nile 179
Atkins, Keletso: The Moon Is Dead! Give Us Our Money! 76, 77–8
Atlantic Ocean
economy/trade 6, 7, 8, 20, 27, 114, 122
slave trade 8, 20, 27, 29, 31–2, 38, 51–2, 58
Austen, Jane 41
Sense and Sensibility 39
austerity, government 159, 246
Austin, Gareth 154, 155–6
Austro-Hungarian empire 138, 139
Azikiwe, Nnamdi 169

Back-to-Africa movements 1
Bacon, Ed 186
Baganda 96, 97, 148, 161
balance of trade 13, 20–21
Bamako 172

Bamba, Shaykh Amadou 89
Bankman-Fried, Sam 205, 215
Baptist Missionaries 79
bar trade 112
Barnard, Frederick Lamport: A Three Years' Cruize in the Mozambique Channel 101
barter 37, 110, 111, 113, 117, 119, 249
Barth, Heinrich 65
Basel (Switzerland) Mission 79
Baten, Jörg 154, 155
Batten, T. R. 135–6, 137–8, 139–40, 147, 245; Problems of African Development 140–43, 149–50, 157–64, 167
bauxite 166
Belinga, Samuel Eno 25
Bell, Henry Hesketh 97
Bello, Mohammed 63–4, 65, 69
Benue River 62, 65
Berlin Agreement (1885) 67–8
Berlin Conference (1885) 83–4, 91, 93, 145
Biafra, Republic of 189–91
Bida, Emirate of 67
bills of exchange 109, 117
Bitcoin 213
'black codes' criminalized behaviours 95
blockchain 214
Blue Books 54, 75
Bohannan, Laura and Paul 219–20
Boigny, Félix Houphouët 246
bond spreads 175
Bonnecase, Vincent 152
Bonny 31, 112
Bosman, Willem 106
Bourdieu, Pierre 87
Brazzaville 99, 100
Bretton Woods Agreement (1944) 168–9, 171, 180, 191–2, 194

bride
  price 223, 229
  wealth 221–3
Britain 2, 28, 32, 175
  Asante, conquest of 108, 109
  Bretton Woods and 171–2
  forced labour and 96
  Gold Coast territories purchased
    from Dutch (1872) 108
  gold standard and 109–10
  industrialization in 77
  inequality in 81
  land value in 92
  mercantilism and protectionist
    policies 21
  minimum wage in 78
  monetization in Africa and 116–19
  Niger Expedition (1841) 60–62,
    65–7, 70
  Poor Laws 51, 55
  primogeniture in 218–19
  settlers in Africa from 20, 23
  silk imports 57
  slavery and 7, 32–3, 34, 37–8,
    39–40, 44, 51, 52, 57, 58–9, 60,
    63, 64, 65, 67–8, 102, 120, 225
  Sokoto, conquest of 68–9
  tariffs and 181–2
  textile industry 181–2
  welfare state 165
  women in 10, 39, 41, 216–17, 225,
    227, 237
British Caribbean 22, 51
British Empire 21, 57, 65, 68, 181
Brussels Act (1890) 68
Brussels Conference (1890) 67–8,
  84
Bryan, William Jennings: 'Cross of
  Gold' speech 130
Buell, Raymond 136; The Native
  Problem in Africa 144–6
Bunkie, Pa 40

Burkina Faso 63, 241, 244, 245–7
Burkinabè 246–8
Burton, Richard 104–7, 110, 124,
  126, 127, 129, 132, 135, 137, 142
  To the Gold Coast for Gold 104–5,
    132–3
  Wanderings in West Africa 106–9
Buxton, Thomas Fowell 3, 43–7, 49,
  56–9, 66, 67, 68, 69, 90, 151, 159,
  204
  The African Slave Trade and Its
    Remedy 43–4, 57–63, 64–5, 70

Calico Acts (1700 and 1721) 48
Cameroon 63, 90, 106, 139, 188
Cape Coast Castle 32–4, 36, 123
capital investment 46, 55, 109, 156–7,
  179, 194
capitalism 22, 85, 125–6, 128, 133,
  146–7, 160, 170, 181, 201, 235
Carlyle, Thomas 72
Caro, Robert 186
Casement, Roger 85
cash crops 14, 89–90, 156, 158, 160,
  175
casino earnings 159
Catholicism 30, 31, 79, 81, 115,
  226
Central Africa 84, 92, 99, 178
Central African Republic 99
central planning 187
ceteris paribus (other things being
  equal) 4–5, 10, 12, 200, 250
Chad 63, 99
Chandos, Duke of 21–2
charities 203–5, 217
child labour 48
China 168, 179, 211, 244, 245
Chiredze, Dorothy 194–5, 205
Christian Aid 217
Church Missionary Society 79, 80,
  86–7

civil wars, African 2, 10–11, 153–4,
    155, 194
'civilized'/civilizing mission 60, 70, 83,
    126, 147
'civilization' 98, 101–2, 159–60
Clapperton, Hugh 65
Clarkson, Thomas 41
'Class B' mandates 139
clinical economics 201
Clinton, Bill 199
cloth 48, 50, 59, 66–7, 111, 112, 116,
    119, 120, 121, 181–2, 227, 229
cobalt 166
cocoa 155, 156, 162, 246
coffee 18, 158, 167, 180, 183
coinage 115–16, 118–19, 120, 122,
    123, 124, 129, 130, 131, 213, 215
Coinage Acts
    Britain (1816) 118–19
    US (1873) 130
Cold War (1946–91) 170, 172, 173,
    180, 182, 191, 192, 193–4, 218,
    219, 246
Collier, Paul: *The Bottom Billion*
    202
colonialism 16
    Africa as last frontier of 165
    colonization on the cheap 99
    debt as another form of 180, 244
    developmental colonialism 166
    neo-colonialism 176–7, 244
    postcolonial Africa 172, 173–4,
        177, 182, 187, 191, 235
    profit and 85
    progressive colonialists 139, 144
Colonial Office, British 40, 75, 95,
    97, 190
Colonial Welfare and Development
    Act, British (1940) 166
coltan 198, 199
commercial finance revolution 36
commodities

commodity currencies 110, 134, 213
    luxury 63, 119, 121, 125
    markets 91, 110, 111–14, 117–22,
        134, 157, 158, 160, 165–7, 172,
        188
    *See also individual commodity
    name*
communism 3, 11, 170, 172, 201,
    210, 243
community development 141
comparative advantage 50, 51, 57, 81,
    151, 173, 183, 198–9
Compoaré, Blaise 247
concession company 99–100
Condorcet, Nicolas de 34
Congo Free State 3, 83–5, 98–102,
    144
Congo-Océan Railway 98–102, 144,
    175
Congo, Republic of 167, 175, 188
conscription 99, 100, 144, 154
conversion rates 111
convertibility 25, 114, 119
convict leasing 95
Cooper, Frederick 91, 190, 195
Cooperative Development Council
    167
cooperative movement 158, 160,
    161–2, 163, 167, 204
copper 166
Cornhill Magazine, The 79–80
corruption 7, 9, 14, 106, 124, 133,
    137, 142, 197, 242, 245, 246, 247
corvée (labour tax) 93
Costello, Jane 159
cotton 21, 59, 60, 64, 65, 66–7, 68,
    69, 90, 121, 158, 160, 161, 167,
    180
COVID-19 116, 209, 213
cowries 35, 115, 116, 117, 120,
    121–4, 126, 128, 129, 130, 131,
    133, 134, 206, 220

credit 36, 90, 109, 113–14, 116, 125,
   131, 160, 161, 163, 169, 174, 179,
   185, 206–8, 211, 243
Credit and Savings Bank, The 160,
   161
cross-cultural trade 114
cryptocurrency 205, 212–15
cultural relativism 126, 127
currency
   Asante government and 107
   commodity currencies 109, 110,
      121, 134, 213
   convertible currency mechanisms
      114
   cowries *see* cowries
   cryptocurrency 205, 212–15
   currency transition (shift from pre-
      colonial currency to one enhanced
      by colonial
   policies) 109–34
   dollar 112, 117, 122, 126, 129–30,
      146, 166, 169, 180, 210
   pound sterling 22, 112, 119, 129
   silver dollar 122, 126, 129–30
   silver standard and 117
   small-currency tokens 118
   transition 109
Curtin, Philip 110

Dahomey 14, 35, 107, 122–4, 128
Dalzel, Archibald 122–3
'danger of a single story' 249
Daughton, J. P. 99
debt 9, 13, 23, 25, 40, 86, 91, 114,
   131, 171–2, 179, 180, 181, 185–6,
   191, 190, 209, 220
   cancellation/relief 194, 242, 243,
      244, 247
   slavery and 249
Decker, Stephanie 190
decolonization 178, 179, 188, 189,
   191, 195

democracy 97, 142, 185, 186, 187,
   193, 249
   development and 185
   representation and 191
Democratic Republic of Congo 179
Department for International
   Development (DFID) 206–7
deregulation 33, 121, 143
'deserving poor' 200
development
   democracy and 185–7, 191
   'developed economy' 170
   development politics 169
   developmental colonialism 166
   economics 11, 16, 171, 196, 201,
      207, 231–2, 234, 236, 231
   effects of on character of colonies
      137
   experts 3, 9, 10, 15, 162, 173
   indicators 10, 239
   infrastructure development *see*
      infrastructure
   microfinance and 207
   as process or goal 247
   return on investment and 202, 206
   self-rule and 164
   women and *see* women
diamonds 180, 198
Dickens, Charles: *A Christmas Carol*
   87–8
direct cash transfers 159
'divide and rule' strategies 170
do-gooders 3–4, 238
domestic slavery 64
Don-Siemion, Thea 50–51
donor money 203, 205
Dovring, Folke 73
Dutch West India Company 32

East Africa 86, 115, 137, 149, 150,
   152–3, 177, 178, 183, 206
East African Federation 178

East India Company 80, 181
East India Company College 80
Ebola crisis (2013–16) 12
EcoCash 211–12
economic growth 2, 3, 6, 21, 39, 89,
  107, 129, 130, 131, 134, 146, 171,
  201, 231–2, 247
economic thinking 200, 237, 240,
  249
economics *see individual area of
  economics*
education
  agricultural 13, 44, 82, 89
  Batten and 135–6, 138, 140, 141,
    143, 159–60
  labour 69
  missionary 71, 80, 81, 86, 225
  poverty and 159–60
  schools 47, 71, 82, 86, 90, 165,
    182, 195, 205, 225–7, 233,
    237–8, 240, 246
  wealth and 149
  women and 225–7, 229, 234,
    236–40
Effective Altruism movement 204–5,
  213, 214
effective occupation 93–4, 145, 147,
  175–6
effectiveness, research into 203–5
Egba Women's Tax Riot (1947)
  230–31
Egypt 28, 90, 93, 94, 145, 168, 172,
  179, 253
electricity 137, 170, 179, 182, 187,
  196, 214, 233
electrification 179, 182, 187, 233
Elmina 31
Emmott, Alfred 68–9
Enlightenment 20, 111
entrepreneurs 82, 156, 203, 205, 206,
  207, 208, 210, 212, 245
exchange rate 115, 129

Exeter Hall, London 60–61
exoticism 18, 126
exports 14, 21, 31, 32, 34, 36, 58, 59,
  60, 64, 89, 90, 91, 128, 151, 158,
  170, 180, 181–2, 189, 191, 199,
  236

factors of production 22
Fair Trade 204
Falconbridge, Alexander 18–19, 27,
  38
Falconbridge, Anna Maria 17–18,
  22–4, 25, 26, 27, 36–7, 39–40,
  41–2, 73–4
Fante 33, 108, 109
farming. *See* agriculture
federalism 178, 188, 190
Female Institution 225, 226
Ferguson, James: *Give a Man a Fish*
  159
Fernando Po 106, 147
feudalism 28, 93
First World War (1914–18) 99, 136,
  138–9, 145–6, 154, 155, 175
Fisher, Irving 127
Food and Agriculture Organization
  (FAO), United Nations (UN) 151
food prices 54, 56, 128–9
Force Publique 84
forced labour 85, 95, 96, 98–9,
  100–101, 145, 149, 153–6
Foreign Affairs 163–4
fossil fuels 6–7
fractional money 115–20
France 7, 20, 138, 145, 167, 169, 175
  Calico Acts and 48
  Congo Free State and 83, 84
  Congo-Océan Railway and 98–102,
    144, 175
  French Equatorial Africa *see* French
    Equatorial Africa
  gold standard and 110

Marshall Plan and 242
Revolution (1789) 218
Sankara and 244, 246, 247
Senegal and 88, 89
silk manufacturer 57
slave trade and 7, 52, 120
sugar and 21, 34
welfare policies 165
Frankema, Ewout 75
Freetown 2, 3, 15, 40, 87, 106, 225, 226
free trade 22, 34–5, 50, 70, 83, 108, 121, 182, 199, 249
French Equatorial Africa 94, 98, 99, 100, 136, 146, 175
Frere, Sir Bartle 153
Frontier Force 93, 146

G8 meeting, Gleneagles, Scotland (2005) 193
Gaddafi, Muammar 244
Gardner, Leigh 175
gatekeeper states 190
GDP 174, 186, 187, 191, 232, 234, 235, 238, 239
Germany 65, 79, 99, 127, 138, 139, 146, 165
Gezo, King of Dahomey 122
Ghana 32, 81, 106, 154–6, 162, 169, 173, 175, 176, 178, 179, 180, 182, 187, 206, 222, 239, 245–6
gift economies 8, 27, 34, 40, 113, 190, 242, 243
GiveWell 203
Giving What We Can 203–5
globalization 128
Global North 205, 210, 250, 251
gold 17, 20, 31, 37, 132, 180
    African reserves of 166
    Burton and search for 104–8
    coins 117–22, 129
    cowries and 115

gold standard 109–10, 112, 124–6, 129, 130–31, 169
slavery and 29, 32–3
washers 106–7, 133
Gold Coast 32, 104, 132, 154
Goldie, George 98, 120
Gorée 31
Gowon, Yakubu 189
Grameen Bank 207
Graphic, The 151
Great Lakes region, East Africa 153
groundnuts 90, 154, 170, 180, 183
guilds 48
Guinea, Republic of 31, 90, 132, 167, 173, 178
Guinea-Bissau 78
Guinea Coast Mining Company 132
guinea coin 118
'guns and gewgaws' 110–11
Gurney, Hannah 45, 46
Guyer, Jane 25; Marginal Gains 152

Hanes, Christopher 220–21
Hanks, Tom 193
Hausa 135, 188, 189
height, average 154, 155
high-modernism 187
Hill, Polly 156, 159, 232–3;
    Development Economics on Trial 235–6
Hodge, Joseph 184
Hogendorn, Jan 120
Hopkins, Tony 253; An Economic History of West Africa 130–31
House Rule Ordinance 94
humanitarianism 7, 8, 9, 15, 36–7, 52, 80, 119, 124, 126, 147, 153
    language of 15
    market-based solutions to poverty and 194, 202–3
    protecting African victims from African bullies and 143–4

technical experts and 163
women and 217
hut tax 92, 97, 145
hydroelectric dams 170

Ifemesia, C. C. 66
Igbo 188, 189
Illustrated London News 152
'image of Africa' problem 249–50
Iman of Zanzibar 101
imports 21, 48, 51, 57, 58–9, 63, 64,
  67, 115, 119–20, 122, 124, 128–9,
  151, 156, 162, 165, 198, 199,
  227–8, 245
  import substitution 178, 181–3
India 48, 51, 57, 68, 74, 80, 116, 121,
  125, 127, 164–5, 168–9, 181–2,
  188, 211
Indian Ocean 115, 121, 152, 154
indirect rule 96, 135–6, 137, 144, 148,
  188, 190
individualism 149, 192
Indochina 165
Industrial Revolution 119
industrialization 8, 77, 81, 181,
  182
inequality 8, 11, 12, 19, 70, 81–2,
  146, 150, 170, 217, 230, 231,
  240–41, 248
inflation 8, 13, 15, 107, 109, 120,
  121, 123–4, 125, 128, 129, 130,
  131, 207
infrastructure 6, 93–8, 100, 102,
  147–8, 155, 157, 170, 176, 181,
  185–6, 214, 232, 243, 251
Inga Dams 179
insecurity 14, 195, 199, 205, 210,
  214–15
insuring against risk 205, 214–15
interest rates 13, 172
International Bank for Reconstruction
  and Development 169

International Labour Organization
  100, 150, 151
International Monetary Fund (IMF)
  169, 183, 193
internet technologies 213–14
Interstate 95 186
investment in a cow or goat 205
inyanga (lunar month) 75
iron ore 164, 166–7, 198
Irvine, James 105, 108–9, 110, 132–3
isiZulu 76, 86
Iteso colonial chiefs 149
Ivory Coast 246, 247

Jevons, William Stanley 126
Johnson, Marion 115

Kano 66, 68
Kanyenze, Godfrey 245
Kariba Dam, Zambia 179
Karonga War (1887–9) 68
kasanvu system 96–7
Katanga Province 188
Kenya 51–2, 149, 152, 178, 183, 206,
  239
Keynes, John Maynard 168, 171, 199
Kingsley, Mary 80–81, 83, 135
Kongkadu 106–7
Kongo, Kingdom of 31
Kongo-Wara rebellion (1928–31) 99
Kung Hsiang-hsi 168

labour
  child labour 48
  concessions 146
  conscripted 99, 100
  contracts 14, 78, 95
  discipline 86, 102
  division of 81, 111, 235
  education 69
  efficiency 84
  food prices and 56

forced 85, 95, 96–8, 99, 100, 101, 145–6, 147, 149, 153–4, 155–6
freedom of 57
household 75, 91–2, 170, 233, 236, 238
indentured 147
land-to-labour ratio 24, 72–5
migration 175
price of things and 56
prison 94–5
question 104–5
scarcity 196, 219
semi-skilled 82
shortages 74–5, 175, 229
slave *see* slavery
supply 196, 219, 250
taxes 93, 94, 95–6, 97, 101, 154, 229
theory of value 50, 126
unskilled 81–2, 83, 170
valuing 78, 92–3
violence 83
wage 28, 72–3, 76, 91, 103, 109, 122, 150, 227–9 *see also* wages
wealth and 20
women and 75, 91–2, 233, 235–6, 238, 239
Lagos, Nigeria 106, 116, 122, 130, 231
Lagos Market Women's Association 231
Lake Victoria 153
Lamizana, Sangoulé 242
land-to-labour ratio 23, 72–5
Law of Demand 4
Law, Robin 128
laziness, myth of African 9, 14, 55, 71–2, 76, 77, 79, 86, 103, 154, 176, 239
Le Fonds d'investissements pour le développement économique et social (FIDES) 166

League of Nations 139, 144, 150, 151
Lend-Lease Program 169
Leopold II, King of Belgium 83–5
Lewis, W. Arthur 171, 196, 231–2
Liberal Ghanaians 173
Liberated African Department 52–3
Liberia 1, 2, 61, 66, 81
civil wars (1980–2003) 2, 10–11
elections, first post-conflict (2005) 2
financing growth in 174–6
forced labour in 144–7
inequality in 146–7
reconstruction of 2
Sierra Leone and, difference between 2–3, 10–12, 15
slavery and 142
tax base 145
women in 217
Lincoln Center, New York 186
Livingstone, David 153
loans 36, 91, 100, 145, 160, 174, 175, 176, 179, 182, 183, 232
microloans 205, 208
London Missionary Society 79
Long Depression (1873) 91, 130
Long, Slow Death of Global Development, The 196
Lovell, Reverend Dr George 135
Lugard, Frederick 68–9, 70, 96, 188; *The Dual Mandate in British Tropical Africa* 69, 136, 137, 144
Lunyole 147

M-Pesa mobile money 206–9, 213
Maathai, Wangari 152
MacAskill, William 203–4, 205
Madaba, R. N. J. 148–9
Madagascar 241
maendeleo (development) 137
Magee, Gary 40
Make Poverty History 193, 201, 215
Makerere College, Uganda 138, 147

Malaya 166
Maldives 121, 122, 123
Mali 172, 173, 178, 216, 239
malnutrition 151
Malthus, Thomas 80, 143
management consulting 203
'mandates', African 139
Mandeville, Bernard: *The Fable of the Bees* 49
Maradi 221
marriage
  bride price 223, 229
  bridewealth 221–3
  market 39, 225
Marshall Plan 165, 242–3, 247
Marxism 181, 235
Matthews, John 112
Mavro currency 212–13
Mavrodi Mondial Moneybox (MMM) 210–15
Mavrodi, Sergei 210–12
McNamara, Robert 200–201
mechanization 48, 58
Melbourne, Lord 60
mercantilism 20–21, 181, 182
microfinance 159, 207, 208, 211, 212
migration 48, 69, 73, 74, 104, 175, 215–16
military-industrial complex, US 170
Mill, John Stuart 72, 74
minimum subsistence 54
minimum wage 48, 49, 78
mining 14, 98, 104–5, 107, 109, 131–2
minority groups 176, 189
mission schools 86, 225
missionaries 9, 44, 52, 54, 71–2, 76, 79–88, 92, 97–8, 103, 106, 126, 135, 153, 159–60, 218, 223, 224–6, 228
Mkandawire, Thandika 201

mobile phones 206–9, 211–14
model farms 13, 38, 60–67, 159
Model Farm Society 62
modernity 10, 22, 136, 150, 153, 169, 231
modernization 170–71, 179, 181, 191, 235–6
Mombasa 153
money
  bills of exchange 109, 117
  coinage *see* coinage
  credit and *see* credit
  currency and *see* currency
  currency transition (shift from pre-colonial currency to one enhanced by colonial policies) 109–34
  donor money 203, 205
  emergence of modern 108–11
  mobile money 206–9, 211–14
  monetization 109–17, 130
  money illusion 127–8
  paper money 109, 125–6, 129, 131
  small change problem 115–20, 206
  time and 79–80, 86–8
  trust and 131, 211–12, 213, 214, 215
Monrovia 1, 2, 15
Moore, Ralph 66
Moradi, Alexander 154, 155
Morel, E. D. 3, 85
Morgenthau Jr, Henry 168
Morgue, James 32
Moses, Robert 186
Mourides, Islamic 88, 89
Musaazi, Ignatius 161, 167

Naidu, Suresh 221
Namibia 99, 192*n*, 245
Napoleonic Wars (1799–1815) 37–8
Natal, South Africa 76–7
national accounting 173–4

National Banking Act (1863) 117
National Council of Nigeria and the
    Cameroons (NCNC) 188, 189
National Health Service (NHS) 165
nationalization, industry 183, 190
natural abundance 13, 19, 55
negro ferocity 44
New York, development of 186–7
NGO reporting to donors 203
Nieboer-Domar hypothesis 73, 74–5
Niger 65, 167, 190, 221
Niger Expedition (1841) 60–62, 65–7,
    70
Niger River 43, 60, 61, 62, 65–7, 70
Nigeria 3, 68, 81, 90, 94, 99, 162,
    169, 182, 214, 215, 216, 219, 249
    Batten and 135–6
    Biafra succession 190–91
    cash crop labour shortages in 175
    cash economy 94–5
    economic development in 137
    exports 182
    federal structure 188, 189
    groundnut economy 170
    independence (1960) 188
    MMM in 211, 212
    oil production 190
    partition 189
    sanitation fines 229–30
    slavery in 120, 220
    Sokoto, conquest of 68–9
    wage labour impact on 229
    women in 221, 222, 227, 229–31,
        235
Nkrumah, Kwame 169, 178; Neo-
    colonialism: The Last Stage of
    Imperialism 176–7
Nnaebue, Ike 215–16
No U-Turn 215–16
Noah, Trevor: Born a Crime 196–7
Nobel Peace Prize 4, 152, 171, 249
noble savage 127

North Carolina Cherokee populations
    159
North, Douglass 4
Northern People's Congress (NPC)
    188
Northern Rhodesia 166
nudge economy 102
nutrition 150–52, 154–5
Nyerere, Julius 179–80, 192

Obikili, Nonso 94
oil production 6, 112, 114. 189, 190,
    191, 199
Ojukwu, Colonel Odumegwu 189
Okadaro 148
Old Calabar 31, 112
Ord, Toby 203
Organisation for Economic Co-
    Operation and Development
    (OECD) 202, 219
Organization of African Unity 243
Ossai, Obi 61–2, 63
O'Swald 122
Ottoman Empire 28, 138, 139
Ouidah 30, 35, 122–3
Oxfam 193–5, 202, 205
    Poverty Report (1995) 194–5, 199
Oxford University 203, 205, 215

PAI (African Independence Party) 241
Pall Mall Gazette, The 104–5
palm oil 53, 54, 67, 90, 99, 105, 120,
    121, 122, 129, 156, 229
Palmerston, Lord 60
Pan-Africanists 178
Paris Declaration on Aid Effectiveness
    (2005) 201–2
Parliament 40, 45, 52, 54, 56, 57,
    60–61, 80, 149
Parliamentary Commission of Inquiry
    sent to Sierra Leone (1825) 52
patronage 40

Peel, Robert 60–61
peer-to-peer schemes 209–10
Perham, Margery 135–6, 137, 144,
    150, 163–4
period poverty 234–5
Personal Responsibility and Work
    Opportunity Act, US (1996) 199
plantations 7, 22, 28, 31, 51, 66, 67,
    69, 76–7, 81, 84, 144, 147, 153,
    220, 221
Pointe-Noire 99
polygyny 220, 223, 229, 230
Poor Laws, British 51, 55
Popp Berman, Elizabeth 200, 237
Portugal 20, 29, 50, 79, 121, 125, 167
Postlethwayt, Malachy 143
Post Office 40, 160
poverty 3, 5, 16, 19, 26, 39, 42, 56,
    82, 91, 119, 124, 140
    education and 159, 160
    Effective Altruism and 214
    growth and 172
    insuring against insecurity and 214
    Make Poverty History see Make
        Poverty History
    measuring 247
    NHS and 165
    nutritional guidelines and 151, 153,
        154
    Oxfam Poverty Report (1995)
        194–5, 199
    period poverty 234–5
    quick fixes for 202–3, 210
    slave-raiding and 153
    term 39, 251
    trap 195, 202
    women and 217, 218, 228, 234–5
prices 4, 48, 54, 56, 127
    bride 223, 229
    commodity 90–91, 110, 111–12,
        118, 157, 160, 161, 166, 172,
        182, 188

consumer price index 75, 124
currency 115, 122, 127–8
exports 128–9, 199
food 54, 56, 128–9
inflation see inflation
labour theory of value and 50, 126,
    127–8
Nieboer-Domar hypothesis 73
Poor Laws and 51
slavery and 34–6, 38, 47, 121, 220,
    223
prison population 45, 54–6, 94–6
private property 23, 24, 149–50
private sector 3, 171, 192, 197
privatization 159, 210–11
productivity 22, 48, 53, 72, 166, 170,
    174, 179
property rights 27, 59, 90, 120
protectionism 21
Protestant work ethic 79
pseudo-gentry 41

Quakers 45
Quirk, Joel 224

Rabba 65, 67
racial supremacy, doctrine of 139
Raisman, Jeremy 168–9
Ransome-Kuti, Funmilayo 230
rare-earth metals 167
raw materials 60, 61, 165, 191, 243.
    See also individual material name
Rawlings, Jerry 246
Reagan, Ronald 200
redistribution 14, 158, 199, 201, 205,
    208, 248
redshirting boys, US schools 237
Reese, Ty M. 33–4
Registrar for Cooperatives 161
rents 73, 86, 149
representation, democracy and 191
Rhodes, Cecil 98, 105

Ricardo, David 50, 57, 81
Rio Nunez 90
Ritchie, Anne Isabella Thackeray: *Mrs Dymond* 79–80
roads 93, 96, 100, 145, 146, 155, 156, 165, 179, 196, 214
Rodney, Walter 178
Roman Empire 29
Rossi, Benedetta 224
Rowan, James 52, 54
Royal African Company 21–2, 112, 145
Royal Navy 59, 106, 112
Royal Niger Company 68, 98, 120
Ruanda-Urundi 139
rubber 84, 99, 120, 165–6
Russell, Lord John 60, 61, 62
Russia 73, 179, 210, 211

Sachs, Jeffrey: *The End of Poverty* 201–2
sadaki (bridewealth) 221
Safaricom 206, 208
Saint-Louis 31
Saint Monday 55
Salau, Mohamed 63, 66
sanitation fines 229–30
Sankara, Thomas 241–7
São Tomé 121, 144
Sargent, Thomas 118
Sass, Julia 225
Saudi Arabia 198–9
Schleicher, David: *In a Bad State* 185–6
Scott, James 187; *Seeing Like a State* 187
Scramble for Africa 15, 80, 83, 145
Second Anglo-Afghan War (1878–80) 68
Second World War (1939–45) 152, 160, 164, 165, 191–2, 200, 242
Sékou Touré 173

self-rule 138–9, 142, 164, 167
Senegal 88–90, 112, 169–70, 183, 222, 253
Senghor, Léopold 169
service-sector jobs 171, 198
settler empire 40, 74
Sexton, Jay 138
Shell-BP 190
Shepherd, Reverend William 85
Sierra Leone 31, 54, 61, 66, 81, 87, 112
     Anna Maria Falconbridge in *see* Falconbridge, Anna Maria
     civil war (1991–2002) 2, 11
     farming in 13–14
     hut tax 92
     independence (1961) 164
     Liberia, differences between Sierra Leone and 1–2, 3, 10–11, 15
     merchants from 90
     Parliamentary Commission of Inquiry sent to (1825) 52
     raw materials and 166–7, 175, 198
     reconstruction in 11, 12
     slave trade and 3, 18–20, 37–8, 41–2, 51, 143
     women in 224–5
Sierra Leone Company 3, 18–20, 37, 41–2, 204
silk weavers 46–9, 57, 66–7
silver 20, 107, 110, 115, 117, 125
silver dollar 122, 126, 129–31
Sirleaf, Ellen Johnson 11
slavery 1, 3, 4, 5–6, 7
     Abolition Act, British (1833) 8, 43, 44, 80
     abolition of trade in (1808) 44, 52
     abolitionism 7, 9, 36–7, 38, 41, 72, 97–8, 105–6, 110, 120–21, 142, 143, 221, 223, 245
     agriculture and 8, 13, 31, 38, 43, 44–5, 57–8, 65, 90–91

allocation of labour to demand and
221
annual gifts given by slave traders to
African states 8, 190
anti-slavery patrols 101, 152–3
Atlantic slave trade 8, 20, 26–32,
38, 51–2, 58
Bello and 63–4
as beneficial to the enslaved 31
Bristol and 41
Britain and 7, 32–3, 34, 37–8,
39–40, 44, 51, 52, 57, 58–9, 60,
63, 64, 65, 67–8, 102,
120, 225
Brussels Conference and see Brussels
Conference
buying power and 38
Caribbean, slave economy of 39
'civilization' and 101–2
commodity currencies and 110
compensation for African
slaveholders, lack of 7–8, 134
compensation paid to Britain's
slaveowners 7, 57
cotton and 64, 59
credit and 36
debt and 249
deregulation of, British government
(1712) 143
domestic slavery 64, 65
doubloons used to pay 107
East African trade 151–3
economic case for ending 72
economic development,
foundational to 247–9
failures of abolition of slave trade to
actually stop slavery 44, 58
farming, replacing slave trade with
59
free trade and 35
French abolish slave trade (1815)
52

incentivizing formerly enslaved
workers 59–60, 71–2
indirect trade taxation and 92
labour shortages and 73, 74, 75
labour theory of value and 50
legality of 30
Liberia and 142, 144
Lugard and 96
Madaba and 148–9
missionaries and 79
poor governance and 143
private property as means of
countering 150
Royal Navy rescues from 106
Sierra Leone Company and see
Sierra Leone Company
slave-raiding 153
Sokoto and 64–8, 69
taxpayer subsidies for slaveowners
52
Uganda and 96
United States and 95
'wealth in people' and 24–7, 35, 38,
39, 42, 73–4, 209, 211, 215, 219,
220, 228, 229
West Indies, abolishment of enslaved
labour in (1833) 43
West African trade opened up to
competition 34
women and 218, 219–20, 221, 222,
223, 224–5, 229, 230
small change problem 115–20, 206
small countries problem 178
Smith, Adam: *The Wealth of Nations*
19–20, 21, 22, 23, 27, 28, 34, 39,
40, 50, 55, 81, 111, 113, 126,
236–7
Smith Bowen, Elenore: *Return to
Laughter* vii
Société de Construction des Batignolles
98
social financial network 211

social mobility 82, 83
Social Science Council Conference, University of East Africa, Dar es Salaam 177, 184–5
socialism 180–81, 191, 241, 242, 244, 246, 247
Society for the Extinction of the Slave Trade and for the Civilization of Africa 60–61
Sokoto Caliphate 63–9, 120
solar panels 214
South Africa 14, 51–2
  black South Africans moved out of cities 186–7
  cash payments in 159
  farming in 71, 76–8
  land value in 74, 90
  missionaries in 85–6, 88
  MMM and 211, 215
  standard of living in 83
  trade unions 245
  UN membership 192*n*
  unemployment in 196–7
South West Africa 99, 139
Southern Rhodesia 175, 178
Soviet Union 168, 169, 170, 173, 210–11, 219, 243
Spain 20, 107, 120, 125, 129, 130, 146
Spitalfields Acts 48, 56, 57
Spitalfields silk weavers 46–8, 56, 67, 181
starvation 148, 152, 171
Stepanov, Mikhail Stepanovich 168
Stephen, James 80
Stephen, Leslie 80
Stephens, Rhiannon 147, 148
Streeten, Paul 178
Strickrodt, Silke 225, 226
strikes 160, 161, 189
Stuff Expat Aid Workers satirical blog 202–3
subsistence

agriculture 64, 91, 150, 174, 180, 184, 196, 219
  levels 54–5, 61, 73, 75, 91
Sudan 68, 77, 88, 94
Sudan campaign (1884–5) 68
sugar 7, 14, 18, 21, 34, 36, 38, 51, 76–7, 180
sumptuary laws 47
Sunday schools 86
supply and demand 5, 51, 55, 62, 111, 112, 127, 250
Swahili 137

Tanganyika 139, 177, 178, 179–80, 192
Tanzania 177, 178, 182, 183, 239
tariffs 14, 48, 49, 108, 174, 181–2, 245, 249
Tawney, R. H. 140
tax 16
  Baganda tax collection agents 97, 148
  collection of 16
  corvée (labour tax) 93
  cowries and 122, 123
  customs taxes 145
  debt interest and 179
  direct taxation of newly occupied territories 92
  effective occupation and 176
  Egba Women's Tax Riot (1947) 230–31
  forced labour as form of 96–7, 101, 153–4
  fossil fuel 6
  guineas accepted as payment for 118
  hut tax 92, 97, 145
  labour taxes/generating low-wage work through 86, 91–6, 101, 102, 109, 154, 228, 229
  migrant groups and 64, 175
  silver and 130

slavery and 52, 63
tax farm 99
trade 14, 92
women and 229, 230–31
Taylor, Charles 11
Temne 17–18, 23, 24, 39–40, 42, 87, 242
Teso 148
Tete-Ansá, Winifred: *Africa at Work* 162
Thackeray, William Makepeace 80
Third Anglo-Burmese War (1885) 68
Thompson, Andrew 40
Thompson, E. P. 77, 78
time use/discipline 77–9, 86, 87–8, 103, 113
Tiv 219–20, 221
Togo 139
Touré, Adama 241
Triangular Trade 31
Triumph of Experts 184
Trotter, Henry Dundas 61–2, 66–7
Truman, Hanbury and Buxton Brewery 45, 46, 47, 49, 58
trust
  money and 131, 211–12, 213, 214, 215
  trade and 114, 117
tungazi ('slave villages' or 'plantations') 67

Uganda 68, 96–7, 99, 136, 138, 147–9, 153, 158, 160, 161–2, 167, 178, 206
Uganda African Farmers Union 161
Ugandan Congress Party 167
Ujamaa (brotherhood) 180
underemployment 82, 196, 198–9
unemployment 8, 15, 196, 236, 239
United Nations (UN) 166, 174, 181, 192, 192n
  Congo intervention (1960) 188

Development Programme 239
  Economic Survey of Africa Since 1950 179–80
  Food and Agriculture Organization (FAO) 152
  former African imperial colonies join (1976) 191–2, 192n
  secessionist claims and 188
  Structure and Growth of Selected African Economies report 183
United States
  democracy in 185–6
  import tariffs 181, 182
  Make Poverty History and 193
  redshirting boys in schools 237
  welfare in 199
University of East Africa 177, 178, 183
University of London 178
Upper Volta 241–7
  People's Development Programme 246–7
uranium 167
urbanization 65, 67, 150
USAID 217
utilitarianism 204

Vagrancy Laws 51, 91
value-based management 203
Vassa, Gustavus (pre-enslavement name, Olaudah Equiano) 55
Velde, François 118
Venn, Jane Catherine 80
Versailles, Treaty of (1919) 138
Victoria, Queen 61, 62
Vinson, Fred 168
Vodafone 206–7, 208
Volta (Akosombo) Dam in Ghana 179

wages 22, 48–9, 50, 51, 56, 57, 71, 72, 74–6, 83, 95, 102, 109, 124, 165, 196, 228–9, 232, 238
Waijenburg, Marlous van 75

Wakefield, Edward Gibbon 73–5,
  82
Washington Consensus 3
welfare 163
  Marshall Plan and 243
  welfare nationalism 195
  Welfare Queen 200
  welfare reformists 199–200
  welfare state 165, 195
Wellington, Henry 52, 54
Wesleyan Missionary Society 79
West Africa 1, 17–18, 19, 24
  bond spreads in 175
  Burton first visits 104, 105–6, 107,
    110–11
  cowries/monetization in 115, 116,
    117, 118, 121, 122, 123, 124,
    126, 129–31, 133–4
  credit systems in 113
  debt in 243
  early-nineteenth-century British
    interventions in 127
  import and export prices 128–9
  Kingsley and 80, 83
  mechanization and 58
  Sierra Leonean traders and 90
  slavery and 29, 32, 34, 153
  women in 225, 232, 236
West Indies 7, 43, 51, 108
White, Harry Dexter 168
Wilberforce, William 47
Williams, Eric 28
Wilson, Woodrow 138–9, 160;
  Fourteen Points 138–9
Windel, Aaron 140
women 8, 10, 15, 217–40, 246,
  249
  biological rate of development
    237–8
  bride price 223, 229
  bride wealth 221–3
  colonial taxation and 230–31

cooperatives and 204
  development, focus on place of
    women in 217
  economic framing of empowerment
    234–5
  economic rescue, origins of African
    women needing 223–4
  education and 225–7, 229, 234,
    236–40
  Egba Women's Tax Riot (1947)
    230–31
  European models of domesticity for
    229–30
  gender equality concept and 234
  gold-washing 106–7
  household work/unpaid labour of
    91–2, 231–7
  market women 226
  microfinance and 207, 211
  patriarchal bargain 224
  period poverty 234–5
  polygyny and 220, 223, 229, 230
  primogeniture and 218–19
  slavery and 220–21, 224–5, 230
  wage labour and 226–9
  wealth-in-people societies and
    219–20
  'women problem', development
    economics (1970s) 232–3
work ethic 9, 14, 55, 71–2, 76, 154,
  176, 239
  natural abundance of agriculture
    and 55
  Protestant work ethic 79
  time use/discipline and 77–9, 86,
    87–8, 103, 113
workers' health 150–51
World Bank 11, 173, 183, 185, 200,
  201, 239
World Economic Forum 234, 235
world system 177, 180, 185
York, Duke of (later, James II) 21–2

Yoruba 188, 230
Yunus, Muhammad 207

Zanzibar 101, 122, 123, 153, 177
Zerbo, Colonel Saye 242

Zimbabwe 192n, 194, 211–12, 245, 253
Zulus 76–7, 86, 88
Zwart, Pim de 83